# THE QUEST FOR AMERICA

# THE QUEST FOR AMERICA

Geoffrey Ashe

Thor Heyerdahl

Helge Ingstad

J. V. Luce

Betty J. Meggers

Birgitta L. Wallace

**Pall Mall Press**    **London**

PALL MALL PRESS LIMITED
5 CROMWELL PLACE, LONDON SW7

FIRST PUBLISHED 1971
© 1971 BY PALL MALL PRESS LIMITED
ISBN 0 269 02787 4

PRINTED IN AUSTRIA BY
BRÜDER ROSENBAUM, VIENNA

# Contents

# Preface

For thousands of years before Columbus tales were told of a 'land to the west'. Recently archaeologists, anthropologists and historians have critically examined these tales with reference to pre-Columbian knowledge of the Americas and have come to some surprisingly different conclusions. This book brings together accounts, by some of these experts, of the major legends of the Old World and of the theories and evidence in the New World for such a knowledge. This is developed by Geoffrey Ashe in his Introduction. Author of *Land to the West*, he has long studied the possibilities of early European contact with the Americas and by analysing the legends and the possible factual clues which they contain he summarizes what ancient civilizations may have known of a western continent. He also concludes the book after a brief account of the 'historical' discovery by Columbus.

The earlier maritime explorations are described by J. V. Luce, Reader in Classics, Trinity College, Dublin and author of *The End of Atlantis*. He then deals with early colonization, shipping, navigation and maps and with Greek myths and legends about the Atlantic.

The one North American site for which there is incontrovertible evidence of pre-Columbian settlement is L'Anse aux Meadows in Newfoundland. It was discovered by Dr Helge Ingstad, the Norwegian explorer and author of *Westward to Vinland*. He considers the voyages of the Norsemen and relates his own search for the North American site where they landed and what archaeology has revealed of their lives there.

Dr Thor Heyerdahl, the explorer and author of *Kon-Tiki* and *The Ra Expeditions*, outlines the opposed views on cultural contacts and cites evidence ranging from the botanical to the ethnographical to support his belief that men from the Mediterranean long ago influenced the early cultures of Meso- and South America. He describes his voyages from Africa to the Bahamas in reed boats which conclusively demonstrated that east-west crossings of the Atlantic were possible millennia ago. He also considers the New World legends, widely prevalent before the Spanish Conquest, of white, bearded gods whose physical attributes were strikingly European.

In North America, there have been numerous claims that Vikings and others had widely explored the continent. The 'evidence' for these claims is authoritatively discussed by Birgitta L. Wallace, a Research Assistant in the Section of Man at the Carnegie Museum.

Dr Betty J. Meggers, Research Associate at the Smithsonian Institution, looks to Asia instead of Europe. She postulates that as well as migrations across the Bering Straits there were trans-Pacific contacts with the Americas and her chapter develops this thesis.

The publishers would like to emphasize that, although the book is designed as an entity, not merely a collection of essays, each author has been at complete liberty to write exactly what he or she wished.

The publishers wish to thank Dr George Dawson of the London School of Economics for his translation of Dr Ingstad's contribution. They also wish to thank the staff of the British Museum and the British Cotton Institute for help in researching the book.

This chart, though based in part on the information contained in this book, is intended less to give exact dates than to provide, in graphic form, a time scale to serve as background to the book. A great many of the dates are conjectural or subject to controversy, their presence here must therefore not be taken as necessarily signifying acceptance by any or all of the contributors.

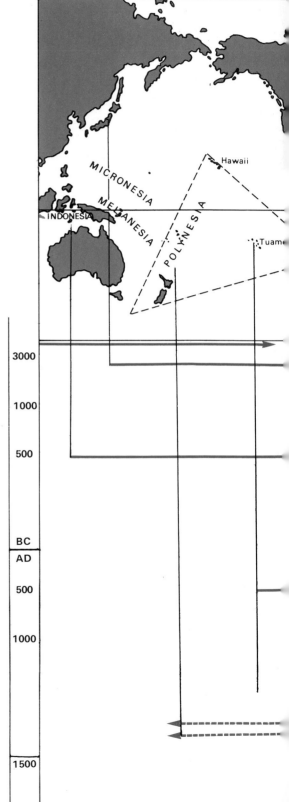

**New World**

*c.* 25000 BC Late Pleistocene Asiatic migrations by land and sea populate the New World

3113 Starting date of Maya Calendar

*c.* 3000 Jomon pottery introduced in Ecuador (Valdivia) from Japan

*c.* 2500 Earliest known use of cotton in the New World (Huaca Prieta)

1200 Earliest known Olmec ceremonial mounds and sculptures (San Lorenzo)

*c.* 500 Indonesian & S.E. Asiatic influence on Bahia culture of Ecuador

475 Discovery of Easter Island by the Peruvians

500 Discovery of Polynesia by the Peruvians

1121 Visit of Eirik, Bishop of Greenland, to Vinland

14th cent. Greenland has a population of about 4000

14th cent. Voyage of Manco Capac to Polynesia

1480 Inca Tupac Yupanqui sails to Polynesia (*Kon-Tiki* 1947)

end 15th cent. Destruction or abandonment of the Greenland settlement

1513 Balboa discovers the Pacific

1517 Córdoba sets foot in Yucatán

1519 Cortés lands at Vera Cruz

1531–2 Pizarro conquers Peru

# General Chronological Chart

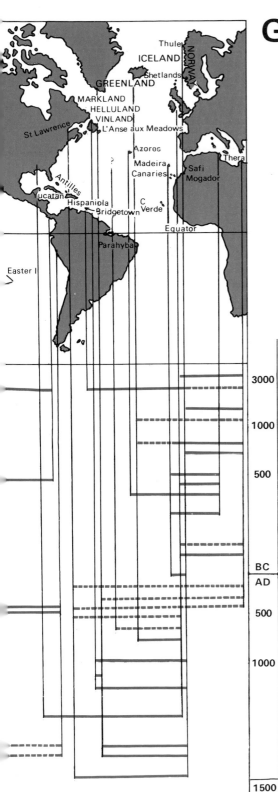

| | |
|---|---|
| 3000 | |
| 1000 | |
| 500 | |
| BC | |
| AD | |
| 500 | |
| 1000 | |
| 1500 | |

## Old World

3rd mill.    Megalithic invasions up west coast of Europe to Shetland Is.

c. 2700    Papyrus sea-going craft in Egypt [AD 1969–70 *Ra I* and *II* (Safi to Barbados)]

1475    Disappearance of Atlantis (Thera)

1400    Mycenaean trade routes to North Europe

1200    Ulysses, according to some, goes to Iceland (Calypso)

800    Homer: *Odyssey*

600    Phoenicians under Necho circumnavigate Africa (Parahyba inscription?)
    Carthaginians discover island of Mogador

525    Phocean *Periplous* quoted by Avienus in *Ora Maritima*, 4th cent. AD

500    Hanno sails south along African coast to Equator
    Himilco sails north up west coast of Europe to Cornwall
    Carthaginians discover Madeira and Azores (Corvo hoard)
    Carthaginian blockade of Straits of Gibraltar till 1st Punic war 264–241
    Midacritus imports tin from Cornwall

450    Herodotus: *Histories* (details on Necho, Hanno and Carthaginians in Atlantic)

350    Plato: *Timaeus* and *Critias* (Atlantis)
    Theopompus: *Tale of Silenus* (description of Hyperboreans, Britons?)

300    Pytheas of Marseilles circumnavigates Britain and mentions Thulē (Norway?)

241    End of 1st Punic war and Carthaginian blockade of Straits of Gibraltar

25 BC–AD 25    Juba of Morocco colonizes the Canary Is.

75    Plutarch: *Face in the Orb of the Moon* (mention of the St Lawrence estuary?)

2nd cent.    Pausanias: *Description of Greece* (voyage of Euphemus into the Atlantic?)

432–440    Proclus: *Commentary on Timaeus* (mention of Antilles?)

539–551    Saint Brendan, reputed voyages around the Atlantic

8th cent.    Islands of the Seven Cities of 'Brasil'

795    Dicuil mentions Irish monks reaching Thulē (Iceland?) and seeing the midnight sun

900–920    *Life of St Brendan* and *Navigatio*

1000    Icelanders under Eirik the Red and Leif Eiriksson reach Vinland (L'Anse aux Meadows)

1075    Adam of Bremen: *Adami gesta Hammaburgensis . . .*, mentions Vinland

12th cent.    Al-Idrisi implies knowledge of Caribs

1130    Ari Frode: *The Book of the Icelanders* mentions Vinland

1159    Abbot Nicholas of Munka-Tvera mentions Markland, Helluland and Vinland

1170    Prince Madoc of Wales reputedly sails to the West Indies and Mobile, Alabama

1347    *Icelandic Annals* mentions Markland

1360    Nicholas of Lynn goes to Greenland

1390    The Zeno brothers sail to Greenland and possibly America

c. 1440    The Vinland Map

1492    Columbus discovers the New World (Hispaniola)

*Ill. 1.* Throughout history and prehistory man always seems to have looked westward to new horizons beyond the sunset. This attitude of mind has not only influenced great explorers and philosophers, but also inspired the myths and legends of centuries. This nineteenth-century painting by Christian Krohg, showing Leif Eiriksson sighting America, typifies the spirit of 'quest' which has always lurked behind man's aspirations to follow the setting sun.

# Introduction

## Geoffrey Ashe

AMERICA IS 'THE NEW WORLD', even to its own citizens: those, at least, with European or Negro ancestry. It is thought of as a region *discovered,* and therefore different from such immemorial presences as Asia and Africa. This view is correct, not only for America's white and dark peoples but for the red also; though in their case the crucial event is farther back.

*Ill. 2*    Who did 'discover' America? That is what this book is about. Yet to define the theme is to restrict it. We do not really mean what we say. We must begin by re-stating the question in relation to the actual discovery, which was certainly made long before history by a party of unnamed savages.

America's aboriginal races are descended from Asian tribes that migrated across the Bering Strait, and perhaps along the chain of the Aleutian Islands. The first of them arrived in the late Pleistocene era, between 25,000 and 35,000 years ago. Huge sheets of ice, still expanding, had absorbed masses of water and lowered the sea-level. An isthmus linked the continents, and people could go over on foot. America was first settled in the same way as Britain was—by a land route over what is now sea—and, like Britain, was not completely cut off until about the seventh millennium before Christ.

The pioneer migrants were true explorers. Man had flourished in the Old World for ages before he found his way to the New. After that, his movement southwards from Alaska was very gradual. Once established in their New World, the incoming tribes developed a character of their own and ceased to be Asians. The break with the ancestral homeland, confirmed by the sea, was total. There is no proof that they retained any traces of distinctively Asian culture or language. At most a claim can be made for a few primitive magical notions. Nor, so far as we know, did anybody in Asia long remember the wanderers' departure, or wonder what had become of them.

Henceforth the two worlds were separate, oblivious of each other. Civilizations grew up in China, India, Babylonia, Egypt, Greece; they also grew up in Mexico and Peru, and on the face of it, independently. The cultures of the Old World can be related convincingly to each other, but not to those of America until 1492. After Columbus there was a general awareness of the New World in larger and larger portions of the Old, and a growing traffic between them. No one can dispute Columbus's credit for that final, irrevocable reunion. But, with the modern study of the Norse 'Vinland' voyages, it has become clear that he was not absolutely the first to resume contact. Moreover we have reason to doubt whether the Norse voyages alone give us the whole truth. The question then is actually this: who were Columbus's forerunners? When and how did anybody at all in the Old World— Norse or others; a minority however tiny, however little regarded— re-open a way to the New after the long divorce?

*Ill.* 1

At the very outset an objection may well be raised. Surely it is presumptuous to put the question this way round without also asking its converse: whether there was ever a reunion from the other side— an ancient discovery of the Old World by Americans, such as the Maya.

We should indeed ask the converse, and when we look to the Pacific it may well raise serious issues, as Thor Heyerdahl and Betty J. Meggers have shown. But historically it is chiefly the Atlantic that counts, and here the converse question leads to the same problems as the usual one, and need not be considered separately. It is cut down at once by the absence of evidence that the techniques required for Atlantic voyages, in any true sense, were known to the American nations. Accidents can happen, of course. Eskimos are said to have drifted over to Scotland in kayaks. There has also been discussion about some so-called Indians alleged by the Roman writer Pliny to have been picked up in a small boat off the coast of Germany about 60 BC (see p. 90). But our only real datum under this heading is a body of legend, mainly Mexican, concerning land over the eastward ocean. And as will appear, the legends never describe Americans as going to these lands; they describe alien, sea-borne visitors as coming from them. If they are evidence, they are evidence for Old World discoverers, posing the question 'Who?' It is in the Old World context that even the New World's clues must be studied. Therefore, the 'discovery of America' does mean that . . . even if we care to speculate about early Americans returning still earlier visits.

But to put Mexican legends in their place, and start resolutely from Columbus's side of the water, is not to get clear of mythological pitfalls. The intercontinental abyss has been a great breeder of dreams, from Atlantis onwards. Much of this debate has been clouded, not only by fantasy, but also by failure to recognize others' fantasies as what they are. Hence an amazing list of claimants. The honour of discovering America has been assigned to various Asian and African peoples—

*Ill.* 2

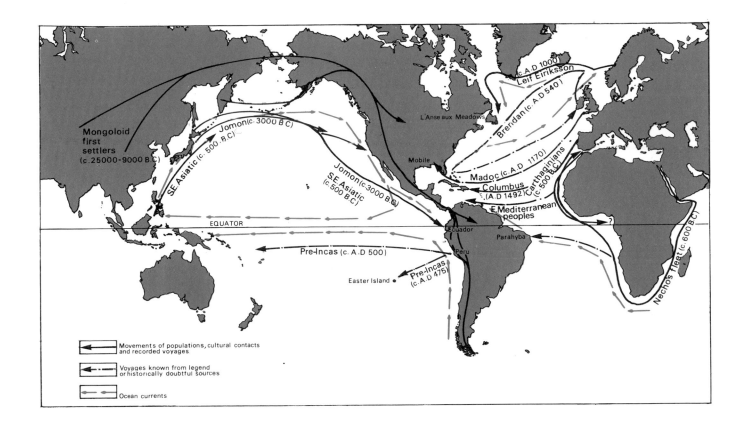

The following labels appear on the map:

Mongoloid first settlers (c.25000-9000 B.C)

Jomon(c.3000 B.C)

SE Asiatic (c.500 B.C)

SE Asiatic (c.500 B.C)

Jomon (c.3000 B.C)

EQUATOR

Pre-Incas (c. A.D 500)

Easter Island

Pre-Incas (c. A.D 475)

L'Anse aux Meadows

Mobile

(c.A.D 1000) Leif Eiriksson

Brendan (c. A.D 540)

Madoc (c.A.D 1170)

Columbus (A.D 1492)

Carthaginians (c.500 B.C)

E.Mediterranean peoples

Ecuador

Peru

Parahyba

Nechos fleet (c. 600 B.C)

Movements of populations, cultural contacts and recorded voyages

Voyages known from legend or historically doubtful sources

Ocean currents

*Ill. 2.* The discovery of America has, at one time or another, been attributed to many different peoples and explorers. This map shows the routes of the main discoverers—known, legendary and inferred—whose claims are the subject of this book.

Chinese, Japanese, Egyptians, Phoenicians, Hebrews, Arabs, Turks—as well as a broad selection of Europeans: Greeks and Romans, Irish and Welsh, Basques and Dutch, English and French and Portuguese. Some of the candidates have a genuine case to back them. Others have none. We must acknowledge not only such obvious factors as patriotic wishful thinking, but also far subtler motives.

The whole theme has a myth-making quality. For thousands of years the centre of human energies moved steadily westwards—from Babylonia to Greece, from Greece to Rome, from Rome to the lands beyond the Alps—so that America, the next step, became (if hazily) a postulate of imagination before it became a fact. As George Berkeley wrote, after the event:

> Westward the course of empire takes its way;
> The first four acts already past,
> A fifth shall close the drama with the day:
> Time's noblest offspring is the last.

When thinking men reached the fringe of Europe and looked beyond, the spell of the sunset, of the mysteries over the horizon, of the inevitable brooding on death and rebirth, would not let them alone. To quote another poet, A. E. Housman:

Comrade, look not on the west;
'Twill have the heart out of your breast;
'Twill take your thoughts and sink them far,
Leagues beyond the sunset bar.

Oh lad, I fear that yon's the sea
Where they fished for you and me,
And there, from whence we both were ta'en,
You and I shall drown again.

Those who know quite well what Housman is speaking of continue to ignore his warning and stare into the gulfs. Even now with its mysteries dispelled, the Atlantic can still be a place of quest and an 'Otherworld'. So it was, and more hauntingly, while its mysteries flourished. The Irish ocean-saga of St Brendan's voyage has perhaps the best claim of any such legend to a factual basis, yet it also has links with the cycle of legends about the Quest for the Holy Grail, and the Passing of Arthur.

For the Europeans who at length built the United States, this particular spell faded out. Their west was land, and they made the most of it. But thanks to their antecedents, the speculative impulse returned nevertheless. America had been discovered: how and when? On both sides of the Atlantic, the urge to believe—to believe in something before 1492 besides untenanted waters—has inspired not only memorable feats of imagination, but a harlequinade of grotesque theories which grab at the frailest props. One recent author, who at least realized that the 'case' for Theory A was as good as the 'case' for Theory B, accepted them wholesale and argued for a full dozen discoveries before Columbus. Another, convinced that South America was reached by Levantine traders centuries before Christ, published an ingenious interpretation of Edward Lear's *The Owl and the Pussy-Cat* under the impression that it was an ancient ballad to which the key— *i.e.* trade with America—had been lost.

Religion too has played its part. Surely nothing but a pre-conceived notion about the 'Chosen People' could have led anyone to contend, as some have contended, for a discovery of America by the Israelites —possibly the least nautical nation of antiquity. (In Jewish eyes, one of the allurements of the New Jerusalem was that there would be 'no more sea', a view angrily rejected by Kipling.) Beyond the more or less sane biblical theories we come to the wilder sort. In 1825 a philanthropist, Mordecai M. Noah, opened a reservation on Grand Island, N.Y., for Jewish refugees. He invited American Indians to join it as well, in the belief that they were the Lost Tribes of Israel. A few years later, Lord Kingsborough did valuable pioneer work on Mexican antiquities with a view to proving the same about the aboriginal Mexicans. The Lost Tribes, it seems, uprooted from

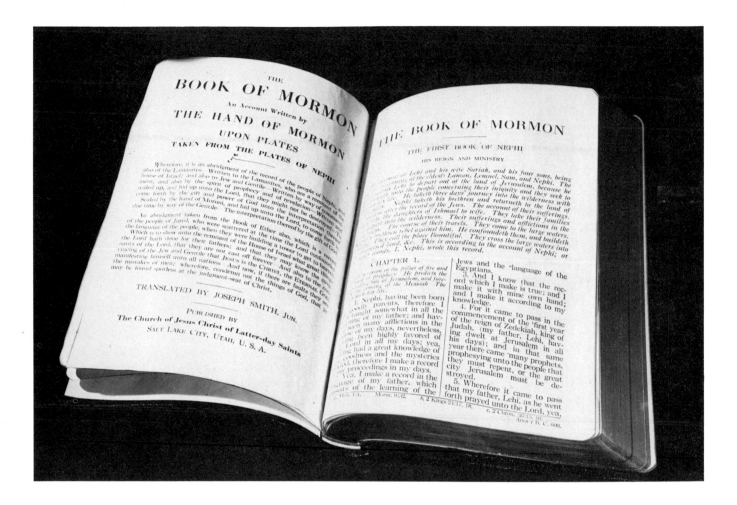

*Ills. 3, 4.* Left, a portrait of Joseph Smith, translator of the *Book of Mormon*, the title page and first page of which are illustrated above. The latter tells how Nephi and his brethren 'crossed the large waters into the promised land'—America.

Palestine in 721 BC, trekked through Asia and crossed the Bering Strait on the ice.

Meanwhile the backwoods prophet Joseph Smith had issued his *Book of Mormon,* which also traces the American cultures back to sea migrations by biblical peoples. Scholars belonging to the Mormon Church have tried to substantiate their prophet's teaching. They rely on the American legends already mentioned, which will be reviewed in their place. But it would be useless to pursue the Mormon 'history', as such, any farther. It is a series of unverifiable assertions. If Joseph Smith did receive a divine revelation, then it is true. If he did not, then it is almost certainly false. The nature of the prophet's experience is outside our present scope.

So much for the kind of theory we shall not be studying at all. But the rest raise difficulties too. Not one is based on objective records such as those that document Columbus's voyages. The Norse sagas come nearest, yet even they are oddly confused by mythical interweavings. One of the classic works in this field is Fridtjof Nansen's *In Northern Mists*. Nansen believed that Norsemen reached Canada in the early Middle Ages. Yet he felt bound to reject almost the whole of the 'Vinland' literature as being too vague, too inconsistent, too suspect in its details, and too much like admittedly fictitious matter from other sources. While later scholarship has taken a kinder view of the sagas, Nansen's book is an impressive witness to the quicksand nature of much of the evidence.

When we turn from Vikings to the more doubtful discoverers, the case is far worse. It should be said at once that we do not possess a single account of an early non-Norse voyage to America which even looks as if it were literally true. We shall seldom be dealing with outright truth or falsehood. We shall be dealing with indirections: for example, signs of an early knowledge of America, which leave us to guess where the knowledge came from. Also we shall be dealing with mythology, or near-mythology: with legends which are not true as they stand, yet cannot be dismissed, because they seem to have truth embedded in them.

The assessment of items of this latter sort is an issue which historians shy away from. They prefer to steer clear of legends entirely. When unable to do so, they often imply that a legend is of value only if it can be construed as having a kernel of truth—as consisting of a literal fact, plus fable and exaggeration which can be pruned away so as to leave the fact exposed. This is sometimes so, but not always. A legend can have historical value with no literal truth in it at all. Unless we grasp that, we may end up as sceptical as Nansen.

Here the classic text is a remark of the Victorian historian E. A. Freeman about the famous legends of Glastonbury, in Somerset: King Arthur's grave, St Joseph of Arimathea, the Holy Grail, and so forth. He wrote: 'We need not believe that the Glastonbury legends are records of facts; but the existence of those legends is a very great fact.' A story may be woven round a delusion, a feeling, a sense of awe, a piece of knowledge which is not explicit in the story itself. Yet the thing at the heart of it is a datum none the less, and perhaps illuminating.

In Freeman's instance, we may accept the verdict of scholarship that the story of Joseph and the Grail has no literal truth in it, and was invented long after the saint's alleged career in Britain. But the mistake of many scholars has been to stop there. The legend, even though factually untrue, points to a fact. It grew round a local tradition that Christians were at Glastonbury extremely early. It rationalized the tradition, so to speak, putting it in terms which people could understand. There is reason to think that Glastonbury's Christian past does go back a long way. There is also reason to think that the investigators who have reached this conclusion might never have done so if the legends, however fictitious, had not maintained an interest in Glastonbury and kept them at work.

The unsolved problem when confronting a legend like this is how to take it seriously without taking it literally. If we take it literally—or even insist on isolating some part of it, and taking that literally—then we may slide into romanticism, and contrive a case which the facts do not warrant. On the other hand, if we refuse to take it seriously, we may well miss important clues which it supplies. Most of the stories hinting at an early discovery of America have this quality.

Over the past hundred years the problem of legend and history has become more acute, and also more interesting, largely because of archaeology. In the 1870s Heinrich Schliemann worked on the site of Troy equipped with a private fortune and a naïve belief that the epics of Homer were true. In the face of academic ridicule he succeeded in digging up Troy, or rather several Troys, superimposed and jumbled. His triumph might have been an exceptional fluke. But in the course of time similar archaeological triumphs followed—at Mycenae and in Crete; in the Holy Land; in China and Mexico and the British Isles. Again and again, places designated in supposedly fabulous tales have turned out, when excavated, to give the tales a kind of support.

But—and this is the crux—only a kind of support. Not confirmation. Archaeology has not tended to promote legends from the status of worthless fiction to the status of historical records; it has tended to put them on a curious, baffling intermediate plane. Bronze-Age Troy does not really agree with the *Iliad*; the heroic civilization of Greece does not fully match Homer's description; and there is no archaeological proof that a single Homeric hero existed. Likewise with the much-exploited archaeology of the Holy Land. Despite all the books averring that 'the Bible is true', nobody has yet proved the reality of a single named biblical character earlier than King Omri of Israel, who comes long after Abraham and Moses and even David.

Schliemann and his followers were less wrong than the iconoclasts, and far more fruitful, even when they were badly wrong themselves. Where excavation can check legends at all, this has been a recurrent outcome. But it would be quite misguided to claim that Schliemann was right, or that he proved Homer to be reliable.

Inevitably, archaeology comes into the American question alongside legend; and inevitably it comes with the same hazards as at Troy and elsewhere . . . only more so. The literary clues used by Schliemann and the rest did at least guide them to exact spots where they could dig. Those concerned with the American question do not point with certainty to a single exact spot in America. Until recently it was hard to see how the archaeological checking process could even begin, unless by a stroke of luck. It does seem to have begun at one point, as Helge Ingstad will show. Otherwise the archaeology involves juggling with at least two unknowns. Mysterious finds, inscriptions, or ruins are noted in the New World. Attempts are then made to connect them with data in the Old, usually with hints at voyages by people who might have been responsible for them. But the hints themselves are at best cryptic, and at worst (to the doubter's eye) imperceptible. We have a mystery at both ends.

Such a situation may well be challenging and exhilarating. It is not scientific. This book will have served its purpose if it defines the problems, and suggests how researches which are not yet scientific may become so. If it points any particular way, I think it will be found to point to a need for concerted instead of disjointed efforts. Sir Mortimer Wheeler has lamented the handicap of specialization even in a far more exact field. The impact of Greek and Roman culture on Asia, he says, is a more obscure story than it should be, simply because the Orientalist may not know a Classical object when he sees it. Likewise, while it may be doubted whether Celtic objects (for example) exist in Mexico, it is all too likely that the Celticists who might recognize them never go there to take a look. They would be afraid of branding themselves as cranks.

As we pursue our multiple theme, we must not be afraid of that. Meanwhile, on the positive side, we should bear in mind the sound and sensible observation of Thor Heyerdahl:

> In order to penetrate ever further into their subjects, the host of specialists narrow their field and dig down deeper and deeper until they can't see each other from hole to hole. But the treasures their toil brings to light they place on the ground above. A different kind of specialist should be sitting there, the only one still missing. He would not go down any hole, but would stay on top and piece all the different facts together.

# The Speculations of the Old World

# 1    Analysis of the Legends

**Geoffrey Ashe**

## The Speculations of Antiquity

MOST OF THE LITERARY MATTER in which the legends occur is European. In order to assess it, the first thing to grasp is the nature of its content. At first, this is not so much factual information as pictures and patterns. Geography dawns as a collective work of art, a portrayal of the world, rooted in myth. Knowledge grows as traders, soldiers, pilgrims exchange reports, and details are filled in. But the pictures and patterns still dominate human minds, almost without exception, for century after century. Statements which seem to be geographical may really reflect some supposed logic in the design. This remains the case, if in varying degrees, right down to Columbus; it is still true, with tragi-comic irony, of Columbus himself; it cannot definitely be called a thing of the past until the eighteenth century.

*Ill. 45*

To embark on the problem by way of ancient Greece, as we must, requires that we start by asking not what the Greeks knew of the world but how they conceived it. For them, the 'Oecumene' (that is, the inhabited earth, the Roman *orbis terrarum*) was a disc of land with a jagged edge. They divided it into three sections—Europe, Asia (meaning as much of Asia as they knew), and Libya (meaning North Africa). Most of the rivers flowed directly or indirectly into the Mediterranean, the Inner Sea, which was itself a kind of super-river, flowing out via the Straits of Gibraltar into the Ocean. Even Ocean was at first conceived as a river, and the greatest of all. From a hidden place in the north it swept all round the Oecumene, past Britain and Spain and Libya, finally going north again round the far side of Asia. What happened in the Arctic to keep it moving was not clear. Most early geographers regarded the Caspian Sea as a bay, with an outlet into the eastern Ocean. Very few—Herodotus was one of the few—understood that the Caspian was enclosed, and that an Asian land-mass lay beyond it.

This picture took shape when the earth was thought of as flat. But it did not change much with the realization that it was round.

*Ill. 5.* Left, St Brendan and his followers stranded on the back of Jasconius, the friendly whale, from the medieval *St Brendan Codex*.

15

Pythagoras achieved that realization as far back as 530 BC. Plato and Aristotle followed him, and so did the Stoic philosophers, and geographers such as Eratosthenes and Strabo. However, when Greeks and Romans grasped that the earth was not only round but far larger than hitherto supposed, they still held to the old image of the world-island with Ocean girdling it; only, the Ocean was now admitted to be more than a mere ring of water.

Even at the earliest stage, when the picture was mainly a projection of myth without knowledge, we find one recurrent belief added to the others. Across Ocean to the westward, beyond Gaul and Spain and Morocco, there was something else. The end of the Oecumene was not the end of all land. Mythology told of the sunny plain of Elysium, and the Isles of the Blest, where heroes beloved of the gods might be translated without death. Out there too lay Erytheia, the Red Island, where Hercules went to capture Geryon's cattle.

*Ill. 6*

More or less in the same quarter was a country of exile to which Zeus, the king of the gods, had banished his deposed father, the Titan Cronus. Cronus had ruled the universe in the lost golden age before the triumph of the lords of Olympus. Atlas was another of the fallen Titans, and the western Ocean was named Atlantic after him. He himself had been turned into a mountain and planted in the nearby corner of Africa, where he upheld the sky on his shoulder. But most of the Titans were somewhere over the Ocean with their dethroned chief. Early myth-makers imagined Cronus in a dark, foggy prison, and the tract of Ocean northwest of the British Isles was sometimes called the Cronian Sea. Later, he was shifted southwards and given a consolation kingdom in the Isles of the Blest.

Such myths, in themselves, may point only to a vague speculative image of 'something there', doubtless influenced by a notion that the region of sunset must be an abode of the dead and departed. Homer portrays Odysseus as sailing out past Gibraltar, and crossing the Ocean transversely against its supposed southward-flowing current, to consult ghosts in the country of the 'fog-bound Cimmerians'. If these Cimmerians are anywhere they are in the British Isles. Britain was probably known dimly to the Homeric world through rumours borne along Mycenaean trade-routes, though it was afterwards lost sight of. Odysseus's crossing of the Ocean implies nothing more far-flung than that. Homer gives no hint of a route to America. (Schliemann thought he did; the last and strangest of the great archaeologist's projects was an excavation programme in the Canaries and Mexico; but he died before undertaking it, fortunately, perhaps, for his reputation.)

In literature nevertheless it was a Greek who did discover America, or rather invent it. Plato's fable of Atlantis, the Isle of Atlas, has inspired a whole library of comment and interpretation. However, its purely 'American' aspect can be summed up without deeper entanglement.

Atlantis, as presented by Plato about 350 BC in his dialogues *Timaeus* and *Critias,* is a philosophic myth. Partly through its general tone, partly through links with the earlier folk-myth of the Titans, it gives a new form to the Greek notion of a lost golden age with a western afterglow. Atlantis, we are told, was a huge island in the Ocean beyond Gibraltar. Nine thousand years ago it was the centre of a rich and glorious empire, wisely ruled by a confederation of kings. The empire extended far into Europe and Africa. But the Atlanteans lost their integrity and declined into imperial greed. They pushed eastwards, conquering nearly all the nations they attacked—but not quite all. The young republic of Athens defeated them and liberated their subjects. Then divine judgement fell on mankind in a tremendous night of storm and earthquake. The Athenian warriors were swallowed up in the earth, leaving a remnant only. Atlantis vanished under the sea. Shallows mark the area where it once was.

Plato (with the Greeks' wars against the Persians in mind) is suggesting in this fable that city-republics have a better moral fibre

*Ill. 7.* Atlas bearing the heavens on his shoulders. Throughout antiquity—and even to this day—the myth of Atlantis, the isle of Atlas, has captured popular imagination.

than empires, and more capacity for courage and regeneration. Few Greeks took Atlantis literally. Beyond reasonable doubt it is chiefly a superb fiction. Plato seems to have put it together by combining traditions about Minoan Crete with others about an Atlantic nation, based, possibly, on the megalithic culture that once spread over the western Mediterranean and the British Isles. The factual basis, so far as Atlantis has one, lies in the second millennium BC, Plato's chronology being a mere fancy or misunderstanding.

*Ills. 8, 9*

In any case there is nothing 'American' about Atlantis itself. But *Timaeus* contains one very odd, gratuitous detail. When speaking of the islanders and their empire, Plato says that their rule extended not only into Europe and Africa but also to a number of lesser Atlantic islands; and that there was a route from Atlantis, by way of these islands beyond it, to the 'opposite continent surrounding the Ocean'. There, also, the Atlanteans had colonies. In other words there was—and still is—a continental land-mass on the far side.

The lesser islands, and the opposite continent, play no part in the story and indeed raise difficulties. They are not liberated by the Athenians, nor do they sink with the parent realm; so even after the disasters, a good deal of the Atlantean Empire remains unaccounted for. Did Plato put them in because they were part of whatever tradition he was using? They curiously recall the actual northern route to America, the island-hopping Norse route via the British Isles, the Orkneys, the Faeroes, Iceland, Greenland.

Crossings in the megalithic era—say between 3000 and 1500 BC—would have been feasible. The megalith-builders did navigate the outer waters, they did come to the British Isles, reports of discoveries farther afield could have lingered on . . . and, at the strictly literary level, that is as much as we can say. Without written records, further guesswork is pointless; and, taken alone, Plato's text hardly even begins to be evidence. But it does begin to be intriguing, at least, when we find two other classical authors looking in the same direction and seeing the same thing. That continent across the Ocean turns up again twice. Both times, it turns up with the motif of a northern transit via Britain: once probably, once explicitly.

The first passage has been suspected of outright parody. Its author is Theopompus, one of Plato's younger contemporaries. The original is lost, but a Roman writer quotes part of it. This extract purports to be a legend about Silenus, the scandalous old comrade of the god Dionysus and the Satyrs. It relates how he visited King Midas (of the golden touch) and spun some extraordinary yarns to him.

Silenus, according to this, told Midas that beyond the known world and across the Ocean there is a continent of indefinite extent. He described its people—men twice our size, living twice as long—and some of its cities, notably Machimus, the city of war, and Eusebes,

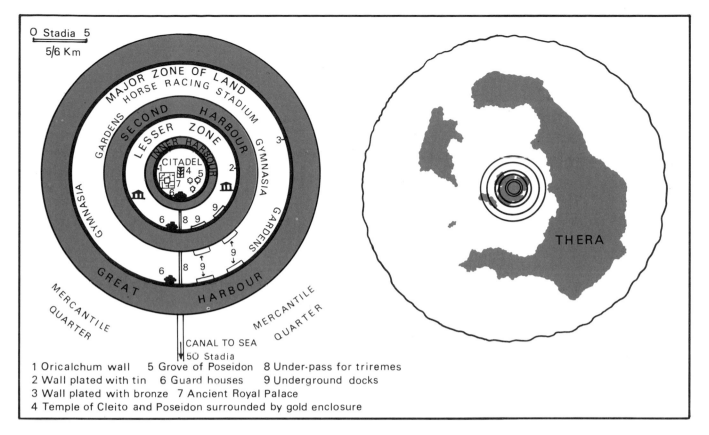

Scale: 0 Stadia 5 / 5/6 Km

MAJOR ZONE OF LAND
HORSE RACING STADIUM
GARDENS
SECOND HARBOUR
LESSER ZONE
INNER HARBOUR
CITADEL
GYMNASIA
GARDENS
GREAT HARBOUR
GYMNASIA
MERCANTILE QUARTER
MERCANTILE QUARTER
CANAL TO SEA
50 Stadia

THERA

1 Oricalchum wall          5 Grove of Poseidon    8 Under-pass for triremes
2 Wall plated with tin     6 Guard houses         9 Underground docks
3 Wall plated with bronze  7 Ancient Royal Palace
4 Temple of Cleito and Poseidon surrounded by gold enclosure

*Ills. 8, 9.* The account of the Atlantis myth by Plato (left) has misled generations of scholars. The destruction of the Minoan island of Thera (modern Santorini) by a volcanic eruption, *c.* 1470 BC, precipitating the downfall of the Minoan Empire, is now suspected to underlie the information given to Solon by the Egyptian priests and misinterpreted by him. The reconstructed map of the centre of Atlantis (above, left) shows the concentric canals and public buildings. Above right, the shape of the present island of Thera is superimposed, to the same scale, on the map of Atlantis as described by Plato (see p. 89).

*Ill. 10*

the city of peace. Among a medley of wild details comes a single arresting touch. The warlike Machimites once fitted out an expedition to invade our own world. They sailed over the Ocean and disembarked first in the land of the Hyperboreans. Thinking their mode of life 'mean and inglorious', they disdained to explore any farther, and returned home.

The point here is that while the Hyperboreans (dwellers-at-the-back-of-the-North-Wind) are speculated about in various ways by various authors, the account that comes nearest to giving them a credible home locates them in Britain. This is by Hecataeus of Abdera, who, like Theopompus, lived about the same time as Plato. Later Ptolemy, the most important of ancient geographers, calls the sea beyond Britain the Hyperborean Sea. Theopompus's story looks like an unfunny burlesque on Plato himself, or on whatever older ideas he elaborated. Yet the hint that the route between the Oecumene and the opposite continent is a northerly one, with a British terminus, fits in with the hypothesis of a dim tradition of northerly crossings somewhere in the Platonic background.

From this point of view, and from others, the third classical version of the opposite continent is remarkable, and deserves more attention than it has had. It occurs in a philosophical dialogue like Plato's, the work of Plutarch, one of the greatest of all sources of information on the Graeco-Roman world. Composed about AD 75, the dialogue professes to be a debate on 'The Face in the Orb of the Moon', but it ranges over a number of topics. In the course of it, a Carthaginian named Sextius Sulla tells a story which he claims to have heard from an unnamed stranger in Carthage.

Every thirty years, he declares, when the planet Saturn is in Taurus, parties of pilgrims set out from Britain to attend a sort of college at a shrine beyond the Atlantic. They sail west from Britain to another island—which is to be identified with Homer's 'Ogygian Isle'—where the midsummer nights are very brief. From there, later in the year, they row a further five or six hundred miles through a sea full of drifting debris and ice, to 'the great continent by which the Ocean is fringed'. They go on into a large bay, its outlet in about the same latitude as the 'outlet' (*i.e.* the misunderstood north end) of the Caspian Sea. Its coast is inhabited by Greeks, who call themselves 'continental' and say they are descended from Herakles. In the area are three islands, equidistant from Ogygia and from each other. One of them is the place of exile of Cronus, the fallen Titan, and is an island of wonderful beauty. Cronus lies asleep in a cave-shrine, dreaming oracular dreams, attended by a mysterious court, and fed by birds on ambrosia. Here the pilgrims pursue their studies. The narrator himself says he studied astronomy and philosophy here for a thirty-year period.

Some of the particulars given in Plutarch's dialogue warn us that we are dealing with matter that is not only largely fictitious but sometimes (where we can check it) impossible. Yet the 'map' remains intelligible enough to be interesting. The voyagers can be regarded as starting from the extreme north of Britain; sailing to southern Greenland; crossing the Davis Strait where it narrows to about six hundred miles; coasting round Labrador into the Gulf of St Lawrence; and landing on one of its islands, such as Cape Breton or Anticosti. The main outlet of the Gulf of St Lawrence actually is in about the same latitude as the north end of the Caspian Sea.

Whatever puzzles it creates, Plutarch's tale is derived from authentic information to some extent. He has not made it all up. Some of his account of the slumbering god in the sunset island appears again in another of his works. It is a genuine piece of British native mythology, collected in Britain. We do not know the god's actual name; the Greeks and Romans had an annoying habit of identifying other nations' gods with their own; but the being whom Plutarch calls Cronus is a Celtic deity, and the myth related of him is Celtic. Much later the British Celts were to adapt it to their half-deified King Arthur, who, it will be recalled, is either sleeping in a cave, or living on in the sunset island of Avalon; he derives from 'Cronus' in both aspects. Plutarch, or the speaker in his dialogue, cites British sources

*Ill. 10.* Head of a sculpture said to represent Plutarch, whose dialogue on 'The Face in the Orb of the Moon' seems to imply knowledge of a land across the western ocean.

for other details. Once again, perhaps, we get an elusive feeling of 'something there'—a hint at a northern voyage-tradition, mixed up with mythology and transmitted very confusedly southwards—but no solid clue.

It may be significant that Carthaginians are brought in; or it may not. As before, we lack the written materials which would be needed to form any opinion. Rome's annihilation of Carthage as a merchant metropolis almost destroyed whatever records existed of the seafaring of its people and their Phoenician forebears. We possess a few second-hand notes on their voyages round Africa, to Brittany, and to the fringes of the Sargasso Sea. The historian Diodorus Siculus mentions their accidental discovery of an island far out from Africa. He exaggerates its size and resources, but it seems to be Madeira. Also, to judge from a reported coin find in the eighteenth century, they may have reached the Azores. But we can get no farther. Various alleged traces of Phoenicians or Carthaginians in the New World will be considered later. For the moment, it must be said that no evidence at the European end takes them anywhere near America, or suggests that they knew even the congenial southern route, let alone the inclement northern one described by the Carthaginian in Plutarch.

Classical literature, therefore, leaves us with irritating bits and pieces which do not fit together, do not supply any verifiable ideas as to who may have reached the 'opposite continent', yet cannot be quite dismissed. The same applies to two further classical texts, by the guidebook-writer Pausanias and the philosopher Proclus, which do not mention the 'opposite continent' but may still have an American reference. However, they are best taken with another hypothesis, from another source altogether.

A detailed analysis of the knowledge of ancient voyagers, and its effect on the contents of the myths and legends outlined above, will be found in Chapter 2.

## The Speculations of the Middle Ages

Thus far, the only pre-Norse 'discovery' by Europeans which has achieved the status of a recognized theory is the Irish one.

Partly owing to advocacy of the wrong kind, based on over-sanguine answers to the wrong questions, this has taken a long time to win even the hesitant respect now conceded to it. Paul Gaffarel, the first thorough historian of the discovery of America, did accept it in 1892. He had few followers. Louis Gougaud, one of the most eminent of Celtic scholars, got as far as a very cautious 'perhaps'. H. G. Wells supported it—perhaps chiefly out of dislike for Columbus and all such devout Italians. Two biographers of Columbus himself, Charles Duff and Jean Merrien, have tentatively favoured the Irish claim; so has the archaeologist T. C. Lethbridge; and it has reappeared in a work by Carl O. Sauer, published under the auspices of a major American university. Its progress may well have been retarded by patriotic excesses, such as the assertion that the basic Irish-American stock is not descended from modern immigrants but from Irishmen settled in America since the dark ages.

The main source is the legend of St Brendan's voyage. Brendan, called 'the Navigator', is the patron saint of Kerry. His name is variously spelt. 'Brandan' is frequent. The highest peak on the Dingle peninsula—Lindbergh's landfall in 1927—is Brandon Mountain. He is a popular saint, widely commemorated in other place-names and in church dedications.

*Ills. 5, 24, 28*

Whatever he did in the way of voyaging, he was certainly a real person, outstanding in Irish church affairs, hardy and long-lived. Born in or near Tralee towards the close of the fifth century, he founded monasteries at Ardfert in Kerry and at Clonfert in Galway. He is said to have visited Wales and Brittany. In his old age he went to see St Columba at the latter's Scottish missionary community on the island of Iona. It appears likely that Brendan was away from Ireland for a long time at some earlier date, and that rumours grew round his absence. At any rate we presently find him described as going on a seven-year quest for a sort of paradise believed to lie over the Atlantic; as wandering far, and exploring many islands; and as finally reaching his goal, which was a vast and marvellous country an immense distance to the west of Erin.

In romantic form, his voyage enjoyed a popular vogue during the Middle Ages. It had, or acquired, mythological links with other Celtic-derived themes, such as the Grail Quest and the Passing of Arthur. In fact it was sometimes counted as part of the 'Matter of Britain' or Arthurian Cycle. Versions of it were composed in French, English, German, Norse, Dutch, Flemish, Provençal and Italian.

Clearly such a story must be approached with extreme caution. Even in its earliest, least embroidered forms, St Brendan's voyage is part of his legendary 'life' as composed more than three centuries after him. It is to be read as such, not as a literal record. The early saints, and especially Celtic saints, attracted masses of pious fable. With few exceptions their written 'lives' give only scraps of biography, almost buried under inflated apostolic exploits, and miracles allegedly worked for them and by them. St Brendan was genuinely famous for seafaring, as far as the Inner Hebrides, if no farther. His legendary 'life' therefore became a tale of sea-marvels as well as land-marvels, and the former, which were unusual, appealed more to audiences and grew to overshadow the rest.

Moreover, the story of the voyage to the great western land was affected by two factors peculiar to Ireland. Both must be understood before it can be evaluated.

*Ill. 11.* The type of ship in which Brendan made his voyages is still in use today off the coast of Ireland, although his boat was undoubtedly larger than this modern curragh. This photograph, looking across Brandon Bay, shows a view similar to the one St Brendan might have seen when he set off from his native country to the 'Land Promised to the Saints'.

*Ills. 11–13*

One was the custom of sea-pilgrimage. Over a period of two or three hundred years, many Irish monks besides Brendan made actual voyages; and as so often in legend-making, the most famous figure came to be credited with deeds not authentically his. Just as the Arthur of legend wins all the British victories against the Saxons, whereas the real Arthur probably won only some of them, so Brendan is made to have adventures which are based on those of other clerical wanderers. He is a hero summing up a whole epoch of Irish exploration.

But the monks' known achievements are striking enough to make an Irish discovery of America a serious issue, even if Brendan himself was not the true discoverer, and even if the true date was somewhat later. The monks originally used the Irish curragh or skin-boat, a seaworthy adaptation of the old British coracle. A light wooden frame was covered with greased ox-hides. The resultant craft, pointed at

23

both ends, could be propelled by oars, and it could also run before the wind with a square sail and probably tack after a fashion. If well handled it could lie low in the waves and ride out storms. The curraghs which are still built today by fishermen are small. In Brendan's time there were much larger ones, for crews of a dozen or more. To reach America in a curragh, and get back again, would have demanded great skill and great luck; but the things which Irishmen did do with these craft show that no arbitrary limit can be set to what they might have done—both in the early days and, still more, later, when they could apply their skill to the wooden ships introduced by the Norsemen.

Monastic sea-pilgrimage was a search for a 'desert': that is, an oceanic equivalent of the land desert where the monks of Egypt and Syria settled. Driven on by the longing to find a haven of peace, to escape from harassment by lay rulers and raiders, and to expiate their sins, Irish ascetics like Brendan pushed ever northwards: not merely into

*Ills. 14, 15*

> . . . the silence of the seas
> Among the farthest Hebrides,

but beyond. They were founding communities in the Orkneys about 579, in the Shetlands by 620, in the Faeroes about 670. The Irish geographer Dicuil describes a reconnaissance in Iceland, and north of it, towards the year 795. At the summer solstice, he says, it was so light throughout the night that the monks could see to pick the lice out of their shirts. At least one unintentional Arctic voyage had been made much earlier. Cormac, a pioneer in the Orkneys, was carried

The Method of Working up yᵉ Vessell used by yᵉ Wilde Irish; taken upon the Place by Capᵗ. Tho. Phillips.

*Ills. 12, 13.* Left, the oldest representation of a curragh carved on a stone pillar near Bantry in southwest Ireland. Dating from the eighth century AD, it is the only contemporary carving which does not show a Viking type of vessel. This boat is riding high on the water and has a long lifting bow with easy curves, very like the modern Irish curraghs (*Ill. 11*). The cross in the stern was still common in the seventeenth century, as can be seen from the illustration of curraghs 'ordinarily used by the wild Irish' (above right).

north by a strong wind for fourteen days. His crew apparently sighted no land, but, on getting home at last, they told of an onslaught by 'loathsome stinging creatures'. These were possibly Greenland mosquitoes, which swarm low over the water.

Besides the tradition of real seafaring by other monks as well as himself, Brendan's legend was influenced by mythology. As we have seen, Europeans who looked west had speculated for ages about the realms of sunset—Elysium, Atlantis, the abode of the banished Titans —but in Ireland these fancies took a more specific turn. With the invention of the curragh came a crop of tales about adventurers who had gone westward and found out. These Sinbad-the-Sailor yarns, the 'immrama', portrayed the Atlantic as full of islands where extraordinary beings lived—giant ants, red-hot pigs, vanishing women, men covered with hair; and where extraordinary things happened— demon horse-races, animals devouring each other, water hurtling overhead with fish tumbling out, choirs singing surrounded by flames.

It has been asserted that St Brendan's voyage is a mere clerical imitation of these yarns, a 'Christianized immram' with no separate interest of its own. This theory, however, fails to stand up under scrutiny. The literary relationship is simply not like that. While the immrama draw on pre-Christian myth, they are not pre-Christian themselves, or even particularly ancient. Of the four that survive complete, only one, the *Voyage of Bran,* is incontestably earlier than the tale of Brendan himself. None of the four is pagan as distinct from Christian, or even 'lay' as distinct from 'clerical'; they all include Christian motifs, and three have Christian characters, including monks; the difference is purely one of emphasis.

Behind the present text of the best-known immram, the *Voyage of Mael Duin* (adapted by Tennyson), there may be an older version which has influenced the Brendan legend a little. But in the text as it

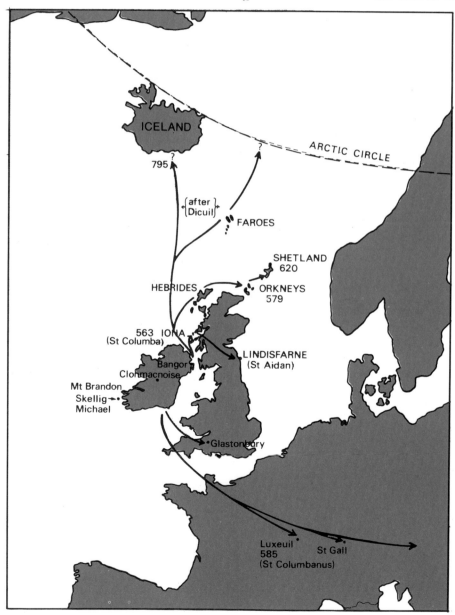

*Ill. 14.* This map shows the considerable distances that the Irish monks travelled in the period between the sixth and eighth centuries AD. In this context, a long voyage by St Brendan seems less improbable.

*Ill. 15.* It was to and from sea-girt 'deserts', such as this rocky island of Skellig Michael, that the missionary Irish monks set out on their voyages of discovery and evangelization.

stands there are plain traces of influence the other way, from the Brendan legend itself, which stands up as an independent work with a character of its own. None of the immrama contain the recognizable sea-lore, or the compass-bearings and kindred details, that give Brendan's alleged seafaring its peculiar interest. With none of them is it possible to draw the map, or identify any of the islands as actual places. None of them would have prompted a theory of an Irish discovery of America.

Because of various literary likenesses, it is not wholly unfair to speak of St Brendan's voyage as a Christian immram. But it is quite unfair to use this label as an excuse for brushing aside the geographic and historical claims that have been made for it. The fact that such claims can be made at all, whereas they would break down instantly if made (say) for the *Voyage of Mael Duin*, is sufficient proof of a difference in kind.

With which preliminaries we may go on to the voyage.

Written allusions to it begin to appear in the ninth century. They grow out of a lost process of oral development, and become fairly plentiful as time passes. For present purposes, however, the texts are three only, and two of these are supplementary to the third, which is the single real document.

First comes a passage in the 'life' of another saint, the Breton Machutus, *i.e.* Malo. This is thought to have been composed between

27

866 and 872. It relates how Machutus met Brendan at a monastery in Wales, and joined him in his search for the Isle of the Blest, called Yma. The account of the voyage is uninteresting, apart from one or two mythological details. But it testifies to a Brendan sea-saga being already familiar outside Ireland by the later ninth century.

Next is the narrative of the voyage given in the main official 'life' of Brendan himself. This exists in the *Book of Lismore* and elsewhere, a good deal enlarged. The original, composed early in the tenth century, has to be disinterred by clearing away all the later embellishments.

*Ill. 16*

It tells how an angel appeared to Brendan at Ardfert with the news that God had granted him a specially favoured retreat beyond the sea. The saint climbed to the summit of Brandon Mountain, and, with supernatural vision, got a glimpse of land far to the west. Putting his monks to work, he built three great curraghs with oars and sails, and they set out—'over the loud-voiced waves of the rough-crested sea, and over the billows of the greenish tide, and over the abysses of the wonderful, terrible, relentless ocean.' For months and years they wandered among islands. (Few of these are described at any length.) Every Easter a friendly whale joined them, and they landed on his back to celebrate Mass.

*Ill. 5*

After five years of futile quest, Brendan returned to Erin. His foster-mother Ita urged that the curragh was an unsuitable type of vessel, since it was made of slaughtered skins, and alien to the holy country which God had promised, where no blood was shed. Brendan moved to Connaught, built a large wooden ship, and set sail westwards from Aran with a crew of sixty. They came to several islands; at the first they were menaced by 'sea-cats', and at the second, by dark pygmies. On a third island they encountered a hermit, who told them the way to the promised land. They reached it at last, and found it 'odorous, flower-smooth, blessed'. Unfortunately there is a gap in the text here. We have no further particulars as to the size or nature of the land, nor do we know how Brendan got home.

This version has a few interesting touches. Thus, a sea-cat is described, and sounds rather like a walrus; while the pygmies recall the 'skraelings' of Norse saga, who are based on Eskimos. It would be rash to press any geographical claims. Yet even here, there is far more awareness of the real ocean than we get in the immrama. The practical detail of the change of boats is utterly foreign to their mad world, even though the reason given is a mystical one. The narrative in itself could not prove anything, and would hardly suggest anything, about a discovery of America. But it has an air of preserving memories and images which are more authentic than immram fantasy. Also it can help, once or twice, in elucidating the third and crucial text. This is the *Navigatio Sancti Brendani*: the *Voyage of St Brendan*.

The *Navigatio* is a Latin prose work written between 900 and 920, by an anonymous Irishman in Ireland. It deals with the voyage alone as a story in its own right, not as part of a complete 'life' of the saint. The author is writing a sort of Irish *Odyssey* round a hero already established as a seafarer, and his biographical pretensions are almost nil. Discussion of the factual basis was bedevilled for many years by misguided attempts to prune away legend and infer, or reconstruct, what the actual Brendan actually did. The true issue emerged only when these attempts were given up, and the correct question was asked: not 'What did Brendan actually do?' but 'What geographical knowledge does the *Navigatio* imply—even if its story is pure fiction?'

Any implied knowledge of America would still be prior to the recorded Viking voyages, and therefore interesting, whether the source of the knowledge was Irish or not. But the 'American' part cannot be isolated from the rest. The value of any alleged proofs must depend largely on our assessment of the *Navigatio* as a whole. We have to consider all the islands which it describes, all the passages between them, all the phenomena on the way, and decide whether or not we get the impression of a map (or something equivalent) underlying the tale. If we do, and only then, its references to land in the remote west are going to be worth scrutiny.

In outline the tale is this.

A monk named Barinthus visited St Brendan at Ardfert and told of a voyage he had made himself, westward through darkness, to the Land Promised to the Saints, 'which God will grant to those who succeed us in the latter days.' A land of unknown but certainly vast extent, it contained the Earthly Paradise. Barinthus's visit had been more or less magical and he did not know, or at any rate did not disclose, the route. Brendan resolved to look for this land. He built a curragh in a creek below Brandon Mountain, and set out with seventeen companions, three of them latecomers taken on as an afterthought.

They embarked about the summer solstice. For twelve days the boat drove westward, but then a change of wind carried it off course. After forty days at sea they sighted a rocky island to the north, with tall cliffs and a single cove. Going ashore with difficulty, they found a deserted building. One of the latecomers, detected in a theft, died and was left there.

Next they came by zigzag courses to the Island of Sheep, where these animals grew to an unusual size. A person lived on it described as 'the Procurator' (a monastic term meaning a kind of bursar or business manager) who gave them advice and food. They wintered on this island. On Easter Sunday they visited a nearby islet which turned out to be a whale, the one Brendan subsequently tamed and said Mass on. His name was Jasconius.

*Ill. 16.* A page from the *Book of Lismore*. The arrow indicates where the reference to St Brendan's voyage begins, which is translated as follows: 'So Brenainn, son of Finnlug, sailed then over the loud-voiced waves of the rough-crested sea, and over the billows of the greenish tide, and over the abysses of the wonderful, terrible, relentless ocean, where they saw the multitude of the furious red-mouthed monsters, with abundance of the great sea-whales. And they found beautiful marvellous islands, and yet they tarried not therein'.

*Ill. 17*

*Ill. 5*

Rounding the south tip of the Island of Sheep, they found another island across a narrow sound to the west, where singing birds abounded. It was called the Paradise of Birds. One of them could talk, and told Brendan that the birds were spirits in disguise—intermediate beings neither angel nor devil. It also prophesied six more years of voyaging.

The monks started off again eight days after Pentecost and 'tossed to and fro' for three months, coming at last to another island. On it was an Irish monastery founded by St Ailbe. The inmates had lived there for eighty years, preternaturally kept alive. Brendan's party stayed for Christmas, left early in January, and drifted until the beginning of Lent. The next island was rich in vegetation, but when they drank from one of its springs, several of them became stupefied.

Three days' sail north brought them into a calm where the sea was like a 'thick curdled mass'. Twenty days' further drift, followed by some sailing with a new wind, bore them back to the Island of Sheep and the assistance of the Procurator. Revisiting the talking bird on the island alongside, Brendan learned that he must follow the same pattern annually—Maundy Thursday on the Island of Sheep, Easter Sunday on the whale's back, Pentecost in the Paradise of Birds, Christmas on St Ailbe's Isle.

From the Paradise of Birds they started westwards again in June, and ploughed steadily on for forty days. A whale threatened them, but was killed by another sea-monster. They put in at a large island where the whale's carcase had drifted ashore, and hacked off pieces of it as food, but were then prevented from leaving for three months by rain and hail. When the weather improved they loaded the boat with herbs and roots, and departed in a northerly direction.

Here the continuity seems to break. No indication is given of the time or distance to the next port of call. We are merely informed that 'one day' the Irishmen sighted another island. It was flat, almost level with the water, and covered with flowers. This was the Island of Strong Men. Its inhabitants chanted hymns, the boys dressed in white, the young men in violet, the elders in purple. They presented the monks with a basket of *scaltae,* huge purple fruit yielding a pound of juice each. The second of the three latecomers remained here by his own wish. After fifteen days of further sailing, Brendan's crew encountered a bird of gorgeous plumage carrying a bough from an unknown tree, with a cluster of red grapes as big as apples. Seven days farther on was an island where the 'grape trees' grew. The trees were very close together. The air was wonderfully fragrant, 'like a house stored with pomegranates'. Many springs welled up. The vegetation was lush and varied, the grass intensely green.

After another gap, unspecified but probably long, the next glimpse of Brendan comes on a feast of St Peter. While he was celebrating

*Ill. 17.* Left, the island of St Kilda in the outer Hebrides would seem to fit the description of the first island that St Brendan came to after leaving Brandon Creek. The cliffs and cove answer to the description in the *Navigatio.*

this at sea, the crew noticed the marvellous clarity of the water below them. They could look down to the sea-bed where shoals of great fishes moved like flocks of sheep. As they watched, and as the saint sang his Mass louder, some of the fishes rose to the surface and circled round. With a steady breeze, the boat glided over this clear water for eight days.

On another day, again after an unstated interval, the voyagers came to a huge column in the sea, made, it seemed, of crystal. It was overhung by a canopy. They passed through an opening in the canopy and examined the column, which they could see stretching downwards into the water.

Leaving the column, they sailed eight days northward without rowing, to a rugged island covered with slag. Giants could be heard toiling at giant forges. One of them came out and threw burning slag at the boat. It fell in the sea and smoke rose up. As the Irishmen turned and fled, more of the giants threw more slag after them. The island blazed, the water seethed, fumes covered the ocean. Brendan said they were on the edge of hell.

After another gap in the narrative—the last—Brendan sights a high mountain in the sea to the north, with smoke belching from the top, and mists hovering round. Here the boat went ashore beside a black cliff. The last of the three latecomers was dragged off by demons. A wind carried the boat south again. Meanwhile the mists were seen to be clearing, and flames were spurting from the mountain.

The monks sailed south for a week and saw a cloud shaped like a man, swaying about on a rock amid ice-floes. It was the spirit of Judas, who, Brendan explained, was allowed a taste of the upper air every Sunday. Passing him by, they continued south for three days more. At the beginning of Lent they came to a circular islet a furlong round, rocky, bare, and steep. There was no place to beach the boat, but Brendan scrambled ashore and climbed with difficulty to the highest part. On a level patch towards the east side were two caves and a spring. Here lived Paul, an Irish hermit, who, like St Ailbe's disciples, was still healthy at an exceptional age—a hundred and forty.

Sailing away south again and then drifting, Brendan reached the Island of Sheep on Holy Saturday, two days late. After Pentecost the Procurator told him to fill his water-skins and make for the Land of Promise. The appointed years of wandering were accomplished. This time he would pilot them himself, and they would get there.

They sailed for forty days (manuscripts differ as to the direction) and entered a thick cloud. Out of this they emerged into sunshine and saw the Land of Promise. It was fruitful and warm, under a perpetual golden autumn. They traversed it on foot for forty days without sighting a farther shore, and arrived finally on the bank of a broad river flowing on beyond. A handsome young man advanced to meet

*Ill. 18.* A volcanic spring in the Furnas Valley on the island of St Michael in the Azores. These mineral waters are notoriously dangerous and this might well be the island where several of St Brendan's companions became stupefied on drinking the water.

them and told them it was time to go back. Christ had kept Brendan on his quest for seven years to reveal the 'mysteries in this immense ocean,' but now he stood on the confines of Paradise, and the pilgrimage was finished. Many years hence, in days of trouble, the Land of Promise would be shown to Brendan's successors as a refuge. Later again it would be made known to all Christendom. So Brendan led his companions back to the coast, loaded the boat with fruit, and sailed off through the cloud, arriving home without mishap.

Such is the scheme of the *Navigatio*. Some of its incidents are variants of incidents in the 'life', which, indeed, occasionally shed light on the meaning. The author, despite considerable skill as a storyteller, betrays that he is rehandling matter which he does not fully understand. Thus the important change of vessel, though dimly implied in one or two phrases, is never explicit in the text as we have it. Also the time-table does not work; or rather, it works only on the supposition that Brendan's quest is in two instalments, as the previous version says but the *Navigatio* never does. Both accounts may derive from an older one in which the saint's seven years of actual voyaging are spread over twelve. The dates that are indicated in the *Navigatio* make sense if Brendan starts out about 539 and attains his goal about 551, with an interval during the 540s.

As a literal exploit, of course, the voyage is incredible, even apart
*Ill. 24*  from its assorted fairy-tale elements; and the wooden ship, realistic in one way, is adverse in another, because there is no evidence that wooden ships were known in sixth-century Ireland. Brendan may have been exploring the Hebrides in 551, but it is most unlikely that

he was exploring the farther Atlantic. However, many students of the legend have been inclined to feel that there is something in it, in the sense that it reflects knowledge as well as dreams. With all its marvels the *Navigatio* is much more sober in tone than the immram romances, and less remote from oceanic realities. Several passages have precise parallels in the *Voyage of Mael Duin*, and in each instance it is the immram that adds really preposterous details.

In the upshot, when the descriptions of Brendan's islands are carefully studied, some of the flights of fancy can be discounted and at least three identifications emerge which are fairly safe. We have at least a toe-hold on the real map.

The Island of Sheep is Streymoy, the chief member of the Faeroes group. The name 'Faeroes' comes from a Danish word for 'sheep'. Since their importation in the seventh or eighth century by Gaelic-speaking colonists, including Irish monks, the animals have been central to the economy. Streymoy has place-names with Irish reference, including Brandansvik, Brandan's or Brendan's Creek.

The Paradise of Birds, across a narrow sound to the west, must then be Vagar. The sound is still called the Vestmanna Sound, the Sound of the West-Men or Irishmen, and Vagar is still noted for its avian life. Fowling is a major industry in such villages as Mykines. From March to August—a season that includes Brendan's visits—the bird-symphony is hard to equal. Guillemots, puffins, golden plovers, meadow-pipits, hooded crows, oyster-catchers, gulls, skuas: at least two hundred varieties have been catalogued. White birds mentioned

*Ill. 19.* Could the flat, almost level island covered with flowers, which the *Navigatio* calls the 'Island of Strong Men', have been one of the islands that make up the Bahamas? The fruit which the monks were offered there, and the description of the flora and fauna of the surrounding islands which St Brendan visited, do seem to hint at a tropical or subtropical climate.

in the *Navigatio* could be the kittiwakes and arctic terns that cover the ground in spring.

Dicuil, the Irishman who described the monks' trip to Iceland, wrote of the Faeroes in 825. The archipelago, he says, consists of 'small islands separated by narrow sounds, on which for about a hundred years there dwelt hermits who came from our fatherland; but even as these islands from the creation until then lay waste, so are they now, on account of the Norse pirates, deserted by these anchorites; but they swarm with innumerable sheep and an extra-ordinary number of sea-fowl.' In other words the essential points about the Faeroes were well known when the *Navigatio* was written, if anachronistic for the historical Brendan.

The Island of Sheep and the Paradise of Birds hint at a source in the general tradition of northward sea-pilgrimage. So does the fiery island inhabited by giant smiths. The description resembles early accounts of Iceland—specifically, the area round the huge active volcano Hekla. The Norsemen regarded this as the region of chaos at hell's gate. The same motif appears in the *Navigatio,* and the giants themselves go back to the classical myth of Etna as the Cyclopean forge, which an Irishman seeking to portray a volcano could have found in Virgil.

*Ill. 20*

For the other places, identification is more risky. Yet often the author supplies a descriptive touch that will fit one Atlantic island, or one zone, uniquely. By collating the work of several commentators, and using all the clues to direction and distance, it has proved possible to reconstruct what is supposed to be happening, in a way which at least arguably agrees with the map.

On this showing Brendan builds his curragh in Brandon Creek on the Dingle peninsula. He leaves about 20 June in, say, 539. After a longish sail he is swept off course and carried round by the prevailing westerlies to St Kilda, the outermost of the Hebrides. The cliffs and cove answer to the description. St Kilda has prehistoric ruins, and a chapel dedicated to Brendan.

*Ill. 17*

The monks then go north, like other sea-pilgrims, and come to the Faeroes and Streymoy. The whale, however strange his conduct, is a proper denizen of Faeroese waters. After Easter 540 Brendan crosses to Vagar and encounters the swarms of song-birds.

The next phase, beginning in June, is long and indefinite. St Ailbe's Isle is the hardest to make even a suggestion about. But in view of what comes after, it seems to be pictured as far south and west, and its long-lived residents give it a 'Fortunate Isle' air. Madeira has been proposed. Anyhow, the sequel takes the boat into the central Atlantic. The island with the bad water could be St Michael's in the Azores, where some of the mineral springs in the Furnas Valley are notoriously dangerous. The 'curdled sea' beyond can be paralleled in classical

*Ill. 18*

authors, and is certainly the Sargasso. The main Sargasso lies west of the Azores rather than north, but the weed spreads considerably. After getting clear of this, Brendan enters the Gulf Stream drift running northeast, picks up a westerly, and returns to Streymoy at Easter 541.

His next foray from Vagar takes him along the northern route to America, but he does not get there. Comparison with the corresponding part of the 'life' narrative (which enlarges on this episode, though putting it later) places him in and near southern Greenland, among whales and walruses. The dead whale's body is washed ashore on one of the many Greenland islands, and the Irishmen carve it up. The three months' foul weather from July onwards is an impressive touch. It is apt to Greenland, but scarcely to anywhere else. The 'herbs and roots' taken aboard are hints at a high latitude.

Brendan departs with wind and current, heading at first into the Davis Strait . . . but here the first break comes. When we rejoin him he is in tropical or sub-tropical seas, with magnificent birds, brilliant colours, opulent fruits. The flat island cannot be any of the mountainous ones in the nearer part of the Atlantic, but it could be in the Bahamas. Long Island, the 'Fernandina' of Columbus (who described it as 'very level'), is a good candidate. Or it might be Grand Cayman in the Caribbean, also extremely flat, and notable for its flowers. The grape island with its closely packed forest, varied vegetation, intense green and fragrant air, could be Jamaica. This

*Ill. 19*

island has more springs than any of the others, and Jamaica is like that: its name is Arawak and means 'abundance of waters'.

After further adventures only vaguely referred to, Brendan returns to Ireland in 543 or '44, and resumes his voyaging in 548 or '49. The undated story of the pellucid sea suggests the Bahamas again, the only extensive Atlantic region where such water is found. Coral dust is the cause, and anglers at Bimini are familiar with the great fish that break the surface—tuna, swordfish, sailfish, dolphins.

The crystal column is accepted by even sceptical commentators as an iceberg, seen, admittedly, through a poetic prism: a large iceberg drifting into warm water, with arches opened in it by melting, and an overhang. It is in the northern Atlantic, and Brendan goes northward from it (not exactly north, but into a higher rather than a lower latitude) in time to witness an eruption of an Iceland volcano.

The second mountain of smoke and fire is sighted in February 551. To judge from the sequel it is very far north indeed—there is still ice in the sea a week's sail south of it—and Jan Mayen may be meant. *Ill. 21* Its chief volcano, Beerenberg, is no longer active, but one of the lower cones was observed erupting in 1818.

Judas's rock is a promontory of eastern Iceland. Paul's steep islet is Rockall, which has no beach for a boat, but can be climbed (just) *Ill. 22* and has a ledge near the summit. The author places it too near Iceland. Hence he starts Brendan off from it in the wrong direction for his passage to Streymoy.

The final trans-oceanic sweep to the Land of Promise, during the summer of 551, unfortunately raises another query about direction. Manuscript evidence suggests that the author gave no compass-bearing, wishing to keep an air of mystery, but that an early confusion led to interpolations which disagree. (The first known transcript of Columbus's Journal mixes up 'east' and 'west' likewise.) However, Barinthus's story at the beginning of the *Navigatio* does say 'west', and it is fair to assume that Brendan goes the same way. The cloud which he sails into can be a fog on the Newfoundland Banks. He passes Nova Scotia and makes his landfall on what is now the Atlantic seaboard of the United States. Some optimists have been more precise, taking him in all seriousness into Chesapeake Bay and up-country to the Ohio River. Anyway, his return to Ireland is direct.

What then shall we conclude about the *Navigatio*? The author's arguable knowledge of the Atlantic is extensive, and does include parts of the New World. It is arguable only, and far from proved. Yet the reconstruction is not selective; it is not confined to a few passages that work, embedded in a mass of nonsense; it covers the whole voyage and accounts for every place visited. The text's implications as to wind and current are acceptable, and most of the distances are as good as those given in early books unquestionably dealing with

*Ill. 22.* Rockall, a lonely, gale-swept pinnacle of rock in the North Atlantic—Paul's 'steep islet'?

real places. They are not stated in miles but in a 'day's sail' unit such as was used by the Norsemen, and its length here can be inferred roughly. Several of the features used for identification, moreover, are exact. They are not generalities that could apply to many islands. The bad water suggests St Michael's and not, say, Bermuda. The flat flowery island has to be in the West Indies area if it is anywhere at all.

*Ill. 23*

Surprising as it sounds, a careful survey of possible sources reveals that most of the implied 'map' underlying the *Navigatio* could have been drawn by a sufficiently learned tenth-century Irishman. Most of it could have been assembled from classical geographers, from previous Irish writers such as Dicuil, and from oral reports of voyages known to have been made. By the tenth century, it should be recalled, an Irishman could consult Norsemen. A query hangs over the Azores; but even there, it is possible to believe in a tradition of some kind, deriving perhaps from the Carthaginians. Dicuil himself seems to allude to the Azores under the mythological name of the Hesperides.

So the case for an active, well-informed mind behind the *Navigatio*, building up the story as a skilful fantasia on a map of the Atlantic, is strong enough to command respect for its 'American' scenes. But enthusiasts for an Irish discovery have tended to stress the wrong ones.

The continental Land of Promise may look temptingly like North America. And yet it remains featureless. We get none of the vivid particulars that make some of Brendan's islands so interesting. The sad truth is that literary fancy would fully account for it, without the need to postulate a discovery. It could derive from Plato, or, more probably, from certain academic notions about a continent 'balancing' the Eurasian land-mass, and an Earthly Paradise over the ocean. Several earlier authors had aired such themes: the chief names are Crates of Mallus, Macrobius, Martianus Capella, and Cosmas Indicopleustes. Macrobius and Martianus, who wrote in the fifth century AD, describe a spherical earth with continents neatly balancing each other. This conception was taken up by such medieval scholars as Bede, Giraldus Cambrensis, Robert Grosseteste. It may of course go back to ancient discoveries, but it may perfectly well be no more than an exercise in symmetry. Minds that were governed by philosophy or theology rather than geography assumed that there 'ought' to be a continent round the other side from Europe and Asia—therefore, God being tidy-minded, there was.

Again, it is quite true that the Earthly Paradise was always located in the east; but if the world is round (and educated Irishmen did know that), then, presumably, one could reach Paradise by sailing west and entering at the back door. This is probably what Brendan is meant to be doing. Columbus himself had the same idea. When he found the Orinoco he conjectured that it was the Gihon (*Genesis* II, 13) and that the Earthly Paradise was in South America.

In other words, Brendan's Land of Promise, however beguiling, can be explained along these lines as a literary-religious figment. The real American interest of the *Navigatio* lies elsewhere, in certain loose ends. The 'West Indian' passages cannot be thus explained. They are oddly adrift, not related to the rest of the map as everything else is. With all their fabulous touches they contain curious hints of observation, at not so very many removes. Some of the features have antecedents in myth, or in immram matter, but some have not. The transparent sea is specially interesting, because in this case we have a specific immram counterpart. Mael Duin also passes over a transparent sea . . . only, with that fictitious hero, it soon becomes blatantly absurd. He looks down at mansions and herds of cattle on the bottom. The Brendan version, which is more or less realistic, must be the original. The immram version has strayed off from the real thing into a fairy-tale. But who reported the real thing in the first place? Could an Irishman have got hold of an authentic account of the West Indies, and if so, how?

The question takes us into a near-vacuum. Conceivably of course, the Vikings began their major exploring earlier than we are led to think, and got to the Indies by Columbus's southern route before the

*Navigatio* was composed. Assertions have been made about weapons found in Central America and a 'rune stone' in Oklahoma. Apart from such Norse guesswork—and it is no more—two paragraphs have occasionally been cited from classical authors as suggesting a knowledge of the West Indies in Graeco-Roman times.

It will be recalled that the disreputable figure of Silenus appears in legend talking of land across the Ocean. Very little can be made of his outpouring to Midas. But in the second century AD Pausanias, author of a sober and valuable *Description of Greece,* reverts to the topic. There was, it transpires, a stone on the Acropolis which Silenus was alleged to have sat on. Pausanias describes it, and then continues:

> The oldest of the Satyrs they call Sileni. Wishing to know better than most people who the Satyrs are I have inquired from many about this very point. Euphemus the Carian said that on a voyage to Italy he was driven out of his course by winds and was carried into the Outer Sea, beyond the course of seamen. He affirmed that there were many uninhabited islands, while in others lived wild

*Ill. 23.* Reconstruction of a map of the North Atlantic showing the various places Brendan visited according to the *Navigatio*. While few exact locations can be deduced with certainty, the text gives general directions from which this pictorial survey (not drawn to scale) has been compiled.

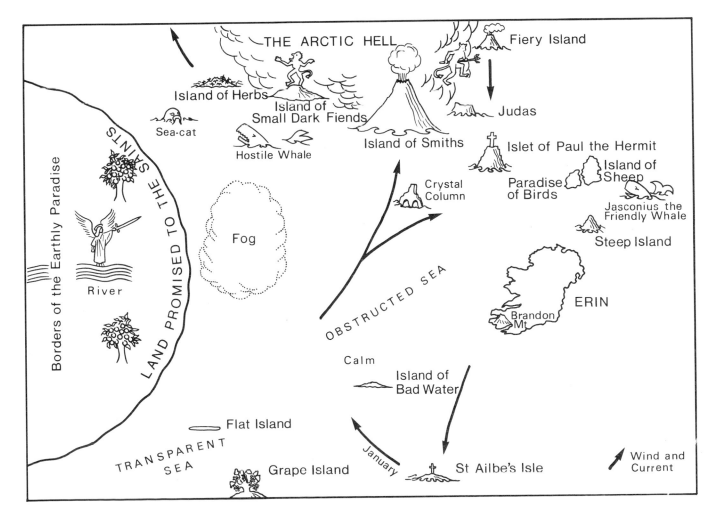

men. The sailors did not wish to put in at the latter, because, having put in before, they had some experience of the inhabitants, but on this occasion they had no choice in the matter. The islands were called Satyrides by the sailors, and the inhabitants were red haired, and had upon their flanks tails not much smaller than those of horses. As soon as they caught sight of their visitors, they ran down to the ship without uttering a cry and assaulted the women in the ship. At last the sailors in fear cast a foreign woman on to the islands. Her the Satyrs outraged not only in the usual way, but also in a most shocking manner.

Far-fetched as Euphemus's misadventure sounds, he could have been swept out of the Mediterranean by an east wind; the same is known to have happened to another Greek seafarer. The Satyr story itself would no doubt always have been dismissed as rubbish if it were not that Lafitau, an early authority on the West Indies, describes the former Carib inhabitants as smearing their heads red, putting on horses' tails, and indulging in brutish orgies. On that ground it has been urged (though not often, and perhaps not very forcefully) that the Satyrides were in the West Indies, being probably the Lesser Antilles.

*Ills. 26, 27*

The second classical text also refers to the Antilles if it refers to anything. Between 432 and 440 AD, the philosopher Proclus composed a commentary on Plato's *Timaeus,* which contains one of his passages on Atlantis. Unlike most of the Greeks, Proclus believed in Atlantis literally. He quotes what purports to be an independent tradition, at third hand or worse, from an ill-located source.

> That such and so great an island [as Atlantis] once existed, is evident from what is said by certain historians respecting what pertains to the external sea. For according to them, there were seven islands in that sea, in their times, sacred to Proserpina, and also three others of an immense extent, one of which was sacred to Pluto, another to Ammon, and the middle (or second) of these to Neptune, the magnitude of which was a thousand stadia. They also add, that the inhabitants of it preserved the remembrance from their ancestors, of the Atlantic island which existed there, and was truly prodigiously great; which island for many periods had dominion over all the islands in the Atlantic sea, and was itself likewise sacred to Neptune. These things, therefore, Marcellus writes in his Ethiopic History.

We may set aside the religious trappings and confine ourselves to geography. The seven smaller islands could be the principal Lesser Antilles, for which seven is a fair round number: say Guadeloupe, Dominica, Martinique, St Lucia, Barbados, St Vincent and Grenada. The three larger ones would then be the Greater Antilles, Cuba, Haiti

*Ill. 24.* Right, among the many ▶ monsters met by St Brendan was this siren, depicted in the *St Brendan Codex.*

and Puerto Rico. By Mediterranean standards they are all big, and the middle one, Haiti, is about a thousand stadia (somewhat over a hundred miles) across. Furthermore, the Caribs and Haitian aborigines discovered by the Spanish had a tradition that many of the Antilles had once been joined up as a single far larger island, but that some ancient cataclysm had split it apart.

Still, neither Pausanias nor Proclus is helpful. The most we can affirm is that *if* they are drawing on any garbled reports from real voyagers to the West Indies, and *if* the quite different *Navigatio* details come from the same source, then the voyagers were not Irish monks. On this ground and others, it is clear that the problem of the Irish discovery of America would be better described as the problem of Irish knowledge of America.

But the champions of Ireland would like to believe that St Brendan, or countrymen of his, did the discovering themselves; and there is a separate clue which they have stressed, although it does not help with the West Indies. Here again they have weakened the evidence by trying to link it up with Brendan in person. Yet it remains evidence . . . of something. The fact is that the same literature which attests the Vikings' exploration of Iceland, Greenland, and 'Vinland the Good' beyond, also attests the Vikings' own belief that Irishmen were ahead of them—certainly for some of the way, and perhaps for all of it.

The *Landnamabok* of the Icelander Ari Frode, written about 1130, says that 'before Iceland was peopled from Norway there were in it the men whom the Northmen call Papar' (*i.e.* Irish clerics), who went away leaving 'Irish books, bells, and croziers'. This tallies adequately with Dicuil's paragraph on the monks who reconnoitred 'Thulē', as he calls Iceland, towards 795 and picked the lice out of their shirts in its lucid summer midnight. Ari refers to Iceland as 'Tili' and speaks of longer intercommunication between Tili and Ireland. An Irish monastery flourished for several decades at Kirkjubaer in the southeast.

As to where the departed inmates went, nothing is known. They may well have fled as the Norsemen approached, after 860; and there are hints that they were thought to have gone farther on, into regions not yet reached by the spoilers. The *Landnamabok* gives the oldest of all reports of a Norse voyage out Vinland way, and this, despite its date, is seldom treated respectfully in debates on Vinland because it raises such acute problems of another sort.

About 983, it declares, while Eirik the Red was studying Greenland, a fellow-Viking made an accidental landfall beyond.

Ari Marsson . . . was driven across the sea by heavy gales to *Hvitramannaland,* which by some is called 'Great Ireland'. It lies westward in the sea near Vinland the Good. It is said that one can sail thither [from Ireland] in six days. Ari could not escape thence,

*Ill. 25.* Left, an Attic red-figure stamnos, *c.* 490 BC, from Vulci. Odysseus is shown tied to the mast as his ship passes the rocky island of the Sirens. The ship is drawn in considerable detail: note the rings at the mast-head for the halyards, the brailing ropes bunched at the stern, and the braces at the end of the yard. A recent suggestion (by A. F. Tilley, *Antiquity* 44, 1970) that the artist envisaged the oarsmen rowing *three* abreast, would explain the discrepancy between the number of heads and the number of oars.

*Ills. 26, 27.* The story of Euphemus as recounted by Pausanias may possibly imply a vague knowledge of the Carib inhabitants of the West Indies. Another tantalizing pre-Columbian mention occurs in Al-Idrisi, the twelfth-century Arab geographer and cartographer, quoted by George Glas in *A History of the Discovery and Conquest of the Canary Islands,* 1764. Speaking of the Atlantic Ocean, he says: 'In this sea is also an island "Saun" in which is found a kind of men like women, having their eye teeth sticking out, their eyes like lightning, their breath like the smoke of burning wood and speaking an unintelligible language. They fight sea beasts and the men

and was baptized there. This was first told by Hrafni Hlymreksfari, who had been long himself in Hlymrek [Limerick] in Ireland. Thorkel Gellisson stated also that Icelanders had told, according to what they had heard from Thorfinn, Earl of the Orkneys, that Ari had been seen and recognized in *Hvitramannaland,* from which he was not allowed to depart, but that he was otherwise held in great esteem there.

The bracketed words 'from Ireland' are of doubtful authenticity. 'Great Ireland' is *Irland-ed-Mikla,* Ireland-the-Great, and its alternative name *Hvitramannaland* means 'White Men's Land'. If Ari was baptized there, it had a Christian population.

The same country appears in the *Saga of Eirik the Red,* written down during the thirteenth century. The *Saga* is one of the chief documents for Norse voyages to various portions of the New World. In 'Markland', probably on the Labrador coast, a Norse party heard from the natives about a land 'on the other side, opposite their land', where men in white garments walked along shouting, carrying poles with cloths attached. This the Norsemen guessed to be 'Hvitramannaland or Great Ireland'. Obviously the white-garbed men could be monks walking in procession.

*Ill. 70*

Also, the *Eyrbyggja Saga* tells of a merchant named Gudleif. While sailing round Ireland on the way to Iceland, he was carried off west are only distinguished from the women by the organs of generation. They have no beards and are clothed with the leaves of trees.' This account, which to its readers would have seemed fabulous, contains some appearance of truth in that the Indians of America have no beards and to those who first saw them smoking tobacco, their breath would have seemed like the smoke of burning wood. These illustrations show a sixteenth-century artist's impression of the Caribs practising cannibalism (left) and smoking and wearing feather or leaf headdresses (right). The men, although resembling Europeans, are shown beardless.

and southwest by a gale. After a long time at sea he reached a coast where he was captured by foreigners whom he 'deemed' to be speaking Gaelic. A tall white-haired Norseman rode up to rescue him, and turned out to be Björn the Broadwicker, who had himself been swept away by a gale from Iceland some years before.

The frequent dismissal of these stories seems to be due solely to their being awkward. As Nansen remarked, Great Ireland rests on just the same sort of testimony as all the remoter Norse discoveries; and the others are accepted. The Ari Marsson report is actually better than the sagas as evidence, being earlier. The name 'Great Ireland' is like 'Magna Graecia', which meant the area of Greek settlement in Italy: it is most easily construed as referring to a colony. The 'six days' sail', even if counted from Ireland, cannot be invoked to discredit the whole story. Several documents show that the Norsemen underestimated the width of the ocean. A statement about an impossibly brief crossing does not invalidate what is said to be at the other end.

Attempts have accordingly been made to trace Irish refugee monks all the way to America, and locate Great Ireland there. It is not beyond credence. The people met by the Norsemen could have been descendants of monks and native women, still nominally Christian and talking a debased Gaelic. However, most advocates of this theory have overlooked a text which explains Great Ireland more simply.

It occurs in the *Description of the World* by the twelfth-century Arab geographer Al-Idrisi. In some notes on Atlantic distances, probably taken from a Scandinavian source, Al-Idrisi says that 'from the extremity of Iceland to that of Ireland-the-Great' (*Irlandah-al-Kabirah*) the sailing time is 'one day'. Al-Idrisi, like the Norsemen, tends to understate. But even if we double or triple his sailing time, it can only point to a single place—Greenland. An identification of White Men's Land as an Irish-founded settlement, not in America but somewhere in Greenland, covers the data well enough. Ari Frode's assertion that it was 'westward near Vinland' merely reflects the fact that Norse Greenland was the point of departure for Vinland expeditions; Greenland does lie 'opposite' Labrador; and while the wind that caught Gudleif did not start him in that direction, he might have picked up a different wind later, and hit Greenland while trying to get to Iceland as he intended. The Great Ireland texts, therefore, fail to support an Irish discovery of America. But they do suggest Irish pioneering beyond Iceland, and strengthen the likelihood that rumours about this part of the world may have gone into the *Navigatio*.

The conclusion is unaffected. The Irish problem is primarily one of knowledge. This remains, even when it is admitted that the case for a discovery by actual voyaging Irishmen is weak.

It has been surmised that other tales of Hibernian ventures (real or fancied) may have coloured the Norse narratives of land to the west. The basic material on 'Vinland the Good', 'Helluland', and 'Markland' is contained in a paragraph from the geographer Adam of Bremen; in the sagas; and—subject to an unresolved query—in the Vinland Map. *Ill. 84*

*Ills. 70, 150*

The whereabouts of these places will be discussed by Helge Ingstad. On literary grounds alone, Markland is the most fully credible, because of the brevity and baldness of some of the allusions to it. We are told of Greenlanders going over to it for timber, very much as a matter of course. It was doubtless in Labrador. There is no longer any doubt that Leif Eiriksson and others did reach North America. Yet even so, *Ill. 1* the peculiarities of Vinland should keep us on guard when dealing with literary evidence. With every allowance made for changes of climate, the descriptions still seem to make it improbably warm, improbably far south, too much like the Fortunate Isles; and according to the Gripla Geography, an Icelandic text, it was believed by some to be part of Africa. Nansen argued that Vinland was a fiction *Ill. 243* based on Brendan's tropical island of grapes, his 'Jamaica'. While this is taking scepticism too far, the saga authors may well have known the Irish tale of a warm western isle, and their portraits of Vinland may have been distorted by the delusion that it was the same place.

(Just as Columbus tried to force his own discoveries into agreement with Asia, presenting Cuba as Japan, Panama as Malaya.)

When we proceed to non-Norse medieval matter, we do find—and the fact is suggestive—that it is Brendan's 'Jamaica', not the Land of Promise itself, which keeps the Irish tradition alive. Rightly, it carries more conviction as an actual place. During the twelfth century 'St Brandan's Isle' begins to turn up in geographical writings and maps. It is always southwest of Europe, and moves gradually farther away with the disillusioning progress of exploration. In 1448 a map by Bianco shows it multiplied as 'St Brandan's or the Fortunate Isles' west of the Azores. In 1492, just before Columbus's sailing, the globe-maker Martin Behaim puts a large St Brandan's Isle near the actual location of the mouth of the Amazon; and the Vinland Map also makes it large, but not so far west.

*Ill. 246*

A second phantasm which seems to be Irish-inspired is 'Brazil', located by medieval charts in various parts of the North Atlantic. It is neither the Hy-Brasil of folklore nor an inspired prevision of the familiar territory, but an island seriously thought to exist. During the 1490s several expeditions sailed from Bristol to look for it. The name may come from the Irish *breas-ail*, meaning 'very good' or 'blessed', in which case we may have nothing more here than a further variation on the Fortunate Isle theme. Both Brazil and St Brandan's Isle are sometimes equated with a supposed 'Perdita', which is constantly being sighted by chance and then lost again. A Spanish romancer even transfers to Brazil the role of the Avalon of Welsh legend, saying King Arthur was taken to it after his last battle.

These fancies are outgrowths of a medieval Atlantic-mythos that dotted the ocean with archipelagoes. It will have become clear that compulsive island-making is a troublesome quirk of the human imagination. Long before medieval Christendom took to it, Plato spoke not only of his Atlantis but of those other islands which belonged to its empire. The Irish *Voyage of Bran* assures us that there are 150 western islands, all bigger than Erin, and Mael Duin visits twenty-nine. The Arab Al-Idrisi puts the figure at 27,000. In this welter of fantasy the traces of solid Irish knowledge fade out. As soon as we leave the *Navigatio* behind, and look at medieval maps or at the popular adaptations of Brendan's adventures, we lose touch with any possible reality. The map-makers and romancers are merely repeating names, episodes and motifs which they do not understand, and confuse beyond redemption. Traditions of Brendan survived to influence Columbus, but as general hints only, not sailing directions.

In the last analysis, while only the Norse case is firmly acceptable, the Irish—if properly stated—retains some importance. Whatever the data imply, they are previous to the known Norse voyages, and hence not derived from reports of them. The same cannot be said of the other pre-Columbian stories, such as they are. Indeed, to the extent that they look to America at all, they are only very doubtfully pre-Columbian.

An essential distinction here is not always drawn. Medieval Europe's fantasies of 'land to the west' seldom or never evoked a continent. They come within our present scope, not because of hints at America which they do not give, but because of their effect on explorers who finally did open up the way across—as will appear. The non-Irish Atlantic mythology is important chiefly as a psychological context.

It expanded, during and after the Middle Ages, to include many other named islands besides St Brandan's and Brazil. Southwest of Erin supposedly lay the crescent-shaped 'Mayda', a Moorish-inspired figment. 'Daculi' was in the seas west of Scotland. Iceland generated two shadows of itself, 'Frisland' and 'Stokafixa'—otherwise 'stock-fish'. There were further islands associated with saints, and some associated with devils. Several 'Green Islands' irresponsibly cluttered the map. In the north was 'Estotiland', which survived long enough to be mentioned by Milton (*Paradise Lost*, x: 686).

Most of these islands were spectral in the last degree. Apart from St Brandan's, the most substantial was the Island of the Seven Cities. In the eighth century, according to a legend which cannot be documented before the fourteenth, seven parties of refugee Christians sailed out of Portugal as the Moors invaded their country. Each party was led by a bishop. On arrival in a western island, the bishops founded seven cities, where the fugitives and their descendants continued to live. The cities were sometimes located in the phantasmal Brazil, but more often in a separate island, 'Antillia'. The Island of the Seven Cities, however conceived, was taken literally and often searched for.

But no one pictured it as a land-mass of continental bulk. In discussing the discovery of America, it must be said again, nearly all these ghost-lands can be consigned to a subordinate place. The last of the dubious 'discoveries of America' are only two in number. Both are suspect because they are never mentioned in writing before Columbus. Besides, with the better-known of the two, the marks of political motivation are palpable.

Richard Hakluyt, the Elizabethan chronicler of 'voyages, traffiques and discoveries', favours a claim that America was reached not only by the Carthaginian Hanno, but also 'by Britons . . . long before *Ill. 66* Columbus led any Spaniards thither'. Behind Hakluyt we can detect a curious medley of wishful thinking largely prompted by the astrologer-royal John Dee, one of the first to employ the phrase 'British Empire'.

In 1578 Dee approached Hakluyt with a theory that Frisland, the ghost-island near Iceland, had been colonized in the sixth century by King Arthur. Subsequent propagandists took the seekers of Camelot all the way to the New World. (The Arthurian Legend provides no basis for this notion.) Hakluyt was not willing to go so far. But he and several contemporaries did endorse a slightly more credible tale, also approved by Dee, which proposed a British discovery of America in the twelfth century. Madoc, son of a North Welsh king, was said to have gone to sea in 1170 to disengage himself from family troubles. He sailed round the south of Ireland, discovered a far-off land with alien people, came home, and left again with a band of Welsh emigrants, but was never heard from. Hakluyt placed Madoc's landfall in the West Indies.

Prince Madoc did exist, and was noted, like Brendan, as a seafarer. But no known account of his American exploit is early enough to have any value. It seems to have been spun out of almost nothing as a British trump for the Spaniard's ace. For over two hundred years Madoc's claim was kept alive, partly by Welsh patriots, partly by the poet Southey, partly by explorers of North America who brought back rumours of a Welsh-speaking tribe. Too often, however, the Welsh Indians turned out to be a little farther up-country than the traveller himself had gone.

When a prize was offered at the 1858 Eisteddfod for the best essay on 'The Welsh Discovery of America', an honest study by Thomas Stephens exploded the whole Madoc story, so far as such a thing ever is exploded. The Eisteddfod judges indignantly disqualified Stephens, and his essay remained unpublished until 1893. Thanks mainly to some residual queries about Welsh-sounding words in the language of the extinct Mandan Indians, Madoc still has a few champions. They include the Virginia Cavalier Chapter of the Daughters of the American Revolution, who, in 1953, put up a memorial tablet at Fort Morgan, Mobile, Alabama, the presumed site of Madoc's landing.

The same documentary stumbling-block stands in the way of any confidence about the final 'discovery' of this kind—the Zeno expedition. The Zenos were two Venetian brothers who flourished late in the fourteenth century. In 1558 a descendant published what purported to be a family manuscript, with a map. About 1390, it was asserted, Niccolò Zeno was wrecked in 'Frisland' and attached himself to the household of a nobleman who rescued him, called 'Zichmni'. Niccolò was joined by his brother Antonio. Zichmni sent out exploring fleets with the Zenos aboard. They visited Greenland. Niccolò died, but Antonio, on another trip, went to the 'island of Estotiland', where he heard of an extensive 'country of Drogio' stretching away south, with various particulars of its natives, such as their custom of human sacrifice.

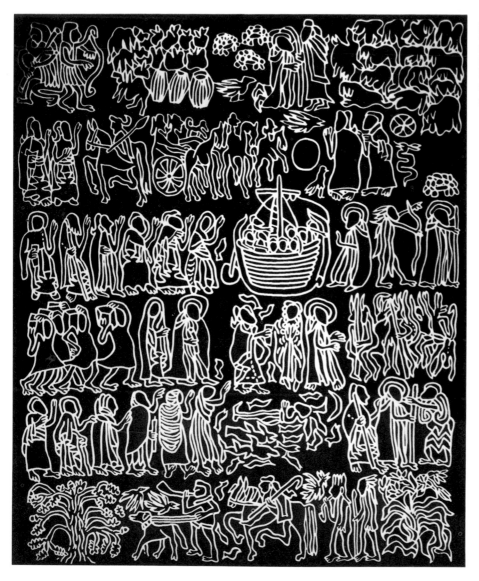

*Ill. 28*. A modern tapestry designed by Louis le Brocquy shows in twenty-four scenes Brendan's leave-taking, journey and arrival in the New World. The scenes should be read vertically from bottom to top and left to right in four columns.

A debate over this manuscript went on sporadically for many years. In 1873 R. H. Major published an analysis in which he tried to make sense of it by arguing that Frisland here meant one of the Faeroes; that 'Zichmni' was a bad transliteration of Sinclair, the family name of the Earl of Orkney; that Estotiland was Newfoundland; and that Drogio was the American continent.

Major has had his supporters and his detractors. But in any case it does not appear that much weight can be given to a manuscript which is not produced till long after the information in it is well known from other sources. *

*The more sober Portuguese claim to have beaten Columbus by twenty years will be treated in the last chapter, where it comes more logically. It is a problem of a different type.

# 2

# Ancient Explorers

J. V. Luce

*Ill. 29*

THE MEDITERRANEAN invites exploration. Cyprus is visible from the Syrian coast; the Cyclades are strung like a necklace across the Aegean; coastal ranges beckon from one side of the Adriatic to the other; Sicily is a central staging-point, and the Balearics form stepping-stones to Spain. Island peaks and mainland mountains signpost the sea-lanes. In their small but seaworthy wooden ships, propelled by oar and sail, ancient seamen, given time, patience, and luck, could cover the 2,400 miles from the Levant to the Pillars of Hercules.

When did explorers first achieve this feat? The answer is bound up with a complicated argument about the development of metallurgy in the Iberian peninsula. Earlier speculations about Egyptian 'colonization' may be dismissed as groundless. But it is now widely believed that prospectors from the Aegean reached southern Spain as early as *c.* 2500 BC in search of new supplies of metal for the advanced civilizations of the Near East. They are thought to have established fortified settlements in the coastal regions of Spain and Portugal, where a number of third millennium sites show features quite distinct from the local neolithic cultures. Slags near one such site in Almeria (Almizaraque) prove that copper, silver, and lead were smelted there. This theory of an influx of Aegean metal-workers, perhaps from the Cyclades, is accepted by Glyn Daniel and J. D. Evans in the revised *Cambridge Ancient History*. A recent carbon-14 date of *c.* 2750 BC for the first Malta temples perhaps charts the passage of these early seafarers.* But it must be admitted that no imports have been found to confirm the theory of direct maritime intercourse between the Aegean and Spain in the third millennium. The complete absence of Cycladic obsidian is certainly odd, and the 'colonization' theory, though plausible, cannot be said to have been finally proved.*

Sea communication throughout the Mediterranean was definitely established by the middle of the second millennium. By that date mainland Greek styles were influencing the local pottery of southern

*For details see D. Trump, *Antiquity* 37, 1963.

*For the main pros and cons see the articles by B. Blance, *Antiquity* 35, 1961, and C. Renfrew, *Antiquity* 41, 1967.

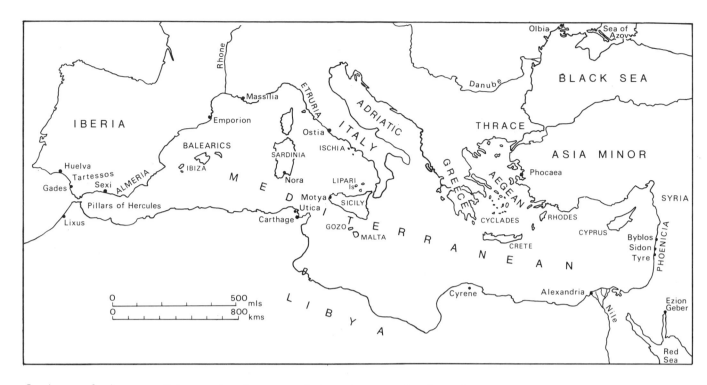

Spain, and Aegean faience beads were being imported, though whether directly or after trans-shipment, we cannot say for certain. The evidence of pottery at least proves that there was a regular trade route from Greece to the Lipari islands as early as 1600 BC, with an extension north to Ischia documented for the fifteenth century. In the Late Bronze Age one may reasonably picture Spain, Etruria (where Mycenaean pottery has recently been found), Sicily and Greece as linked in a nexus of trade, with the mineral resources of the west as the main magnet for Aegean mariners. A ship wrecked off southern Turkey about 1200 BC was carrying a cargo of bronze scrap and ingots of copper and tin, and the crew were using a mixture of Cypriot, Syrian and Mycenaean pottery.* The copper ingots in shape and marking are very similar to ingots found in Sardinia and dated to the same period.

Passages in Homer and the Old Testament tend to confirm this picture of a far-reaching Mediterranean metal trade in the Late Bronze and Early Iron Ages. In the *Odyssey* (I, 184) there is a casual reference to sea-borne commerce in iron and copper, possibly between the Adriatic and Cyprus. And if, as many (but not all) scholars suppose, the Biblical Tarshish is to be equated with Tartessos in southwest Spain, Phoenicians from Tyre were trading there at least as early as the seventh century BC for silver, iron, tin and lead (see p. 78).

The merchant-venturer risking his life at sea for the sake of financial gain became a stock type for Greek and Roman moralists. Trade was

*Ill. 29.* Map of the Mediterranean, showing the principal places mentioned in the text of this chapter.

*Ills. 30, 31*

*This important wreck was excavated in 1959, and has been fully published by G. F. Bass, *Cape Gelidonya: A Bronze Age Shipwreck,* American Philosophical Society, Philadelphia 1967.

*Ill. 41*

*Ill. 32*

54

*Ills. 30, 31.* An oxhide copper ingot (top), and a well preserved portion of a wicker basket (bottom), perhaps used as a container for scrap metal. These are two of many objects recovered from a ship wrecked off Cape Gelidonya, southern Turkey, about 1200 BC. The finds provide first-hand evidence for Levantine metal trading towards the close of the Bronze Age.

the first, and virtually the only motive, for ancient maritime exploration. There are two records of ancient voyages whose prime purpose seems to have been the extension of geographical knowledge (see p. 78 and p. 85), but these are very rare exceptions to the general rule. The modern motive of adventure for adventure's sake cannot, I think, be documented from factual accounts of ancient voyages, though it does figure to some extent in poetical treatments of the voyage of the Argonauts. Tennyson's Ulysses, purposing to 'sail beyond the sunset', displays a romantic pioneering spirit, but his classical prototype showed no such desire to launch out into the unknown. His wanderings started when he was blown off course, and his one desire thereafter was to get himself and his goods safe home to Ithaca. In general, ancient mariners were as resourceful and adventurous as their trade demanded, but they preferred to sail on known waters, and any pioneering of new routes was either accidental, like the case of Colaeus (p. 84), or state sponsored, like that of Hanno (p. 81).

Ancient colonization, like modern, tended to follow the routes pioneered by the merchants, the obvious way to secure a lucrative trade route being to plant colonies at strategic points along it. There were, of course, other pressures at work, particularly in early Greek colonization. The urgent need to acquire new land for surplus populations has often and rightly been emphasized. But it is significant that the earliest Greek colony in the western Mediterranean was founded by Euboeans before 750 BC on the rugged island of Ischia off the Bay of Naples. This move was not designed to appease land-hunger, but rather to establish an advanced base for the exploitation of the mineral wealth of Etruria.

From about 750 BC onwards the Greeks flocked west to found a new Hellenic world in south Italy and Sicily. At the same period the Phoenicians were also thrusting to the west, occupying Malta, Gozo, Motya in the west of Sicily, and, most significantly, founding Carthage to dominate the channel between Sicily and north Africa. From these

*Ill. 32.* The hazards of early Greek voyaging are vividly depicted in this unusual shipwreck scene on a Late Geometric vase from Ischia (eighth century BC). Note the upturned boat on the right, and the corpse being swallowed by a large fish on the left.

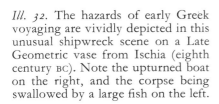

bases they pushed on swiftly and purposefully for the Straits of Gibraltar, and archaeological evidence shows that they had passed into the Atlantic and founded trading-posts at Gades (Cadiz) and Lixus before 700 BC. Greek tradition assigns a foundation date *c.* 1100 BC for these places, and also for Utica, a tradition which may reflect pre-colonial voyages. A stone with a Phoenician inscription from Nora in southern Sardinia may date from the late ninth century BC. But permanent occupation is nowhere evidenced much before 700 BC. The sailing route to Spain was consolidated by a colony on Ibiza, traditionally dated 654 BC, and a recently excavated cemetery near Sexi indicates Phoenician presence in the early seventh century.

Herodotus noted that from the earliest times the Phoenicians were prepared to undertake 'long voyages'. Certainly in the seventh century BC they outstripped the Greeks in the race to the west. While the Greeks were consolidating their hold on southern Italy and Sicily, the Phoenicians were beginning to grasp the opportunities of lucrative trade along the Atlantic coastline. Their motives and methods are clearly set out in a passage of Diodorus Siculus (first century BC):

> This land [Spain] has about the finest and most extensive silver mines of any . . . The use of silver being unknown to the natives, the Phoenicians, on learning of its presence through their trading ventures, purchased it in exchange for other goods of little value. They then transported it to Greece and Asia Minor and all other countries, and acquired great wealth . . . . As they prospered greatly over a long period through this commerce, they sent out many colonies, some to Sicily and its nearby islands, and some to Africa, Sardinia, and Spain. (V, 35)

Ancient voyages are studied in more detail in a later section (p. 70). Here I confine myself to some general remarks about the size and

*Ill. 35.* Right, a drawing of a wall-relief in gypsum from the palace of Sennacherib (705–681 BC) at Kouynjik (Nineveh), showing part of the Phoenician fleet off Tyre in the Campaign against the Assyrians in 701 BC. Two types of ship are represented: 'long' ships with ram and mast, and 'round' ships (*gauloi*) with no mast and a less elevated deck. Both types have two banks of oars.

*Ills. 33, 34.* A seventh-century BC krater showing (on left) a Greek ship with ram about to engage a larger sailing ship. The vase is probably of West Greek origin, and may depict a clash between Greeks and Phoenicians (or Etruscans). The line on which the armed men stand may, by artistic convention, represent a raised gangway amidships. Note the armed man in the crow's nest and the spare spears at the stern of the Greek ship.

operational qualities of the vessels with which the Greeks and Phoenicians opened up the Mediterranean and penetrated into the Atlantic.

It is important to distinguish between war-ships and merchant-ships. War-ships were long and slim, and relied mainly on oars for propulsion. They were easily manoeuvred, but their shape and comparative lack of storage space made them less seaworthy and less capable of long voyages, especially across open stretches of sea. Ancient historians thought it worthy of note that the Phocaeans used war galleys rather than 'round' ships on their pioneering expeditions to Spain.

*Ills. 33–35, 38*

Merchant-ships were 'tubbier', and consequently slower and more awkward to row. Aristotle, thinking in terms of oar-propulsion, compares them to bees, with wings barely adequate to carry their stout and bulky frames. War-ships on this comparison are birds, with a very different ratio of wing to body area. But of course ancient merchant-ships relied mainly on sails for motive-power. With a favouring wind they could cross long stretches of open sea. They carried smaller crews, and had much more storage space, so provisioning was much less of a problem. Their more elaborate decking made them much more seaworthy in bad weather. Obviously they were far more suitable for trade and exploration—hence Hesiod's advice to praise a slim ship, but to put your goods in a fat one. Mainly because of their lack of glamour pictorial and written evidence about them is comparatively scanty.

*Ills. 25, 36*

To judge from an Assyrian relief, the Phoenicians seem to have developed fairly substantial merchant-ships by 700 BC. Their standard type was the decked and rounded vessel known to the Greeks as *gaulos*. This word, which in Homer means 'pail', is thought to be a Semitic loan-word. Later, by the same transference as in English, it came to be applied to the ordinary merchantman or 'tub'. Herodotus describes a 'large *gaulos*' fitted out in Sidon for a reconnaissance trip

*Ill. 35*

*Ill. 37*

through Greek waters, and filled with 'all manner of good things'. A character in Aristophanes called Euelpides (the name means Hopeful) dreams of acquiring a *gaulos* and making his fortune with the aid of long-range weather forecasts by the birds. The interior of a *gaulos* is described in Xenophon, and the passage is worth quoting for its unusual detail. The speaker, an Athenian named Ischomachus, is recalling a visit he made to the vessel when she was in port, presumably at the Piraeus:

> The best and tidiest arrangement of gear that I ever saw, Socrates, was when I went on board that great Phoenician merchantman. I saw a vast quantity of stores all packed separately in very small containers. A ship needs a lot of spars and cables, a lot of rigging, a lot of devices for defence against hostile craft, and plenty of weapons for its crew. Besides, there was the equipment for its messes, not to mention the merchandise. All was stowed in a space not much larger than a good-sized dining-room.* All the items were so arranged that they could be located at once and removed quickly if needed. The mate knew by heart the location and quantity of every item, and spent his spare time checking over the stores. 'When a storm comes on at sea,' he told me, 'that's no time to start looking for things, or to produce them in bad order. God punishes the lazy.' *(Oec.* VIII, 11 ff.)

*From the evidence of houses excavated at Athens and Olynthus, this would imply a space about twenty feet square.

This rare glimpse below deck on an ancient ship confirms that the high reputation of Phoenician seamanship was not unjustified.

From excavations of the dockyard slips in Piraeus we know that the fourth-century BC Athenian trireme measured 125 feet by 20 feet, but there are no comparable data for the merchant-ships of that time. Homer twice mentions a type of 'broad' ship with mast and twenty oars, but gives no dimensions. The coaster wrecked off Cape Geli-

*Ill. 37.* A terracotta model of a *gaulos* from Amathus, Cyprus. It shows housings for a helmsman, oarports, deckboards and four thwarts.

donya about 1200 BC was 35–40 feet long with a quite narrow beam, and was carrying a ton of copper and tin ingots and two hundred-weight in ballast stones. About 600 BC the average Phoenician *gaulos* must have been appreciably bigger, and may not have fallen far short of the Portuguese caravels of the fifteenth and sixteenth centuries, about 50–100 tons' burden. According to Casson, fourth-century Athenian merchantmen averaged 130 tons' burden. Later, a 'ten thousand talent ship' became a stock phrase for a large merchantman, which would imply a cargo capacity of up to 250 tons, and this may be taken as the normal upper limit.

*Ills. 30, 31*

Larger ships could be built for special purposes. Ptolemy IV (222–205 BC) had a prestige galley said to have been 420 feet long with a crew of 4,000 rowers and 2,850 marines. In the reign of Caligula (AD 37–41) a special transport vessel conveyed the Vatican obelisk and pedestal, almost 500 tons, plus a ballast of 800 tons of lentils, from Egypt to Italy. But ships of this size were never in regular use. However, the Romans did develop an impressive fleet of grain ships which plied between Ostia and Alexandria. An eye-witness account of one of these 'outsize' ships is given by Lucian, who states her measurements as: length 180 feet, breadth a little more than one quarter of length, depth from deck to hold $43\frac{1}{2}$ feet. The 'ship of Alexandria' in which St Paul was wrecked had a complement of 276 besides cargo.

## Ancient Navigation

When out of sight of land ancient navigators had no means of fixing both co-ordinates of their position. For latitude they could measure the sun's inclination with pointer and hemispherical bowl, or take the altitude of stars against mast or rigging. But lacking reliable chronometers they had no practical method for reckoning longitude. In any case, observations of latitude and longitude are only of use in

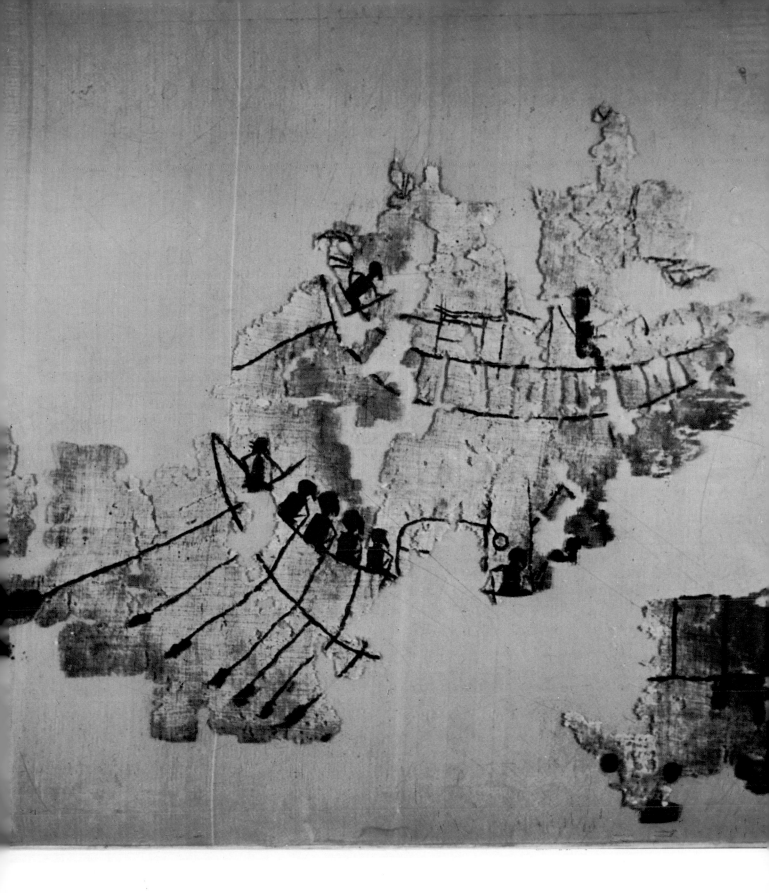

*Ills. 40, 41.* Left, a beautiful gold cup from a Wessex culture burial at Rillaton, Cornwall. The cup is three and a half inches high with a riveted handle. It is so Mycenaean in technique that it may well have been an import from the Aegean. Below, a delicately wrought piece of gold jewellery from the so-called 'Tartessian' treasure recently found at El Carambolo (Seville). The jewellery in the hoard, which may date from the eighth century BC, is Iberian in style, but shows the influence of Phoenician technique.

relation to standard maps and charts. Their art of navigation was therefore based on very different methods from those in use today. Orientation was obtained by observation of sun and stars—the crew of St Paul's ship gave up hope when neither was visible for many days. It was counted a merit of the Phoenicians' seamanship that they determined north from the Little Bear rather than the Great Bear. Other directions were related to named winds which were assumed to blow from fixed points of the compass. Distance covered was calculated by dead-reckoning based on the length of an average day's sail. No wonder Aristotle remarks that more 'deliberation' is needed in navigation than in gymnastic training 'because it has not been reduced to such exact rules'. Obviously the ancient methods were more suited to the Mediterranean than the Atlantic, depending as they did on clear skies, a regular wind system, and the absence of tides. A Mediterranean pilot would have been very much 'at sea' in the changeable weather and swift currents of northern seas. He would also miss the many landmarks provided by islands and lofty coastal ranges.

It is an interesting question to what extent ancient mariners relied on maps and written manuals. Homer describes Proteus as knowing the 'measures of the sea', which seems to imply a lore of accepted distances on the sea-lanes. But at this early date such lore was in all probability oral rather than written. By the classical Greek period written manuals called *periploi* were coming into use. The Greek *periplous* was the ancestor of the medieval portulan. The term means a 'sailing-round', and could be applied to the narrative of an individual voyage of exploration, but generally it meant a *seriatim* description of coasts and ports with detailed information on trade and navigation. The earliest extant *periplous* dates from *c.* 350 BC, and bears the name of Scylax, a noted sea-captain of an earlier age. It describes the Mediterranean, the Black Sea as far as the Don, and a stretch of the African coast south from the Straits. Gades is briefly noted, and beyond it 'there are many Carthaginian trading-posts, and mud, and high tides, and open seas'—a significant example of Carthaginian propaganda designed to discourage Greek incursions into the Atlantic. Other extant *periploi* are the *Periplous of the Erythraean Sea* (first century AD; routes from Egypt to India and East Africa) and the *Stadiasmus Maris Magni* (perhaps fourth century AD). Like modern *Pilots*, these works give detailed information about harbours, anchorages, watering-places, etc. Distances are sometimes given in stades (ambiguous, because either eight or ten to the mile), sometimes in terms of a day's sail.

A day's sail may be interpreted as the distance which the average merchant ship would travel with a favourable wind in a twenty-four hour period. From data in various authors this can be calculated as

between 100 and 150 miles. An ancient merchant ship, then, could do up to 5 knots, but the average pace was probably closer to 3 knots.

It is often said that ancient ships could only sail with the breeze astern, but this is undoubtedly to underestimate their capacity. The yards could be swung and braced fore and aft, and the set of the sail adjusted appropriately. A procedure for sailing into the wind is clearly described in a passage of Aristotle's *Mechanica* (7, 851b 6). He explains how the sail is drawn down in front of the mast to 'make a foot', and the aft portion reefed to reduce the ship's tendency to luff. This rig virtually transforms the square sail into a triangle with the point down and forward. 'The wind then drives the ship forward, and the steering oar turns it into a favourable wind by pulling against it and using the sea as a lever.' He even describes the sailors leaning out to windward to trim the vessel. A fleet tacking is also described quite nautically by Virgil:

> Together they all made a foot (*fecere pedem*), and they let out right-hand and left-hand folds of the sails alternately [*i.e.* as they went about on the other tack]. Together they brace the lofty yards this way and that. The fleet holds on its way with a wind it has made its own.
>
> (*Aeneid*, v, 830–2)

Morrison and Williams are right to deduce from these passages 'a practice of tacking prevalent in the Mediterranean from at least the fourth century BC'.

The main handicap of the ancient mariner was his lack of precision instruments.* He had no log for measuring his rate of speed, no sextant for determining his position, no compass for finding his bearings. He did however share one useful item of equipment with his modern counterpart, the lead and line for taking soundings. Herodotus describes soundings taken on the approaches to the Nile delta, and the sailors in the *Acts* began to cast the lead when they

*Ill. 42.* A relief from a third-century AD Roman sarcophagus. A boy has fallen from a skiff into a rough sea near the entrance to a harbour (probably Ostia). The two ships on the left are coming out to rescue him, sailing on the port tack with a following wind. The ship on the right is about to enter the harbour on the starboard tack, and a collision appears imminent. The forward placed mast and the fore-and-aft rig of the middle ship are notable.

*A unique and complicated machine was recovered from a wreck off Antikythera dated *c.* 65 BC. An input axle turned pointers at various speeds on a number of dials through a complex system of gear wheels. It has sometimes been called a navigational aid, but this seems most unlikely in view of the study published by D. J. de Solla Price in *Scientific American*, June 1959, 60–63. Price interprets it as an 'astronomical clock' showing lunar, planetary and sidereal cycles, and designed for mounting and exhibition in a public place on land.

suspected they were nearing land in the dark. The rapid shoaling showed this to be the case, and made them drop anchor at once and wait for dawn. The taking of soundings might even be implied by the Homeric formula 'he who knows all the deeps of the sea'. Sounding rods appear on ancient Egyptian reliefs, and the practice is doubtless of great antiquity in Mediterranean navigation.

In regard to provisioning, a passage of Homer describes what may well have been standard practice. Calypso is stocking the small boat which Odysseus has built for the voyage back to Ithaca. She puts in goatskins of wine and water, staple foods in a leather bag, and 'many agreeable relishes'. The description could be more explicit, but it may be assumed that the staple food was cereals, and the relishes may have included cheese, salt fish, and perhaps olives and vegetables. Aristophanes mentions garlic, olives, onions, and anchovies as among the Athenian fleet's provisions. The skin bags would have been reasonably water-tight. Later we hear of pitch-lined chests for water storage, and cargo was often conveyed in earthenware jars. In general, provisioning for a voyage posed more problems then than now, and regular stops would have been necessary for small boats to replenish supplies of food and water. There is no hint of precautions against scurvy, and it is perhaps significant that Odysseus describes a successful open sea passage as made 'without disease'.

One final limitation on ancient voyages of exploration may be briefly mentioned. On their western voyages Greeks and Phoenicians were making contact with peoples at a much lower level of civilization, but they could never count on military superiority over hostile natives. Odysseus' men were driven off by the Kikones, and he lost all his ships except one in the Laestrygonian ambush. To overcome the Cyclops he had to use his precious Thracian wine—an ancient equivalent of the trader's 'rum-bottle'. Such experiences must have been typical in the westward movement of Greek expansion.

In the light of all these factors, we can both admire the achievements of ancient maritime exploration, and understand its failures. The Greeks acquired a thorough knowledge of the whole extent of the Mediterranean and the Black Sea, and planted hundreds of colonies around their shores. They helped to open up Arabia, the Persian Gulf, and the western coasts of the Indian peninsula. Their greatest explorer Pytheas circumnavigated Britain, and perhaps got as far north as Norway (pp. 85–87). The Phoenicians concentrated on the route to Spain, but one isolated expedition may have circumnavigated Africa (p. 78). Carthaginian admirals explored the Atlantic coastline as far north as Brittany and as far south as Sierra Leone (pp. 81–84). From about AD 50 on, Roman ships went regularly from the head of the Red Sea to south India and Ceylon. On reaching the Gulf of Aden they used the southwest monsoon to cut straight

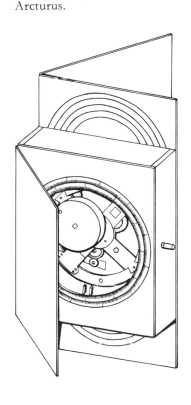

*Ill. 43.* The function of this machine is discussed in the note opposite. It consists of a box with dials on the outside and a sophisticated assemblage of gear wheels inside mounted eccentrically on a turntable. The input axle is on the right. The cogs of the bronze wheels are precisely cut to an angle of 60°. An inscription on the casing refers to the rising and setting of prominent stars, *e.g.* Arcturus.

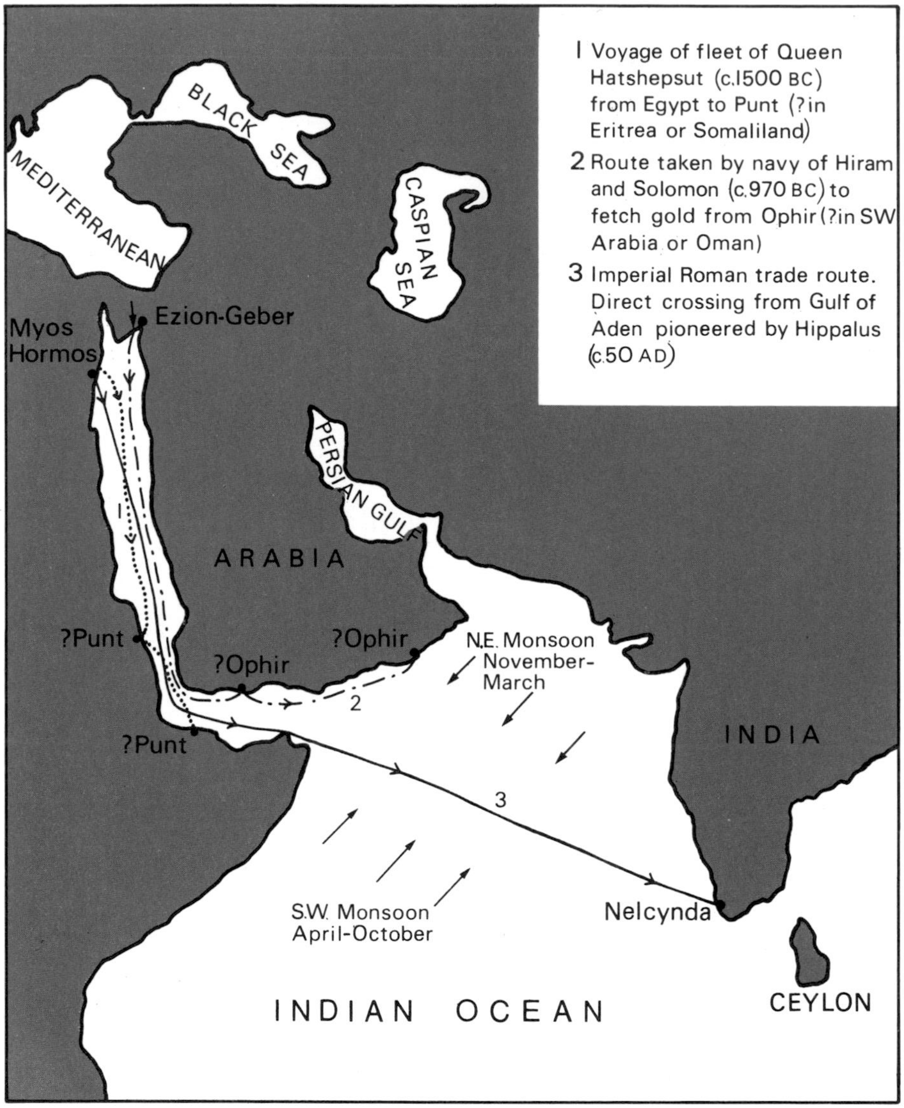

Within the map:

1 Voyage of fleet of Queen Hatshepsut (c.1500 BC) from Egypt to Punt (?in Eritrea or Somaliland)

2 Route taken by navy of Hiram and Solomon (c.970 BC) to fetch gold from Ophir (?in SW Arabia or Oman)

3 Imperial Roman trade route. Direct crossing from Gulf of Aden pioneered by Hippalus (c.50 AD)

BLACK SEA

MEDITERRANEAN

CASPIAN SEA

Myos Hormos

Ezion-Geber

PERSIAN GULF

ARABIA

?Punt

?Ophir

?Ophir

N.E. Monsoon November–March

INDIA

?Punt

3

2

S.W. Monsoon April–October

Nelcynda

CEYLON

INDIAN OCEAN

across the Indian Ocean, a passage taking five to six weeks. They returned by the same route in the late autumn using the northeast monsoon. This route was pioneered by a certain Hippalus, and the round trip amounted to about seven thousand miles. Some went even further. Chinese annals record the arrival of a Roman 'embassy'— probably merchant-venturers—in AD 166.

There can, therefore, be no doubt that the developed ships of the Roman period had the capacity to cross the Atlantic and back. But there is no evidence that anyone tried to emulate Hippalus as a trail-blazer in the Atlantic. The main reason for this lack of enterprise in western waters must have been fear of the unknown. The northern

*Ill. 44*

and eastern shores of the Indian Ocean had been explored by coast-wise traffic before Hippalus, and south India was known as a desirable market. Its approximate latitude, distance, and direction could be roughly plotted on a map, and a navigator could estimate his chances in a direct passage relying on seasonal winds. None of these conditions obtained in the North Atlantic. Its wind system was much less predictable, and there was no knowledge of any land lying beyond it. Therefore there was no commercial motive for risking a voyage, and the fear of getting completely lost in a boundless expanse of waters must have acted as a very potent deterrent on exploring zeal.

*Ill. 45*

The Phoenicians were very secretive about their maritime knowledge, but the Greeks published what they discovered, and they were the first nation to attempt scientific mapping. A record of what they knew or surmised about the 'inhabited world' *c.* 200 BC may be seen in the reconstruction of the great map of Eratosthenes. The map is controlled by the parallel from Gibraltar to Rhodes (both of which are in fact almost on the same latitude), and the meridian through Rhodes extending south along the line of the Nile and northwards through the Hellespont and Bosphorus to Olbia (Odessa). This north-south line is not so accurate as the east-west parallel, and has caused some distortion in Thrace and southern Russia. In general, the coasts and islands of the Mediterranean are given with reasonable accuracy. Distortion and ignorance increase markedly towards the extremities. Nothing is known of the great southward extension of Africa. The Indian peninsula and Ceylon (Taprobane) are barely recognizable. The Caspian Sea opens on to the northern Ocean. Britain and Ireland are tilted too much to the northeast. Some knowledge of the Asian land-mass had come from Alexander's campaigns, but this had not been properly co-ordinated with the maritime data on the Indian Ocean. The defective mapping of northwest Europe was largely the result of the Carthaginian blockade of the Gibraltar Straits which virtually denied Greek seamen access to the Atlantic from about 500 to 250 BC. Europe north of the Alps was not really opened up for geographical survey until the time of Julius Caesar.

*Ill. 47*

If Eratosthenes' map be compared with the world map of Ptolemy compiled in the second century AD, many improvements in detail will be noticed (p. 69). The Caspian Sea has become an inland sea, for example, and much more is known about the Far East. But the basic structure is that established in the heyday of Alexandrian science. It was not to be improved upon until the fifteenth- and sixteenth-century discoveries, and most medieval maps are infinitely crude by comparison.

From the Hellenistic Age onwards geographers envisaged a spherical earth. The hypothesis that the earth is a globe had appeared in Greek thought in the fifth century BC, and may go back to

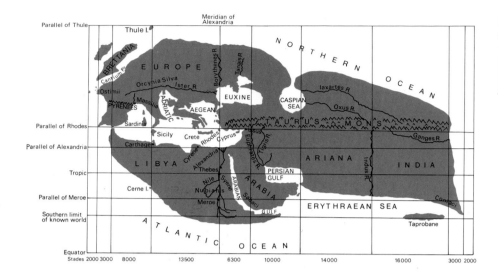

Parallel of Thule

Thule I.

Meridian of Alexandria

NORTHERN OCEAN

BRETTANIA

EUROPE

Carryium P.

Orcynia Silva

Ister R.

Borysthenes R.

Tanais R.

EUXINE

Iaxartes R.

CASPIAN SEA

Oxus R.

Ostimii

PYRENES

Massilia

ADRIATIC

AEGEAN

Parallel of Rhodes

Sardinia

Sicily

Crete

Rhodes

Cyprus

T A U R U S  M O N S

Ganges R.

Euphrates R.

Tigris R.

Parallel of Alexandria

Carthage

Cyrene

Alexandria

ARIANA

INDIA

Tropic

L I B Y A

Thebes

Nile

PERSIAN GULF

Indus R.

Parallel of Meroe

Cerne I.

Nubians

Syene

ARABIAN

ARABIA

Sabael

ERYTHRAEAN  SEA

Conneci.

Meroe

GULF

Southern limit of known world

A T L A N T I C   O C E A N

Taprobane

Equator

Stades 2000 3000     8000          13500        6300     10000          14000          16000     3000 2000

*Ill. 45.* A map of the inhabited world according to Eratosthenes (*c.* 275–194 BC). Eratosthenes was head of the Library at Alexandria and has been called 'the first systematic geographer'.

Pythagoras. It was certainly held by Plato, and Aristotle supports it with the sort of arguments still used in every geography primer.

From observations of the angle of the sun's rays made simultaneously at Syene (Aswan) and Alexandria, Eratosthenes (*c.* 275–194 BC) calculated the circumference of the earth sphere as 252,000 stades. If he used the 'short' stade, his result is less than 200 miles out—an astonishing performance. Indeed, the theoretical measurement of the globe may be regarded as the culminating achievement of Greek science. Strabo warns readers of his *Geography* (composed between 9 and 5 BC) that they must have made a study of the 'globe and its circles' if they are to follow his treatise. 'It is this lack of preliminary training', he continues, 'that makes the work of the authors of the so-called *Harbours* and *Coasting Voyages* incomplete. They fail to supply the relevant mathematical and astronomical details.'

Eratosthenes reckoned the length and breadth of the known world to be 78,000 and 38,000 stades respectively. When these figures were plotted on the surface of a sphere 252,000 stades in circumference, it became obvious that the 'inhabited world' covered only a small portion of the globe's surface. This led to speculation about unknown continents south of the equator, and also in the temperate zone in our hemisphere. Eratosthenes himself seems to have thought that one could sail west to India 'if the width of the Atlantic sea did not prevent it'. Strabo, however, supposed that there could well be two or more 'inhabited worlds' beyond the ocean in the northern hemisphere.

As early as *c.* 385 BC Plato had expressed his belief that the dimensions of the settled areas round the Mediterranean and the Black Sea were very small in relation to the surface of the whole earth. He conjectured that the Mediterranean was a small inlet from

*Ill. 46.* A reconstruction of the Globe of Crates. Crates of Mallos was head of the Library at Pergamum in the second century BC. Strabo implies that the globe he constructed was at least ten feet in diameter. In addition to the known 'inhabited world', it depicted three other hypothetical land-masses symmetrically disposed and separated by broad belts of ocean.

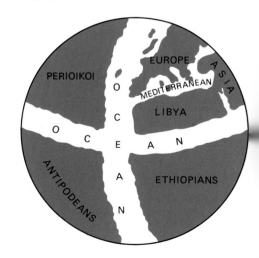

PERIOIKOI

EUROPE

ASIA

MEDITERRANEAN

LIBYA

OCEAN

ANTIPODEANS

ETHIOPIANS

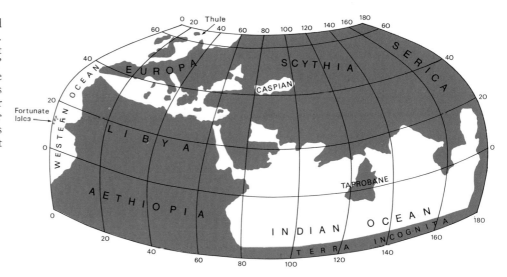

*Ill. 47.* The map of the world according to Ptolemy (*c.* AD 150). Ptolemy calculated the east-west extension of the 'inhabited world' as 180°, reckoning from a base meridian at the Fortunate Isles (Canaries). Despite some major errors, like the enclosing of the Indian Ocean, the map represents the culminating point of ancient cartography.

*A summary based on *Phaedo,* 109 a–b, and *Timaeus,* 25a.

*Ill. 46*

*G. Pillot, *Le Code secret de l'Odyssée,* Robert Laffont, Paris 1969.

the 'true ocean', *i.e.* the Atlantic, and that beyond the ocean lay a vast continent many times larger than the little world of the Greeks.* This was simply an *a priori* assumption. Plato had no geographical information on which to base it. But the speculation appealed to the imagination of the ancient world, was taken up by subsequent myth-makers and romancers, and was never entirely forgotten through the medieval period.

Crates of Pergamum (second century BC) took up the conjecture in the light of Eratosthenes' work. He is credited with the construction of a large-scale model globe, perhaps ten feet in diameter. He posited a broad belt of water extending all round the equator, and crossed at right angles by a similar belt from pole to pole. These ocean belts encircled four distinct land masses, one of which was the known world of Europe-Asia-Africa. The other three were peopled by him with hypothetical Ethiopians, Antipodeans, and Perioikoi ('dwellers-round'). Crates applied his conception to problems of Homeric geography. In particular, he thought of Odysseus' wanderings as taking place largely in the ocean gulf beyond the Straits of Gibraltar. Thanks to Macrobius, these fanciful notions coloured the geographical imaginings of medieval Europe, and perhaps influenced the design of the royal orb. A recent French writer has revived Crates' thesis about Odysseus in the Atlantic, and locates Aeolus in Madeira and Calypso in Iceland.* But this, like Crates' globe, is very speculative.

The speculations of philosophers and globe-makers seem to have had no effect on ancient exploration, though they did colour several Utopias, and influenced one of Plutarch's myths (see pp. 20 and 89). No one set out to find land in the west, or a westward route to India. But the ideas filtered down to Columbus through Roger Bacon's *Opus Maius* (1267) and Cardinal D'Ailly's *Imago Mundi* (1480). Seneca had spoken airily of India as only a few days' sail from Spain with a favourable wind, and Columbus was impressed by the fancy.

The tradition of the ancient map-makers was more explicit if less optimistic. Ptolemy had projected the known world to cover 180° on the parallel through Rhodes. The actual figure from the Canaries to Indo-China is 126°, so he considerably over-stretched his material. Marinus (*c.* AD 110) made it 228°, an estimate preferred by Columbus. After taking into account the great eastward extension of China revealed by Marco Polo's travels, Columbus reckoned that only about 78° of the globe's circumference remained to be explored west of the Canaries. Since he wrongly took a degree to be only 50 miles he envisaged that only 3,900 miles lay between him and the known Far East. There is still considerable controversy about his ultimate aims and preconceptions, but there can be no doubt that his initial voyage was encouraged by traditions derived from ancient Greek science. Even on his last voyage he still thought he had reached parts of Asia or India. Thus, as J. O. Thomson puts it, 'the most important thing in ancient geography was an error which caused the unconscious discovery of America.'

*Ill. 47*

## Some Records of Ancient Voyages

In Egypt, as in Mesopotamia, boats had been equipped with sails before the end of the fourth millennium, but perhaps only for use on rivers or lakes. The earliest positive evidence for sea-borne commerce is found in a laconic inscription recording among the events of the Fourth Dynasty (*c.* 2600 BC) the 'bringing of 40 ships filled with cedar wood'. The wood was put to good use, for another inscription relating to the same period reads: 'shipbuilding of cedar wood, one Praise-of-the-Two-Lands ship 100 cubits long' (over 170 feet). In 1954 this inscription was strikingly confirmed by the discovery of a well preserved cedar-wood boat 143 feet in length in a vault beside the Great Pyramid of Cheops. The Cheops boat and the *Praise-of-the-Two-Lands* may have been for use on the Nile only, but the '40 ships'

*Ill. 48.* Clay model of a boat found at Eridu, southern Mesopotamia, *c.* 3500 BC. There is a sturdy round socket forward to amidships and a hole drilled through each gunwale. This arrangement seems designed for a mast and supporting stays. Eridu was at that time a coastal town.

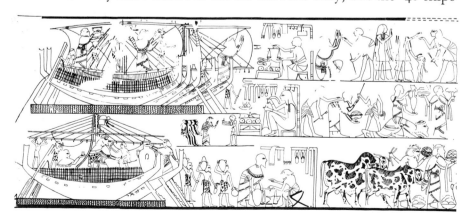

*Ill. 49.* A drawing from a painting (now destroyed) in the tomb of Kenamun in the Theban necropolis (Eighteenth Dynasty). It shows the arrival of ships from Canaan in an Egyptian port. The lines of the ships may be compared with those of the Phoenician 'round' ships in *Ill. 35.* Note the fencing round the cargo space and the two sail yards.

Ill. 50

*Ill. 50.* A relief from the mortuary temple of Queen Hatshepsut at Deir el-Bahari. About 1500 BC, the Queen commissioned a fleet to fetch incense and other rare goods from Punt. One of the trading galleys is here shown in splendid detail, with the prows and sails of two others behind. Note the baboons on the hogging truss and the exotic Red Sea fish below.

must have made the passage from some port on the Levant coast, probably Byblos. 'Byblos ships' are mentioned in Egyptian records from the Sixth Dynasty on, but such ships, like the timber, may have belonged to the West Semites of Lebanon.

Crete came under Egyptian influence in the third millennium, but the evidence for direct contact is slight, and the main link may have been through Byblos and the Palestine coast, with Minoans and Canaanites as active in the commerce as Egyptians. The Ipuwer papyrus refers to a breakdown of trade between Byblos, Keftiu (Crete), and Egypt, probably in the unsettled period after the collapse of the Old Kingdom (2200–2100 BC). Breasted thinks that Egyptian interest in seafaring gradually declined until in the second millennium they could describe Asia Minor as a 'cluster of islands'.

A notable revival occurred in the reign of Hatshepsut, *c.* 1500 BC, when an Egyptian expedition, utilizing seasonal northwest and southeast winds, sailed down the Red Sea to Punt, and returned safely with incense trees, ivory, cinnamon wood, apes, gold, and myrrh. The commemorative inscriptions and reliefs show that this was regarded as a notable achievement. If Punt, as seems probable, is to be located near the southern end of the Red Sea (either in Eritrea or Somaliland), the round trip was about 3,000 miles, the equivalent of a voyage from the Delta to Corsica and back.

But there is no evidence that the ancient Egyptians ever traded further west than Crete. From records extant from the Old, Middle, and New Kingdoms, we can derive a coherent enough picture of their geographical horizons, and these always remained very limited,

*Ill. 51.* The great Victory Stele set up by Tuthmosis III in the temple complex at Karnak, and now in the Cairo Museum. It records his conquests in all foreign countries in the first half of the fifteenth century BC, and mentions the subservience of the 'western land' of Keftiu (Crete) in line 16, and of other islands in the 'Great Green' (eastern Mediterranean) in line 18. In the two symmetrical panels at the top, Tuthmosis is seen making offerings to Amun, attended by the goddess of the Theban necropolis who (on the left) carries his bow and arrows, and mace.

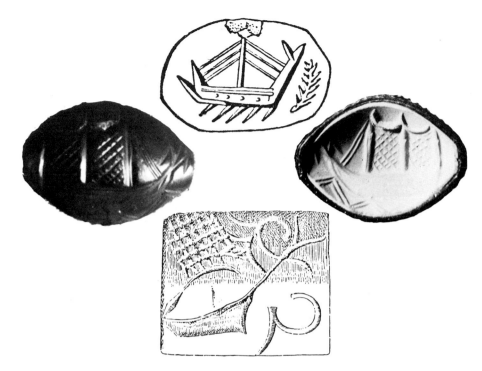

*Ill. 51*

*Ills. 52–54.* Some representations of ships from Minoan seal stones: top, a merchantman from about 2000 BC, with mast and stays, oars, and high prow; to the right, an olive spray. Centre, a seal (on left) and its impression, of uncertain provenance but dated *c.* 1450 BC. A two-masted ship is shown, with rectangular patterned sail. Below, a ship with long forked prow under full sail, *c.* 1500. The style is unusual, but conveys a fine impression of movement. Note the curling bow wave and the indication of rigging attaching the patterned sail to a bowsprit. The mast was perhaps represented by a metal strip which has become detached from the seal, itself a flattened cylinder of bronze.

*The full text in translation may be consulted in J. B. Pritchard, *Ancient Near Eastern Texts,* Princeton 1955, 373–5.

*Ills. 52–54*

*Ill. 52*

especially to the west. The Ipuwer papyrus uses the phrase 'as far away as Keftiu'. The prelude of the great Victory Hymn of Tuthmosis III (first half of the fifteenth century BC) is more explicit. It celebrates the submission of 'the earth in its length and breadth', and 'all lands . . . as far as the four supports (or pillars) of heaven'. The Hymn itself makes it clear that Crete for the Egyptians lay at the western limit of the world.* Because of its lofty mountains Crete may well have been imagined as one of the four sky pillars at the corners of the world. There is no evidence that the ancient Egyptians ever looked, much less went, any further west. Speculations about Old Kingdom 'explorers' and 'colonists' diffusing Egyptian culture far and wide have no basis in fact, and are most implausible given that the Egyptians never even explored their own river to its upper reaches.

Minos was remembered in Greek legend as a ruler of the sea. The long peaceful evolution of the unwalled palaces of Crete, all of them close to the sea, shows that the Minoans were immune from invasion, and so enjoyed naval superiority in the Aegean. Recent excavations in Cythera, Kea, and Thera have tended to confirm the tradition of a maritime 'empire' by revealing prosperous overseas bases and colonies. Ships are frequently depicted on Minoan gems and sealstones, and a type with a sail and fixed rudder can be traced back to the middle of the third millennium. Later, two-masted and even three-masted ships are depicted. On a clay impression from Knossos the sign for ship is grouped with the olive spray, a clear indication of an export trade in olive oil.

From 2000 BC onwards Crete was trading busily with Greece, Cyprus, Syria and Egypt. Did her ships also sail westwards? There is some evidence that they did. The earliest Italian metal daggers of the Remedello type seem to copy early Minoan exemplars. In Malta an underground tomb-sanctuary is decorated with spirals very like those on Minoan vessels of *c.* 2000 BC. Cycladic vases dating between 2000 and 1600 BC have been found in the area of Marseilles and in the Balearics, and may have been carried in Minoan vessels, though they could also indicate a continuance of earlier Cycladic trade with the western Mediterranean. Ship graffiti on the stones of a temple at Tarxien in Malta were first noticed in 1956, and have been tentatively dated to *c.* 1500 BC. Ships of a number of different types are depicted, and their finder has made the reasonable suggestion that the drawings are votives commemorating the safe arrival of the mariners of a number of nations.* This suggestion might be supported by the Late Bronze Age statuette of the Phoenician god Melqart recovered from the sea by fishermen near Sciacca in southwest Sicily in 1955. Unfortunately the experts differ about its date, some placing it as early as the fourteenth century, others close to 1100 BC. There is also the ancient tradition of an expedition of Minos to Sicily. Some recent historians have been very sceptical about this tradition, but it is at least certain that southern Italy and the Lipari islands were much frequented by Mycenaean ships from 1600 BC to the close of the Bronze Age. This is proved by the pottery found in these areas, and one Italian import found in a merchant's house at Mycenae—a winged-axe mould of a type completely foreign to the Aegean world but familiar from the culture area of north Italy and the upper Danube basin.* The Minoans were perhaps always more interested in controlling Aegean trade with the Levant, and allowed the Mycenaeans a freer hand in the west to continue earlier Cycladic mercantile activity.

It has long been held that there was commercial interchange between the Aegean and northwestern Europe during the second millennium BC. One can point to the very numerous finds of Baltic amber from graves at Mycenae and elsewhere in the Peloponnese, mostly dating from before 1400 BC. It is also claimed that the segmented faience beads, which occur at various sites in Britain and Ireland, are imports from the eastern Mediterranean. But it by no means follows that contact between such widely separated regions was effected by traders using the long sea route through the Mediterranean and up the coasts of Spain and France. The amber was almost certainly brought down through central Europe to the head of the Adriatic, or possibly to a Black Sea port near the mouth of the

*D. Woolner, *Antiquity* 31, 1957.

*Ill. 55*

*F. H. Stubbings, *Annual of the British School at Athens* 49, 1954, 297–8.

74

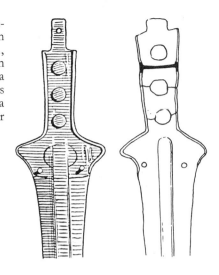

*Ills. 56–58.* Left, a flange-hilted bronze sword from Ørskovhedehus, Jutland, which appears to copy Aegean types of *c.* 1400 BC from a chamber-tomb at Ayios Ioannis near Knossos (right) and a chamber-tomb at Mycenae (far right).

*R. G. Newton, C. Renfrew, *Antiquity* 44, 1970.

*S. Piggott, Sborník Národního Muzea V Praze (Acta Musei Nationalis Pragae) 20, 1966.

*Ill. 40*

◀ *Ill. 55.* Left, a Late Bronze Age statuette of the Phoenician god Melqart, bearded and in Asiatic pose, but wearing an Egyptian crown, found in the sea off Sicily.

*Details and references in A. Snodgrass, *Early Greek Armour and Weapons*, Edinburgh 1964.

*K. Randsborg, *Acta Archaeologica* 38, 1967.

Danube. As for the British faience beads, spectroscopic analysis now indicates that they were manufactured locally, with centres of production located in Scotland and Wessex.* The technology of their firing is quite sophisticated, and one could still argue that the 'know-how' must have been diffused from the Levant, but the beads themselves can no longer be regarded as proof positive of commercial intercourse.

However, the case for some kind of trade nexus between Mycenaean Greece and the British Isles rests on much besides the faience beads.* Gold cups and zigzag bone shaft inlays from graves in Wiltshire and Cornwall have close counterparts in the shaft graves at Mycenae. Gold-mounted amber discs from Wessex have Minoan and Cypriot parallels. In both areas amber necklaces occur with spacer-plates perforated in such a complex and distinctive way that the similarity virtually demands the assumption of reciprocal trade. Of course it still remains a question how many links there were in the chain of contact, and the route remains hypothetical. In this last instance, similar finds in south Germany and Austria indicate a central European route.

The Mycenaeans wanted valuable raw materials, copper, tin, gold, amber. In return they supplied jewellery, weapons, and, it has been suggested, wine. The influence of their more advanced technology may be seen in bronze corslets of allied type found at Dendra (Argolid) and Čaka (Slovakia), and in related bell-type helmets from Knossos (*c.* 1400 BC) and Beitzsch (north Germany).* There is also a remarkable flange-hilted bronze sword found in a tumulus at Ørskovhedehus in southwest Jutland in 1905, and recently submitted to intensive analysis.* The shape of the tang, and the number and placing of the rivet holes, find their closest parallel in a type of Aegean sword well known from Crete and the Argolid around 1400 BC. Metal samples from the Ørskovhede sword, and from two from the Argolid, were tested, and significant differences in tin content and in the method of manufacture were revealed between the Danish and Greek swords. It seems reasonable to conclude that typical products of Aegean metallurgy were being copied in southern Scandinavia in the fourteenth century BC. In this case the contact route may have been through France (a sword of a similar type is known from Lyons), or through eastern and central Europe (close imitations of Mycenaean swords have been found in Bulgaria and Rumania).*

The implications of the so-called Mycenaean dagger carving at Stonehenge are as unclear as the representation itself. That it indicates the presence of a Mycenaean mason or architect seems rather unlikely. It could have been incised long after the completion of the monument, and might more plausibly be explained as the token of a gift to the shrine. A dagger from the Aegean could have passed through a number of hands, as perhaps did the bronze dagger of Mycenaean III C type discovered at Pelynt in Cornwall in 1845. The Wessex rulers who reconstructed Stonehenge (between *c.* 1500 and 1400 BC on the generally received dating, though this has been challenged recently*) are credited with trade connections at least as extensive as Mycenae. Goods could have been exchanged at the mouth of the Rhône or the head of the Adriatic, and there is no need to posit Mycenaean trading expeditions to the British Isles. The activities of Mycenaean merchants can be established only as far west as Sicily and Etruria.

*Ills. 56–58*

*S. Piggott, *art. cit.*

*Ill. 59*

*Ill. 61*

*C. Renfrew, *Annual of the British School at Athens* 63, 1968, would put back these dates by as much as 300 years.

*Ills. 59, 61.* Left, part of stone 53 of the sarsen trilithons at Stonehenge showing (to the left) a carved dagger of Mycenaean type, first observed, with other similar carvings, in 1953. It should be compared with the bronze dagger of Mycenaean III C type (twelfth century BC) found at Pelynt in Cornwall in 1845 (right).

*Ill. 60.* A drawing of a ship (partly restored) from fragments of a Middle Helladic vase from Iolchos, *c.* 1600 BC. Note the bow ram. The oval with enclosed zigzag amidships is thought to be a decoration, but it could represent the rowers' benches as though viewed from above.

*For which see E. D. Phillips, 'Odysseus in Italy', *Journal of Hellenic Studies* 73, 1953.

The Greek epic tradition preserved memories of early voyages in strange waters, notably in the saga of the Argonauts and the story of Odysseus' wanderings. Jason launched the Argo at Iolchos, and it is a pleasing coincidence that the earliest known representation of a Greek ship comes from this site. The Argonauts sailed eastwards, and so are not of direct concern in the present study. But Odysseus and his fleet were blown westwards from the southern Peloponnese, and for more than two thousand years Homeric scholars have argued about the identification of his subsequent landfalls. Many interesting suggestions have been made, notably by Victor Bérard and R. Hennig, but no agreement has been reached. Homer's account has some obvious inconsistencies in its geography, quite apart from the magical powers attributed to Circe and Aeolus which are appropriate to the denizens of a poetic fairyland. But the 'deep sea yarns' may not be all fiction. Many scholars believe that Homer inherited some distant memories of the hazards of Mycenaean penetration into the waters round Sicily. The Messina strait still contains a whirlpool which could be the source of the Charybdis story. And even though there were no one-eyed giants nearby, there must have been many savage tribes ready, like the Laestrygonians, to inflict severe losses on traders or colonists. Such suppositions remain conjectural, for Greek contact with the west seems to have been severed for at least two centuries after *c.* 1100 BC, and Homeric references to Sicels probably stem from the early colonial movement of the eighth and seventh centuries. But the wealth of Odysseus legends in Italy* shows that the colonists themselves believed that they were returning to an area where their ancestors had been before.

The Phoenician homeland on the coastal plain below the Lebanon range had been occupied by Semites since the third millennium, and was rich in traditions of ship-building and commerce. The name 'Phoenician' embodies the early Greek awareness of them as 'red-men' (either from the colour of their skins or their murex-dyed textiles); to the ancient Hebrews they were Canaanites. Their ethnic origins are obscure, but by 1000 BC they are recognizably a nation with their main power concentrated in four or five ancient harbour towns, of which the most important were Tyre and Sidon.

About 970 BC Hiram of Tyre manned a fleet for Solomon with experienced sailors, who fetched gold, almug trees and precious stones from Ophir. We also read that 'a navy of Tarshish with the navy of Hiram' brought 'gold, and silver, ivory, and apes, and peacocks' (I Kings IX, 26–8; X, 11, 22). The port of departure was Ezion-Geber (Eilat at the head of the Gulf of Aqaba), and Ophir is to be looked for in southwest Arabia, or further east in Oman, where the peacocks (if they are not a later interpolation) might have been available. Some take the ships as far as India for they came 'once in three years', but such far-flung trade is very unlikely for Solomon's time.

'Ships of Tarshish' is a recurrent and disputed phrase in the Old Testament, Tarshish being identified either with Tarsus in Cilicia* or with Tartessos in Spain. In the context of Solomon's enterprise 'navy of Tarshish' (if not anachronistic) seems to refer to the type of vessel, not the destination, and probably implies sturdy freighters used on long voyages. But when Jonah took ship to Tarshish he was trying to go as far west as possible. 'Tarshish ship' may well have altered its meaning as the Phoenicians extended their trade to the western Mediterranean. Ezekiel's picture (Chap. XXVII) of the trading connections of Tyre shows what a great emporium it had become by 600 BC: 'All the ships of the sea with their mariners were in thee to occupy thy merchandise . . . Tarshish was thy merchant . . . with silver, iron, tin, and lead they traded in thy fairs.' Here the association of Tarshish with silver and tin tells in favour of the Tartessos identification.

Solomon was not the only potentate to call on Phoenician naval expertise. About 600 BC the Pharaoh Necho commissioned a Phoenician squadron to attempt the circumnavigation of Africa from east to west. Herodotus tells us how they fared:

> The Phoenicians set out from the Red Sea and sailed into the sea to the south. Whenever autumn came, they would put in, and sow a crop at whatever point of the coast they had reached. After waiting for the corn to ripen they would harvest it and sail on. In this way two years went by, and in the third year they sailed in through the Pillars of Hercules and arrived back at Egypt. They reported—I do not find this credible, but some do—that in circumnavigating the continent they had the sun on their right. (IV, 42)

This brief account has occasioned a vast amount of discussion. The round trip would have been over 15,000 miles. Allowing an average day's sail of 30 miles, the journey would take two to three years, as Herodotus reports it did. Winds and currents would be favourable as far as the Bight of Benin, and the sun *would* be on their right as they sailed westward round the Cape of Good Hope. This detail rings true and tends to authenticate an otherwise almost incredible feat. It is hard to see how it could have been invented. Scepticism about the achievement was expressed in antiquity, and a number of modern authorities refuse to credit it. There are serious objections, notably the deficiency of detail, the fact that no leader is named, the hazards of navigation over such an immense distance, and the lack of recognition by ancient cartographers. But no single objection is decisive. It can hardly be doubted that the expedition did set out. Necho was an enterprising ruler who tried to dig a canal from the Nile to the Red

*For this less orthodox interpretation see R. D. Barnett, *Journal of Hellenic Studies* 73, 1953, p. 142, and for a recent survey of the problem W. Culican, *The First Merchant-Venturers*, London 1966, pp. 114–16.

*Ill. 64*

*Ill. 63*

*Ills. 62, 64.* Below, a potsherd, *c.* 700 BC, from Tell Qasile, South Palestine, bearing the inscription: 'Gold of Ophir for Beth Horon, shekels III'. Horon was a Canaanite god. Right, a stone from Nora (Cape Pula), Sardinia, with a Phoenician inscription, the first line of which has been read as *b' Tršš*, 'in Tarshish'. Ninth to eighth century BC.

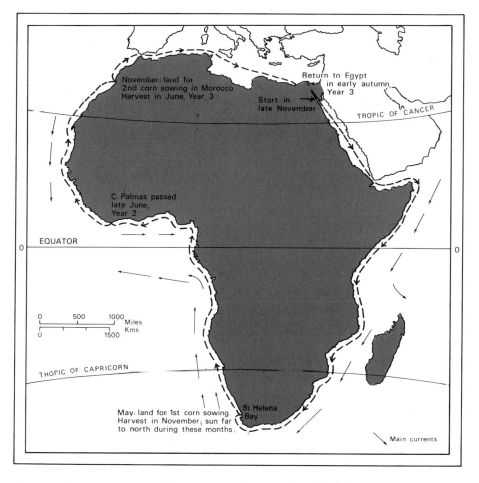

*Ill. 63.* A map giving a conjectural reconstruction of the possible stages of the Phoenician circumnavigation of Africa, *c.* 600 BC, within the overall time for the voyage as recorded by Herodotus.

Within the map:

November: land for 2nd corn sowing in Morocco. Harvest in June, Year 3

Return to Egypt in early autumn, Year 3

Start in late November

TROPIC OF CANCER

C. Palmas passed late June, Year 2

EQUATOR

May: land for 1st corn sowing. Harvest in November; sun far to north during these months.

St Helena Bay

TROPIC OF CAPRICORN

Main currents

Sea, and was interested in promoting trade with the Mediterranean. When his canal failed he would naturally think of exploring an alternative route between the 'northern' and 'southern' seas, and would turn to the Phoenicians as the most experienced mariners of the time. Their ships were hardly less seaworthy than those in which Drake and Magellan sailed round the world. The line of the coast would serve them instead of a compass. The voyage was within the bounds of possibility, and although it cannot be proved beyond doubt, I am inclined to agree with those who accept it. The details were either not fully reported—the Phoenicians were notoriously secretive about such things—or else were forgotten because the voyage did not suggest any practical possibilities for trade. But it did establish that Africa was surrounded by continuous sea, the point that claims Herodotus' main attention. This fact was never forgotten by the Carthaginians, though not all subsequent Greek geographers were aware of it. A vague memory of it, perhaps contaminated with garbled versions of Hanno's voyage (for which see p. 81), survived the Middle Ages to inspire the plans of Prince Henry the Navigator.

On such a lengthy voyage the main risk was that the ships would lose touch, or be blown so far from land that they could not make their way back again. If this happened off Angola the southeast trade winds might have impelled part of the squadron irresistibly towards the coast of Brazil. Obviously this possibility was an important factor in the case of the notorious Parahyba inscription, allegedly discovered at Pouso Alto in northeast Brazil in 1873. The inscription, said to have been on stone, is extant only in a transcription. The monument itself was never produced for inspection. Professor Cyrus Gordon, who has recently argued in favour of its authenticity, translates it as follows:

> We are sons of Canaan from Sidon, the city of the king. Commerce has cast us on this distant shore, a land of mountains. We set [= sacrificed] a youth for the exalted gods and goddesses in the nineteenth year of Hiram, our mighty king. We embarked from Ezion-Geber into the Red Sea and voyaged with ten ships. We were at sea together for two years around the land belonging to Ham [= Africa] but were separated by a storm [lit., 'from the hand of Baal'] and we were no longer with our companions. So we have come here, twelve men and three women, on a . . . shore which I, the Admiral, control. But auspiciously may the exalted gods and goddesses favour us!

Despite Professor Gordon's ingenious pleading, one must agree with the general verdict of scholars (strongly reaffirmed by Professor F. M. Cross) that the inscription was a clever forgery designed to appeal to the antiquarian tastes of Dom Pedro II. *

The Carthaginians were the first to make a systematic exploration of the Atlantic coasts of Africa and Europe. Their purpose was to consolidate and extend their trade, especially in gold and tin. Herodotus gives a vivid picture of their 'dumb barter' with native tribes on the Moroccan coast, perhaps based on the island of Mogador, which they had reached before 600 BC:

> When they reach these peoples they unload their goods and set them out along the beach. Then they re-embark and send up smoke signals. The natives on seeing the smoke come to the place, put down gold against the goods, and retire. Then the Carthaginians land and examine it, and if they think it represents a fair exchange, they take it and leave, but if not, they go back to their ships and wait. The natives return and put down more gold until it reaches a satisfactory amount. (IV, 196)

In this traffic, cloth, pottery and trinkets must have fetched many times their value. B. H. Warmington considers that 'exploitation of this source of gold, with similar methods of acquiring silver and tin

*Ill. 65.* Transcription of the Parahyba inscription.

*See their articles in *Orientalia* 37, 1968.

in northern Europe, were the foundation of the Carthaginian Empire from the late fifth century onwards'.

About 500 BC a Carthaginian named Hanno led a large expedition to colonize and explore the coast south from Gibraltar. His official report survives in a Greek version, of which some extracts are given below:*

*The Greek text, with translation and commentary, is conveniently accessible in C. Kaeppel, *Off the Beaten Track in the Classics*, 27–61.

*Ill. 66*

> The Carthaginians decreed that Hanno should sail beyond the Pillars of Hercules and found colonies of Libyphoenicians. He set out with 60 pentecontes, men and women amounting to 30,000 in all, besides corn and other gear. [The figure must be greatly exaggerated even allowing for extra transports besides the warships.]
>
> After passing the Pillars we founded the first colony called Thymiaterion, two days' sail beyond, and sited in a large plain . . .
>
> We came to the Lixus [probably the Draa], a large river flowing from Libya. The Lixites, a nomad people, were pasturing their flocks beside it. We stayed some time with them and gained their friendship . . .
>
> Taking interpreters from them we sailed south along a desert shore for two days, and then east for one day. There we found a small island in the recess of a bay, less than a mile in circumference. We established a colony there called Cernē. Our sailing time from Carthage to the Pillars equalled that from the Pillars to Cernē, so we reckoned that it lay on a line with Carthage.

Herne island, off Rio de Oro not far from Villa Cisneros, is often identified with Cernē. It lies at the required distance from the Straits, but if Hanno regarded it as on the same latitude as Carthage, or due south of Carthage (as some of the ancient writers took it), he was of course very astray in his mapping. This important new colony then served as a base for further exploration southwards, as Hanno goes on to describe:

> We coasted south for twelve days. All the land was inhabited by Aithiopians who fled at our approach. Their language was unintelligible to our Lixite guides. We anchored under high mountains, forest-clad, with perfumed and variegated trees . . .
>
> After taking on water we sailed on for five days until we came to a large bay, which the interpreters said was called West Horn. In it was a large island with a saltwater lake in which was another island where we went ashore. By day we saw nothing but forests, but at night a blaze of many fires, and we heard a sound of pipes, and the clash of cymbals and drums, and an infinite clamour. Fear then seized us, and the soothsayers advised us to leave the island . . .

81

During four days' sailing we saw the land at night ablaze with fire. In the middle was a towering flame reaching, as it seemed, to the stars. By day this appeared as a very lofty mountain called Chariot of the Gods. Coasting on for three days past rivers of flame we reached a bay called South Horn, where was an island like the last one, with a lake containing another island full of savages. Most of them were females with hairy bodies whom the interpreters called Gorillas. All the males eluded capture, taking to the rocks and hurling stones at us, but we did take three females who bit and tore at their captors as they were dragged away. We killed them, skinned them, and brought the pelts back to Carthage. This was the limit of our voyage as our stores began to give out.

This very early and remarkable travel document has generated an immense literature, and almost every detail is the subject of controversy. But despite the difficulties, a convincing picture of a great pioneering voyage emerges from the text. How far did Hanno go? Some bring him past the Niger to the Cameroons, stressing the 'gorillas' and the lofty volcano 'Chariot of the Gods' identified with Cameroon Peak (13,000 ft.). But this does great violence to the sailing data. Besides, gorillas in our sense would have been too savage to capture, and there is no need to interpret the fires as volcanic. The nocturnal 'rivers of flame' may be plausibly interpreted as lines of burning grass and bush set alight by the natives—a practice noted by many explorers, and still current in Liberia in this century. The 'gorillas' will then be chimpanzees. If this is correct, Hanno will have reached Sherbro Sound near the border between Sierra Leone and Liberia, less than 8° north of the equator, after exploring more than 2,000 miles of the African coast, an achievement not surpassed until the fifteenth century. His report, it seems, was published as a tribute to his venture, but with some details deliberately distorted, and a total suppression of all mention of the gold trade for which Cernē must have been a key market.

At about the same time as Hanno's voyage, another expedition was sent out under Himilco to explore northward along the Atlantic seaboard. The purpose was again commercial, to establish control of the tin trade, the chief mines being in northwest Spain and Cornwall. Previously this trade had been in the hands of the Iberians of Tartessos,* but after 500 BC they were supplanted by Carthaginians operating from Gades. Cornish tin may have been reaching the Mediterranean world from as early as 1500 BC, but there is no evidence for Mediterranean traders on the Atlantic route before the Carthaginian take-over pioneered by Himilco.

Unfortunately his own report of his voyage is not extant, and we have to rely on late and scanty references.* He described the sea

*The Greeks variously used the name Tartessos for a kingdom in Southwest Andalusia, for the River Guadalquivir, and for a trading-town near its mouth whose exact site has not been located.

*The most important are in Avienus, *Ora Maritima* 108–129 and 380–9.

82

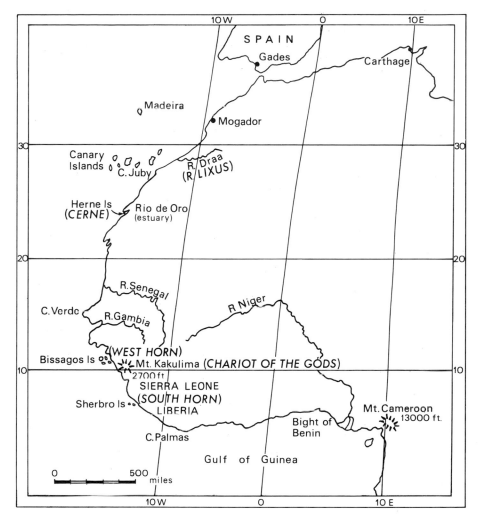

*Ill. 66.* A map to illustrate the voyage of exploration made by Hanno the Carthaginian, *c.* 500 BC. The names in brackets are those given in the extant account of the voyage. Their identification with modern place names is a matter for conjecture.

*Ill. 40*

beyond the Pillars as interminable and empty, and reported difficulties from sluggish, shallow, weed-clogged waters. One thinks of tidal estuaries which would have seemed so strange to Mediterranean sailors when first encountered. References to clogging seaweed are found in other ancient descriptions of the Atlantic, and have been incautiously inflated by some writers into a 'terrible sea of weed', and then equated with the Sargasso Sea, but there is no basis for this identification. Himilco also emphasized the fogs, the absence of wind (surprisingly), and the terrifying sea-monsters (predictably). We are told that his voyage lasted four months, and it seems likely that he penetrated at least as far as Brittany, if not to Cornwall, and spent some time organizing commercial contacts.

From their trading down the African coast the Carthaginians must have known about the Canaries, for Fuerteventura can be seen from Cape Juby, but there is no evidence that they settled there. The archipelago was not thoroughly explored until Juba, king of Morocco *c*. 25 BC–AD 25, sent an expedition.

They may also be credited with the discovery of Madeira. Diodorus (V, 19–20) tells how a Carthaginian ship was blown off course and found a large island several days' sail west of the African coast. The island was mountainous, with fruitful valleys and fertile plains. The climate was mild, with game and fish in abundance, and there were navigable rivers. 'It seemed like a dwelling place for gods, not men.' Madeira lies about 400 miles out, and being 40 miles long by 15 broad would be large by ancient standards. It suits Diodorus' description well, except for the navigable rivers.

It is an open question whether the Carthaginians reached the Azores, which lie about 1,000 miles west of Portugal. A find of nine gold and copper coins of Punic type was reported by J. Podolyn from Cuervo island in 1749, but unfortunately the hoard was never properly authenticated, and has now disappeared.* Plutarch reports that some sailors from Gades made their way to certain 'Fortunate Isles' where soft breezes brought a gentle rain from west and south. Two islands are mentioned, and their distance is given as 1,100 miles from the African coast. They have been identified with the Azores, but on the whole the description probably suits the Madeiras (700 miles southwest of Gades) better, since there are ten islands in the Azores, but only two habitable ones in the Madeiras.

*R. Hennig, *Terrae Incognitae* I, 109–19, defends the authenticity of the find.

The first Greek known to have sailed on the Atlantic was Colaeus of Samos. About 630 BC he was trying to get from Cyrene to Egypt, but was blown back by a 'levanter' which eventually carried him through the Straits of Gibraltar to Tartessos. There, in an 'untapped market', he was able to exchange his wares for so much silver that he made his fortune out of this one voyage.*

*The story is in Herodotus IV, 152.

Over the next hundred years the tough sailors of Phocaea in Ionia established a route to Tartessos from Sicily and Italy via Sardinia and the Balearics. They also explored the Gulf of Lyons, and founded Massilia (Marseilles). From there, Greek traders penetrated up the Rhône to profitable markets in Gaul, and colonies were established down the east coast of Spain, notably Emporion (Ampurias) *c*. 550 BC. A certain Midacritus is recorded as being the first Greek to import 'white lead' (*i.e.* tin) from the 'Tin Island' (probably Cornwall), but his date and city are unknown.

Some definite knowledge of Atlantic coastlands was acquired from these activities, and was summarized in a *periplous* by a Massilian captain about 525 BC. This work is not extant, but it formed one of the sources used by the late Roman poet Avienus in his *Ora Maritima* (fourth century AD). Avienus mentions a promontory Oestrymnis, lofty and facing south, and scattered Oestrymnid islands rich in tin and lead—probably a general reference to Ushant and the coasts of

Brittany and Cornwall with their off-shore islands. He knows that the 'Sacred Island' (Ireland) is two days' sail from Brittany, and mentions Britain under its pre-Celtic name Albion.

About 500 BC the Carthaginians established a blockade of the Straits, and Greek traders were effectively excluded from the Atlantic until the Carthaginians lost their naval supremacy in the first Punic War (264–241 BC). Greek knowledge of the Atlantic littoral declined so rapidly that Herodotus could doubt the existence of the 'tin islands' (*i.e.* the Scillies and Cornwall). Not until about 300 BC did a Greek captain slip through the Straits again. This was the celebrated

*Ill. 67* Pytheas of Massilia, whose voyage of exploration in northern waters was the outstanding scientific expedition of the ancient world. Pytheas may have been financed by Massilian merchants eager to locate the sources of tin and amber, but his own interests lay in the advancement of geographical knowledge. A competent astronomer (he calculated the latitude of Massilia to within $\frac{1}{2}$ per cent of the correct figure), and the first Greek to associate tides with the moon, he set out to trace the coastline of Europe to its furthest limits. Later Greek cartographers relied greatly on his reports and observations of latitude, which he published in book form. Pytheas was unjustly written off as a liar by Polybius and Strabo, and his works have not survived, so the detailed reconstruction of his voyage depends on quotations and references, and is somewhat problematical. But there can be no doubt that he circumnavigated Britain for he defined its triangular shape and named its three main promontories, Belerium (Land's End), Cantium (North Foreland) and Orcas (Duncansby Head). From shore excursions he was able to record particulars of life in Britain: the use of chariots in warfare, the primitive wattle or log cabins, the storage of grain in roofed barns, and the carting of tin-ingots at ebb tide to an 'island' off the Cornish coast. Pytheas literally put Britain on the map, being the first writer to use the name. He also knew of Ireland as another large island lying beyond Britain but does not seem to have visited it.

His most sensational report concerned the land of Thulē which he regarded as the most northerly part of the British archipelago. He placed Thulē at six days' sail north of Caithness, and close to the 'congealed [frozen?] sea'. In Thulē the inhabitants lived on millet (a mistake for oats?), wild herbs, fruits and roots; they made a beverage from honey, and threshed their corn in barns because of the rain and lack of sun. Pytheas also reported that in mid-summer the nights in Thulē were of only two or three hours' duration—a clear indication that he reached at least latitude 61° N, the parallel of the Shetlands and Bergen. He also seems to have heard of the 'midnight sun', though we cannot be sure that he actually went as far north as the Arctic circle.

Strabo poured scorn on one detail in his account. He claimed to have encountered near Thulē conditions in which air, earth, and sea blended into a mixture which he compared to a 'sea-lung', and which prevented any further progress. The meaning of the 'sea-lung' has not been satisfactorily explained, and we cannot be sure what he was trying to describe. He may have encountered ice-floes. If so, he was at least as far north as the Faeroes. Perhaps the most plausible explanation is that he met a dense and chilling sea fog off the Norwegian coast.

Pytheas' Thulē has been variously identified with Iceland, with Shetland, and with Norway. Iceland is probably ruled out by not having bees (for the honey drink), and in any case was probably uninhabited at this time. The Shetlands or Norway seem more plausible candidates, but we have not enough detail to settle the

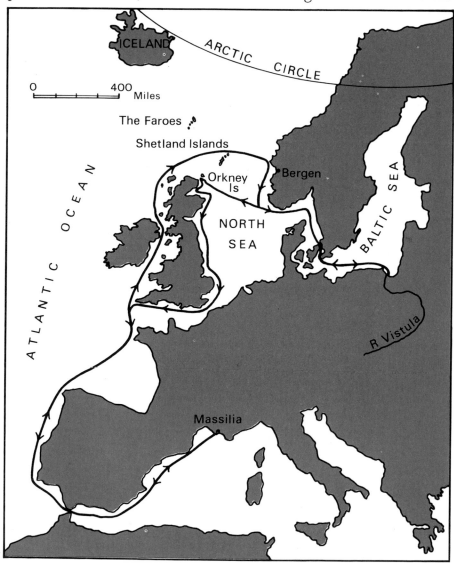

*Ill. 67.* A reconstruction of the voyage of Pytheas of Massilia, *c.* 300 BC.

*For a recent discussion, see R. Dion, *Revue de Philologie* 40, 1966.

issue between them. It is at least likely that Pytheas rounded the Shetlands, struck east to Norway, and followed the Scandinavian coastline as far as the Kattegat. He may even have explored the Baltic as far as the Vistula. *

Pytheas' round trip totalled about 8,000 miles, further than Columbus on his 1492 voyage. As Kaeppel remarks: 'In matters of endurance and daring there is little to choose between them.' No other ancient navigator approached Pytheas in scientific accomplishment, acute observation, and persistent penetration into unknown and formidable seas. We may fittingly close our account of ancient westward exploration with this summary of his voyage.

## The Atlantic in Greek Myth and Legend

The extent of ancient voyaging can be safely determined only on the basis of archaeological data or from the accounts of ancient historians or geographers. A journey once certified may be linked with a mythical landscape, but the myth in isolation should not be used as evidence that a discovery was made. This caution is particularly necessary in regard to 'western islands' or 'isles of the blest'. Like the terrestrial paradise of the Middle Ages, such islands lay always beyond the horizon of the explored world. If Homer describes Elysium with its cooling Ocean breezes 'at the end of the world', this is no proof that Minoans or Mycenaeans discovered remote Atlantic islands in the Bronze Age. It only confirms the tendency of the religious imagination to look beyond the sunset for the paradise of the departed. The remoteness and security of an island lying beyond an expanse of water made it a suitable symbol for the place of the dead. Secluded islands were also suitable abodes for gods and goddesses, and so the island of Cronus, or of Circe, or of Erytheia the Hesperid (the 'sunset-pink island in the west') lived in the popular imagination and entered into the currency of poetry.

But what if a living man had to visit such a place and return to his own kind? In such cases the poet tended to merge the known with the imaginary landscape to make the transition to 'fairyland' more credible. This process may be seen in Homer's account of Odysseus' voyage to the Land of the Dead (*Odyssey* 10, 508–12 and 11, 13–19). Homer and his hearers pictured the world as a circle of inhabited lands surrounded by the 'river' Oceanos. From somewhere in the western Mediterranean Odysseus sails to this 'river', a term that may imply a vague knowledge of the merging of Atlantic and Mediterranean at the western Straits. He then crosses the Ocean stream to a sunless land 'shrouded in mist and gloom'. This land contains 'groves of Persephone' and the 'house of Hades', so from one aspect it represents the 'other world'. But it is also inhabited by a community of Cimmerians who are quite distinct from the ghosts of the departed.

Such touches of 'local colour' may be plausibly explained as based on rumours of the uncouth inhabitants of northwest Europe and the cloud and gloom of northern winters. But when later in the *Odyssey* (24, 11–14) the dead are pictured on their journey to Hades past the 'Rock of Whiteness', it is going too far to identify this with the Cliffs of Dover!

A similar merging of fact and fancy may be seen in the saga of Herakles. His quest for the golden apples from the Garden of the Hesperides symbolizes the hero in search of immortality, which can only be won by overcoming the dragon guarding the 'tree of life'. Poets handling this myth felt obliged to give it a local habitation, and so in one version we find Herakles looking for the apples in the Caucasus. But as the Greek horizon expanded westwards the exploit tended to be located in northwest Africa, and then Atlas of the Atlas mountains was brought in to lend the hero assistance.

The roots of Greek mythology are very complex. It is quite possible that some ill-defined geographical information passed with the amber and tin along the trade routes of Bronze Age Europe, and so filtered into the pool of early Greek legend. In this way one could explain Homer's 'sleepless' herdsman, able to earn double pay where 'the paths of day and night are close together' (*Odyssey* 10, 84–6). This obscure phrase is perhaps best understood as embodying an awareness of the short nights in high latitudes, though it has recently received a much more mundane and Mediterranean explanation.* There is a passage in Hesiod (*Theogony,* 729–745) which also perhaps reflects a dim awareness of northern wastes and desolation. Hesiod, too, pictures flocks of clamorous swans on the banks of the stream of Ocean (*Shield of Herakles* 314–17). If the swans are whooper or whistling swans (*cygnus musicus*) we have here some indication of a knowledge of Baltic or North Sea fauna, for this species, nowadays at least, is a rare migrant in Mediterranean lands.

*L. G. Pocock, *Classical Quarterly,* N.S. 18, 1968, refers it to the meeting of two herdsmen, one bringing home sheep in the evening and the other taking out cattle for night pasturage.

But the game of putting Homer (and Hesiod) on the map has all too often been overplayed. For example, Calypso has been located in many an island from Malta to Tenerife. There is simply not enough evidence to support any of the proposed identifications to the exclusion of all others. In the 'white calm' and 'sheer cliff' of the Laestrygonians' harbour Bérard detected an ice-covered Norwegian fjord. But ruffled water is 'black' to Homer, so calms are naturally 'white', and there is no shortage of cliffs in the Mediterranean. With move cancelling move the game usually ends in an inconclusive draw.

It would be a long task to sift Greek mythology for possible fragments of Atlantic geography, and the results would be disappointingly inconclusive. I shall confine detailed analysis to two legends, Plato's story of Atlantis—derived from his ancestor Solon—and Plutarch's account of the land of Cronus. These are not traditional religious myths or anonymous travellers' tales, but distinctive productions by well-informed individuals. Both undeniably gave rein to their creative imagination for many of the details, but did their basic framework of islands in the Atlantic and a land beyond the Ocean owe anything to valid geographical information? That is the problem most relevant to the present enquiry.

*Ill. 8*

*Ill. 9*

Plato's Atlantis legend may be read in his *Timaeus* and *Critias* (see p. 17). The question of Atlantis has recently been much discussed in the light of discoveries on the volcanic island of Santorini (ancient Thera), which lies in the Aegean about 70 miles north of Crete. I am one of those who take the view that the legend embodies a distant and garbled memory of the great eruption of Santorini between 1500 and 1450 BC. The resultant earthquakes, tidal waves, and fall-out of ash caused great destruction in Crete and the surrounding islands, and fatally weakened the Minoan sea-empire, which then collapsed before the rising power of the mainland Greeks.

If this interpretation is correct, the historical prototype of Atlantis was really Minoan Crete and its island dependencies. It is quite possible that Solon coined the name Atlantis for the island described by his Egyptian informants (which was really Crete, though neither he nor Plato recognized it as such). The name means 'island of Atlas'. To Plato and his contemporaries this inevitably implied a connection with the 'sea of Atlas', *i.e.* the Atlantic Ocean, for the mythical Atlas had by then become associated with the Atlas range of Morocco, and so with the waters beyond.

*Ill. 7*

In the present context our concern is not with the ultimate origins of the legend, but with the use that Plato made of his materials. What information, then, did Plato have about the Atlantic? He would have known about the great Carthaginian outpost of Gades, and in fact introduces this name into his story. From his visits to Sicily, where Greek territory adjoined Carthaginian, he may have heard some report about the explorations of Hanno and Himilco. His emphasis on the shallowness of the waters beyond the Straits, and his statement that 'the sea in those parts is impassable and impenetrable' appear to reflect Carthaginian propaganda. Indeed, such a statement really underlines Plato's ignorance of the Atlantic. We cannot therefore take seriously his reference to the vast continent lying beyond Atlantis and its adjacent islands. As explained above (p. 68) this was simply an *a priori* assumption in keeping with his belief in the great size of the globe, which must, he thought, contain other land masses even greater than the known portions of Europe and Asia. It was a lucky guess based on no empirical information.

*Ill. 66*

*Ill. 10*

Had Plutarch any better information for the remarkable story which he incorporates into his treatise on 'The Face in the Orb of the Moon' (p. 20)? The 'continental' Greeks and the delectable island with its schools of science and philosophy are obviously fabulous. Moreover, Plutarch is clearly drawing directly on Plato's *Timaeus* for his conception of the continent beyond the ocean. But his geographical picture is more explicit, notably in regard to the chain of islands and the gulf on the latitude of the Sea of Azov. This picture may easily be related to the Faeroes, Iceland, Greenland, and the Gulf of St Lawrence. In fact Ortelius in 1593 cited this text to prove that the ancients had discovered the North American continent, and this has been a long-lived belief shared by Kepler and many others down to our own day.

Is there any independent evidence to support it? Knowledge of northwest Europe had increased greatly in the five centuries from Plato to Plutarch. The Roman conquest of Britain was completed in Plutarch's lifetime, and in the generation after his death Ptolemy was able to draw a tolerably good map of the British Isles. A jug of grey ware with a Latin inscription, brought up by a trawler from near the Porcupine Bank 150 miles west of Ireland, raises interesting questions about ancient trade routes in this area.* The Shetlands and Outer Hebrides must have been visited, but we have no evidence for voyages in this period even as far as the Faeroes, much less to Iceland or Greenland. Plutarch's King Cronus asleep in his island paradise has a flavour of Celtic mythology about him. But this does not mean that the Celts were in possession of any reliable information about any 'land to the west'. I cannot believe that Plutarch's story has any valid geographical content. In my opinion he was, like Plato, merely speculating about a further continent and a possible route to it, and it is only coincidence that some of his description can be made to fit some of the facts.

*Ill. 68*

*Reported in the *Journal of Roman Studies* 24, 1934, 220–1.

A number of other ancient romancers handled the theme of Atlantic islands and a continent beyond, and were duly satirized by Lucian in his *Vera Historia*. The hero of this tale sailed from Gibraltar, and after a lengthy voyage fetched up at an island with a river of wine. He was swallowed by a whale, and went up to the moon, and finally ended his lunatic cruise in 'the continent opposite us'.

The basis of all these tales remains the same: Plato's theorizing about the 'true continent' beyond the 'true ocean', in combination with the mythical theme of a paradisal island, the latter a little amplified and coloured by sailors' yarns about actual visits to Madeira or the Canaries. They provide no evidential basis for the belief that the ancients discovered America.

Paradoxically, the suggestion that Red Indians 'discovered' ancient Europe may rest on a slightly less flimsy basis. It goes back to a curious incident in the life of Quintus Metellus Celer, governor of Cisalpine Gaul in 62 BC, and governor designate of Transalpine Gaul prior to his death in 59 BC. Presumably he had interests and con-

*Ill. 69*

*Ill. 68.* An *olla* of Roman grey ware which was dredged up by a trawler near the Porcupine Bank, 150 miles west of Ireland. On the bottom is a rudely scratched drawing of an animal, possibly a bear, and above this a graffito inscription: C PISCI FAGI, possibly the owner's name.

*Pomponius Mela III, 5; Pliny *N.H.* II, 170. The MSS. vary widely about the name of the forwarding tribe. Readings include *Boiorum, Suevorum, Baetorum.* Migrations were such a feature of the Celtic and Germanic worlds that we find Boii in Bohemia *and* central France, Suevi in northeast *and* southwest Germany. The Baeti were in southwest Spain, which seems very remote from the provinces associated with Metellus. A shipwreck of the 'Indians' near the mouth of the Rhine, and their passage as slaves up the river and across the Alps perhaps suits the data best.

nections north and west of the Alps. At all events, a chieftain from somewhere beyond the Roman frontiers was moved to make him a present of some shipwrecked sailors who must have been regarded as a 'nine days' wonder'. After interrogating them Metellus formed the opinion that they had been blown by a storm from 'Indian waters' and eventually cast up on the coast of 'Germany'. He related the incident to his friend Cornelius Nepos, and Nepos included it in a geographical work (now lost), whence it was cited by Mela and Pliny.* These writers all used the information as proof that the ocean extended continuously round the north of Europe to India. One thing at least is certain: no one from India could have taken this route at this date. It is also hardly conceivable that Indian merchants could have been blown round Africa to be wrecked in northwest Europe. Where, then, did the castaways hail from? Scholars have variously argued that they were Laplanders, Balts, Britons (woad-dyed to an *indigo* colour!), African negroes, and Red Indians. Obviously the evidence permits no certain conclusion. It seems they must have been dark-skinned, and remote enough to be entirely foreign to the chieftain who sent them on to Metellus. Beyond that one can hardly go, though one wonders how they communicated with the Roman governor, and why he formed the opinion that they had come from Indian waters.

A better authenticated incident in AD 1508 lends a little support to the conjecture that they could have been Red Indians. In that year a French ship sailing near the British Isles encountered a small boat manned by seven men of medium height, darkish skin, and broad features, who spoke an unintelligible tongue. Six of them died, but one survivor was taken back and presented to Louis XII—a curious parallel to Metellus' 'Indians'. The detail which seems to clinch their North American origin is that their boat was made of tree bark over a light osier framework.*

*The incident is recorded by Cardinal Bembo (1470–1547) in his *History of Venice*.

## Conclusion

In the second millennium BC the peoples of Europe had risen well above the level of barbarism. Goods were exchanged freely, and achievements like Stonehenge imply a high standard of social organization. Metals were mined from Spain to Ireland and from the Danube to Cornwall. The spread of megalithic monuments from Spain to Scandinavia seems to indicate coastwise shipping from at least the middle of the third millennium, and possibly earlier. By 1500 BC Aegean objects were reaching the British Isles, and Baltic amber had been brought to Greece.

Against this background, it is not unreasonable to suppose that some miscellaneous and ill-defined information about western Europe filtered through to the Mycenaean world before the end of the Bronze Age, and was incorporated into Greek mythology and the epic tradition. But there is no evidence to show that early traders from the Aegean ever sailed as far as the British Isles. A part of southeastern Spain may have been colonized from the Cyclades as early as c. 2500 BC, but the impetus of this movement—if it occurred—was not sustained, and Mycenaean pottery has not been found in any quantity further west than Sicily and the Lipari islands. By the Late Bronze Age the Iberians presumably had their own shipping and brought their goods to the central Mediterranean for exchange and trans-shipment. It is not unlikely that Minoan and Mycenaean skippers occasionally sailed to the Straits of Gibraltar—they had the capacity for such a voyage—but they have left no evidence of occupation west of Sicily.

Greece lapsed into a Dark Age between 1100 and 900 BC, and all detailed information about the westward sea routes is likely to have been lost. Only a vague memory of the seas round Sicily survived in the Odysseus saga.

Decline was less marked in the Levant where vigorous 'sea-peoples' established themselves on the coastal plains of Canaan. Minoan refugees went to Syria and Palestine, and some of their naval expertise

*Ill. 69.* In 1859 a French savant, ▶ M. Egger, suggested that this Roman bronze (right), now in the Louvre, might be a portrait of one of the 'Indians' interrogated by Quintus Metellus Celer, c. 60 BC. This conjecture seems most implausible. There is no reason to connect the bronze with the 'Indians', and the physiognomy of the bust is much more Roman than Red Indian.

The object has its own interest. It is a bucket (*situla*) in the form of a human head. The projection on top is the handle, and the cranium is hinged to open like a lid. It might possibly be a divining urn. Such urns were sometimes filled with water prior to the placing in them of the lots.

may underlie the Phoenician maritime expansion which was well under way by 1000 BC. In Greek tradition the Phoenicians 'colonized' Utica and Gades by 1100 BC, but probably this implies no more than occasional trading trips, for archaeology has revealed no trace of their occupation of these sites earlier than the eighth century BC. Thereafter they steadily became the dominant maritime power in the western Mediterranean.

In the sixth century Phocaean enterprise brought Greek traders into Atlantic waters, and definite information about the Atlantic coastline up to Ireland is now recorded in writing for the first time. Herodotus is the first author to use the name 'Atlantic Sea', around 450 BC, but he knows very little about it because by this time the Greeks were confined within the Straits by the Carthaginians. He does, however, know that the Atlantic is continuous with the Indian Ocean because of the Phoenician circumnavigation of Africa around *Ill. 63* 600 BC. That astonishing voyage opened no new trade routes, and its implications were never properly appreciated by ancient geographers.

From Gades the Carthaginians monopolized Atlantic trade until their defeat by Rome. They planted a colony a thousand miles down the African coast, and explored as far south again. They certainly discovered the Canaries, probably Madeira, and possibly the Azores. Northwards they traded with Brittany and Cornwall. They must have acquired much information about long stretches of the Atlantic coast, but published little apart from an account of Hanno's voyage.

The only Greek explorer of note in the Atlantic was Pytheas, who *Ill. 66* sailed round Britain about 300 BC, and reported on an 'island' of *Ill. 67* Thulē much further to the north. His report suits Shetland or Norway rather than Iceland, but nothing definite was ever found out about Thulē by the ancients. It remained *ultima Thule,* the notional northern limit of the world.

After the Roman conquest of Britain the British Isles became quite well known to the geographers, but were never used as a base for further exploration in Atlantic waters. The main thrust of Roman commercial expansion went eastwards. From about AD 50 a regular trade route was established from the Gulf of Aden direct to southern India and Ceylon. Occasional merchant-venturers penetrated the Bay of Bengal, and reached the Malay peninsula, and even China.

There can be no doubt that Phoenicians, Carthaginians, Greeks and Romans all had ships capable of making an Atlantic crossing. The circumnavigation of Africa (if it occurred) was over 15,000 miles; Hanno's voyage was 6,000 miles; Pytheas travelled nearly 8,000 miles; and the pepper run to the Malabar coast involved an ocean passage of some 2,000 miles out of sight of land. But there is no evidence that an Atlantic crossing was ever achieved, or even attempted, by any ancient captain.

*Ill. 46*

Talk of a continent beyond the Atlantic begins with Plato. He had no evidence for the suggestion; it was simply an inference from the new doctrine of the earth as an immense sphere. Later, Crates thought up three hypothetical continents to fill the blank spaces on his globe. No one set out to test these hypotheses by voyages of exploration. A torrid zone was thought to cut off access to the southern hemisphere, and the Atlantic lay as an impassable barrier to the west. Composers of Utopias imagined inhabitants in these unknown lands, much as a modern writer of space fiction might picture life in another galaxy. Plutarch's story of the land of Cronus is a comparatively sober essay in this genre. But in default of other evidence no ancient legend of 'land to the west' can establish a pre-Columbian discovery of the New World.

The most that can be allowed is that such a discovery could have occurred accidentally as a result of Carthaginian trading down the west coast of Africa. We know that a Greek trader was blown perforce from Cyrene to Tartessos, a distance of over 1,700 miles. Similar accidents may have happened off the Moroccan coastline. Once a ship reaches the Azores or the Canaries, it is all too easy to end up in the Caribbean. In 1731 a boat with six men and a cargo of wine travelling from Tenerife to Gomera fetched up in Trinidad. Did something similar happen in antiquity? Ancient sources can provide no answer to this question. An answer can only be based on an assessment of the evidence for trans-oceanic influence on the cultures of Central and Southern America.

But it is certain that the skill of Greek map-makers and the large vision of ancient thinkers laid the foundation and provided the inspiration for Columbus's first expedition. Seneca prophesied better than he knew when he closed his fine chorus on seafaring with the famous lines:

*Venient annis saecula seris*
*Quibus Oceanus vincula rerum*
*Laxet, et ingens pateat tellus,*
*Tethysque novos detegat orbes,*
*Nec sit terris ultima Thule.*

The years run slow, but yet shall come
A time when Ocean frees our bonds,
When vast new worlds shall stand revealed,
Nor Thulē be the last of lands.          (*Medea*, 375–9)

# Norse Explorers ⠀⠀⠀⠀⠀⠀ 3

Helge Ingstad

THE BACKGROUND TO THE NORSE DISCOVERY OF AMERICA is that remarkable period in history which has been called the Viking Age, a time when practically the whole of Europe was exposed to attacks from the peoples of Scandinavia. It began somewhat before the ninth century with sporadic raids along the coasts of England, after which time activity increased with almost explosive force. Fleets of Viking ships sailed to new countries, bent now not only on plundering but also on conquest.

The Norwegian Vikings often sailed to the islands of northern Scotland, and then further south to England, Ireland, France and eventually deep into the Mediterranean. The Danish Vikings were no less active, sailing mainly to England but also southwards to France and beyond. The Swedish Vikings concentrated their activities in the Baltic lands and to the south, down the great rivers of Russia to the Black Sea, Byzantium and Baghdad. In many of the conquered areas the Vikings established their own kingdoms.

There was, however, one route which the Norwegian Vikings had largely to themselves (later they were joined by Icelanders) and that was the 'Western Route' or *Vestervegen, i.e.* the western sailing route across the North Atlantic. With Norway's long ranging coastline facing this ocean, this was a natural development. With the passage of time, these seafarers discovered one island after another as they proceeded further and further west until Norse ships landed on the coasts of North America. The Western Route was finally completed.

The belligerence of the Viking period has done much to overshadow this other aspect of Viking activity: the discovery of new lands where the Norse\* people built settlements and where hard work was more important than brandishing swords. Nor have other aspects of the Viking culture received their fair share of attention: these headstrong 'Northerners' developed their own legal system, their own oral literature, a magnificent art of wood carving and a mastery of runic script.

*Ill. 70*

\*Translator's note: Norse is here used in its original sense of referring to the Western Vikings, *i.e.* those who sailed to the west.

96

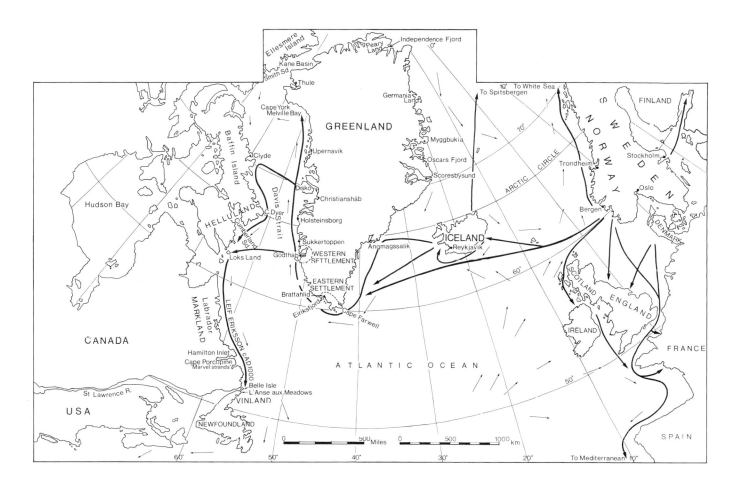

*Ill. 70.* Map showing the sea-routes of the Norsemen in the Viking age, including the so-called 'Western Way' from Norway to Iceland, the Norse settlements in Greenland and then on to North America—Helluland, Markland and Vinland.

*Ills. 75–77*

The people along the coast of Norway eventually achieved a high standard of seamanship and of ship-building. The Gogstad Ship (see pp. 100, 101), dating from about the tenth century, which was discovered in a burial mound in southern Norway, attests to these facts. It is built of oak and is 23·8 metres long, the breadth midships being 5·1 metres. With crew and full equipment on board, it would have drawn about one metre of water. The mast was hefty and intended for square sail. The ship also had side-oars, sixteen on each side. It was not only a strong and flexible ship, but striking with its fine lines and the high slope of the bow. In 1893, a Norwegian, Magnus Andersen, sailed a reproduction of the Gogstad ship across the Atlantic, making important observations on the voyage. It became obvious that the vessel had remarkable seaworthiness in all kinds of weather; it held to an average speed of about 5 knots and under especially favourable weather conditions reached a speed of 10 knots.

On the westward journeys of the Norwegian Vikings, the Shetland Islands, the Orkneys, the Hebrides and the Faeroe Islands were reached relatively early. In these places the Vikings made their homes

97

and had their own chieftains. Iceland was discovered in the middle of the ninth century, and the discovery was followed by rapid emigration there. It began from the west coast of Norway, and was mainly from there, but eventually a number of emigrants arrived from the Norwegian colonies on the islands of northern Scotland and from Ireland. Iceland became, in 930, an independent state.

Further to the west there lay still another island, the huge expanse of Greenland which was as yet an unknown land, although reports of its existence had come from a man called Gunnbjörn, who told of having sighted it. The next person to become involved in this pattern of expansion was Eirik the Red, a leader surpassed by few and one of the most remarkable personalities of the Viking Age. He was born in Jæren, in southwest Norway, about AD 950 and eventually followed his family to Iceland and settled there. He was, however, a quarrelsome character and came into sharp conflict with the powerful local families, as a result of which he was condemned as an outlaw. In secret, Eirik equipped his ship (in 982) and sailed in a southwesterly direction—he wished to find the land which Gunnbjörn had sighted. He discovered Greenland and in the course of three years he systematically explored the southwestern part of the country. He then returned to Iceland where he organized one of the most remarkable polar expeditions ever known. It was to comprise emigrants who would settle down in this new country, to which Eirik had given the name Greenland (Graenland), as a further encouragement to prospective settlers to undertake the voyage.

In the summer of 985 (986) a fleet of twenty-five square-sailed ships departed from the west coast of Iceland for the dangerous ice-ridden waters of Greenland. On board there were some four hundred persons, including women and children; in addition there were horses, cattle, sheep, goats and the simple equipment of the Viking Age. Only fourteen ships reached southwestern Greenland; the rest disappeared or returned to Iceland. Once there, the emigrants set

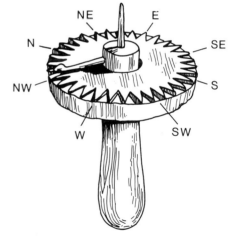

*Ills. 71, 72, 74.* Aids to navigation in the Viking age: the wooden half-disk (left) was found at Unartoq (Siglufjord), Eastern Settlement, in Greenland and is thought to be part of a Norse bearing-dial (above). Right, a Norse 'Solskuggsfjol' which was used to measure the shadow of the sun.

*Ill. 73.* Wreck I of the Skuldelev ships, the only example yet found of a Scandinavian 'knorr'. It was discovered in Denmark. The 'knorr' was a broad-beamed merchantman and probably the sort of vessel used by the Greenlanders on their voyages of discovery.

*Austerbygden and Vesterbygden, the Eastern and Western Settlements, are both on the west coast of Greenland. Their names reflect their relative position, the former being to the southeast of the latter.

about eking out a living in this new polar land. There were two settlements, Austerbygden in the south and Vesterbygden further north.* Eirik chose the most propitious area—Austerbygden—for himself; settling at the head of Eiriksfjord (Tunugliarfik) he built a homestead which was named Brattahlid.

The conditions in Greenland do much to explain the Norse voyages to North America. It was from this land that the 'Vinland voyagers' sailed to the New World; and Eirik the Red and his children, not least of them Leif Eiriksson, played central roles in these expeditions. An objective evaluation of these journeys requires that the society and the living conditions in Greenland be kept constantly in mind, and a short description of the most important aspects of the country and the people is therefore vital.

The emigrants' new land was mountainous and wild. To the east, the vast icecap plateau rose to about 10,000 feet, while along the coast the polar stream from Siberia carried the ice masses northwards. On sheltered mountain slopes, however, there grew wind-warped birch trees and along the fjords there were the rich grassy plots where the people mainly settled. It is probable that the Norsemen were alone for a considerable time in this part of the north, though Eskimos seemed to have been there before and disappeared, and apparently they did not reach the settlement again before the fourteenth century, when a branch of the Thulē Eskimos moved down the west coast. All told

*Ills. 75–77.* The Gogstad ship was excavated from a Viking burial mound in southeast Norway in 1880 (left). It dated from the middle of the ninth century, and it was in this ship that a Norwegian king was probably buried. The general arrangement of the ship can be seen below: it is 77½ ft. long and 17 ft. broad at its widest point. Right, the bow of the Gogstad ship.

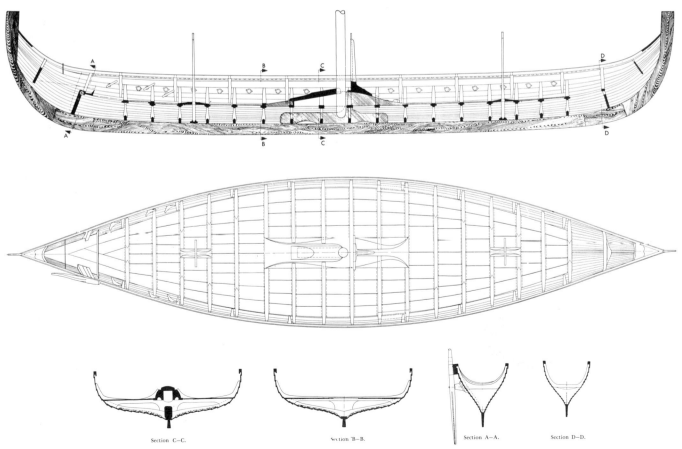

Section C–C.    Section B–B.    Section A–A.    Section D–D.

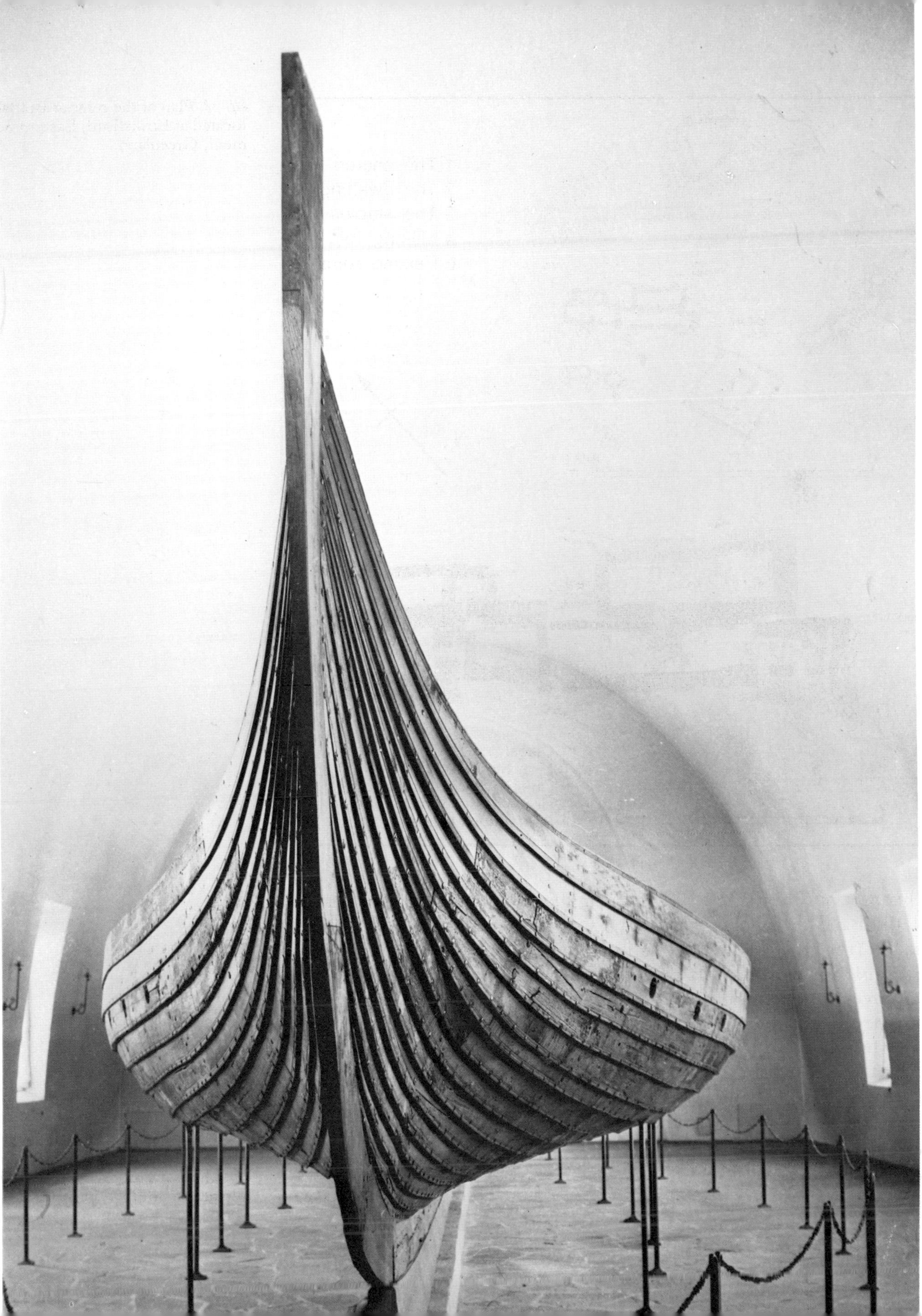

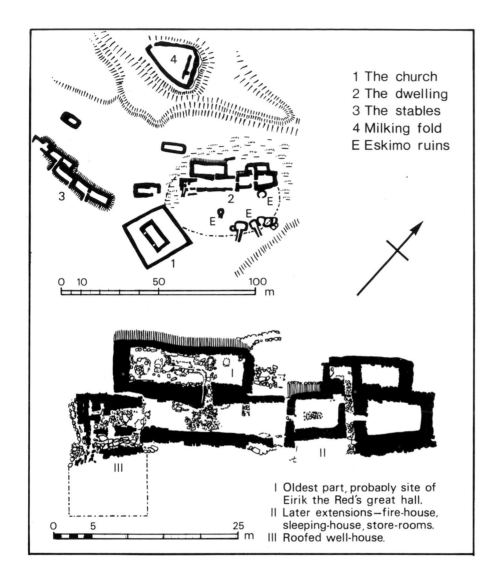

*Ill. 78.* Plan of the ruins at Brattahlid, located at Eiriksfjord, Eastern Settlement, Greenland.

1 The church
2 The dwelling
3 The stables
4 Milking fold
E Eskimo ruins

I Oldest part, probably site of Eirik the Red's great hall.
II Later extensions—fire-house, sleeping-house, store-rooms.
III Roofed well-house.

this part of Greenland was a polar-influenced zone where the climate a thousand years ago (according to pollen analysis) did not differ much from that of today, and it was one which necessitated a bitter struggle for existence. It thus becomes easy to understand what the discovery of the more fertile lands of North America must have meant to the Greenlanders. These circumstances must be given particular weight when evaluating the written sources which give information about the 'new lands' to the west. It must not least be taken into consideration that in Greenland the sole building material for ships was driftwood, whereas the forests of Labrador lay only a fairly short sailing distance away.

They built their houses of turf and stone, tended their herds, fished, hunted caribou, seals, walruses and polar bears. They made their own

*Ill. 79.* Right, a Norse woollen ▶ garment with a headcovering, both of which were excavated at Herjolfsnes in southwestern Greenland.

iron from bog-iron. The women wove. The many fascinating excavations carried out by Danish archaeologists show that Norse culture persisted on this polar island.

A direct route from Greenland to Norway and back was quick to develop, and Bergen became the chief terminal port. Among items exported were skins, furs, blubber, dried fish, walrus tusks, live polar bears, and white falcons.

About the year 1000 Christianity was brought to Greenland and thereafter churches were built. In 1124 the Greenlanders received their first bishop, who from 1153 came under the authority of the Norwegian archbishop of Nidaros (Trondheim). Greenland was, at first, an independent republic, but in 1261 voluntarily accepted the suzerainty of the Norwegian king and became part of the Norwegian empire, which then comprised the Shetland Islands, the Orkneys, the Hebrides, the Isle of Man, the Faeroes, Iceland and Greenland.

It is astonishing how relatively large the population of Greenland must have been. Ruins have been found of about three hundred farms, seventeen churches, a bishop's residence, two monasteries and various other buildings. At its height, in the years of the thirteenth century, the community probably comprised 4,000 inhabitants. Furthermore, various factors indicate that this community was still extant as late as about the year 1500. Among other things, the remarkable finds by Danish archaeologists of woollen garments and head coverings in the half-frozen ground at the churchyard at Herjolfsnes demonstrate its survival and connection with Europe. Characteristically European hats, which were the fashion of the fourteenth century, and the tall head coverings which were used in the time of Charles the Bold of Burgundy at the end of the fifteenth century, were found in the excavations at Herjolfsnes.

After this time something drastic must have happened. When ships later reached the Greenland settlements none of the people of Norse origin were to be found. Ruins of farms, churches and monasteries witnessed what once had been—but a whole community had vanished. What was the fate of this people? The theories have been many but no one knows with certainty what ultimately happened to this extraordinary Norse civilization which had lived for about 500 years on that distant Arctic island.

With the colonization by Eirik the Red of southwest Greenland, North America had become a neighbour. The Davis Strait was all that separated the two lands and this at its narrowest point was a mere 250 nautical miles wide. To cross this strait was only a modest voyage for Norse seamen who maintained a direct route to the west coast of Norway—a distance of about 1,500 nautical miles over the North Atlantic. It was probably fairly soon after the settlement of Greenland that the ambitious hunters on that island realized there was more land to the west. Ancient Icelandic sources mention voyages far north of the settlement areas to the so-called 'Northern Hunting Grounds' (Norðersetur) for the purpose of hunting, fishing and gathering driftwood. The hunters probably went at least as far as Disko Island at 70° N, sailing along a coast where there would be large catches of walrus, whales, seals and caribou. It would be strange if during such voyages they had not glimpsed, at some time or other, Baffin Island's high mountains with their glittering glaciers.

If we consider that the Greenland community survived for nearly 500 years, we are surely justified in assuming that the Greenlanders could hardly have avoided discovering North America. This would be a reasonable conclusion even if there were no written sources with which to verify it.

We are fortunate, however, in having written sources which tell us about new lands west and southwest of Greenland, discovered about the year 1000 and named Helluland, Markland and Vinland. On the one hand, there are a number of scattered and relatively short sources, and on the other the Icelandic sagas, namely *The Greenlanders' Saga* and *Eirik the Red's Saga* which directly relate voyages to the new lands.

Of the former sources only the most important will be mentioned. The oldest written source is contained in the work of the German, Adam of Bremen, *Adami Gesta Hammaburgensis ecclesiae pontificum*. The work was written about 1075—only a generation after the voyages of the Greenlanders to Vinland had taken place according to the Icelandic Sagas. His information is reportedly obtained from the Danish king and he states among other things:

> Moreover, he also mentioned another island which many have found in that great ocean, which is called Vinland, since there grow wild grapes and they give the best wine. That place has also an abundance of self-sown wheat, and we know this, not from legend but from the reliable report of the Danes . . . . Beyond this island, there is to be found no habitable land in that great ocean, but everything else beyond is filled with intolerable ice and terrible mist.

This constitutes remarkable information from Germany at such an early period. It is the case, however, that Adam's work in many instances is unreliable and we would agree with various eminent scholars such as Sven Søderberg and Fridtjof Nansen that his description of grapes, wine and self-sown wheat is an addition which has no factual support, but arises from a misunderstanding of the name Vinland (see pp. 175 ff). Substantively, however, there remains the fact that many people had reportedly come upon a new land which was called Vinland.

No less interesting is the first Icelandic mention of Vinland, to be found in the *Book of the Icelanders*, written by the reliable Icelandic historian Ari Frode (1068–1148). He lived not long after the time of the Vinland voyages (*c.* 1000), and in a milieu which should have given him more accurate information about the lands to the west than most. He first relates Eirik the Red's discovery and colonization of Greenland and continues:

> . . . both to the east and west [Eastern and Western Settlements] they found dwelling-places, the remnants of boats and stone implements which made them realize that the same sort of people had lived there as in Vinland and whom the Greenlanders called Skraelings [which refers to the natives of North America].

The most important thing about this passage is that it is not written to tell about Vinland: it simply uses a name connected with Vinland in order to explain something else. It presupposes an awareness of what Vinland was, or in other words posits the discovery of that land as part of accepted knowledge. On its own distinctiveness, this source stands out as a remarkable piece of evidence that the Greenlanders knew of the existence of North America.

An old Icelandic description of the world from the fifteenth century, which probably originated from the widely-travelled Icelander, Abbot Nicholas of Munka-Tvera (died 1159), tells of three lands to the west, Helluland, Markland and Vinland, and adds that it is no great distance from Markland to Vinland.

Most of the evidence mentioned probably relates to the voyages to these lands which took place about the year 1000 according to the Icelandic Sagas. How much later did they persist? It would be very strange if the Greenlanders had not renewed their journeys to these richer lands in the course of their nearly five centuries of civilization, especially when the route was known and they could get hold of valuable furs, walrus tusks, and timber for ship-building. Some sources indicate that such voyages did take place. In the Icelandic annals preserved in fourteenth-century manuscripts, the following piece of information for the year 1121 can be found:

> Eirik, Bishop of Greenland, went in search of Vinland (*fór at leita Vinlands*).

With this account, the Greenland bishop disappears from history and we are left with the questions: what was the purpose of his journey and what happened? Several scholars suggest that Eirik acted as a missionary to the natives of America, but it seems highly improbable that a Norse bishop at this stage would become involved in such a venture in a strange land among hordes of wild Indians and Eskimos. The most natural explanation seems to be that Bishop Eirik intended to pay a visit to a Norse community on the coasts of North America.

Icelandic annals have, in addition, recorded for the year 1347 an event which demonstrates that North America was known at that time. They state:

> Then there came a ship from Greenland which was smaller than the small Icelandic vessels. It put in at outer Straumsfjord, and had no anchor. It had 17 (some say 18) men on board. They had sailed to Markland but had since been storm-blown here.

This source has a marked ring of authenticity. Markland, which in all probability is Labrador, is used without further explanation and the presumption is that it was the familiar name of a known country.

Amongst the other sources mention should also be made of a few very old maps. First, there was the so-called Skálholt map of 1590, charted by the Icelander, Sigurdur Stefansson. Most scholars are convinced that the map was prepared, according to the descriptions in the sagas, as a rough sketch and that it lacks any geographical value. To this one must counter two arguments. The first was proposed by the English scholar, G. M. Gathorne-Hardy, who declares that there is scarcely another map giving such a realistic delineation of the northern regions of North America for that period. Secondly, the settlements—Austerbygden and Vesterbygden—are both indicated by distinct bays on the map and have been given correct locations

*Ills. 80, 81.* Below left, the famous Skálholt map which dates from AD 1590. The original has been lost and this copy was drawn in 1670. The long and narrow peninsula on which is written *Promontorium Winlandiæ* seems to correspond to northern Newfoundland. The Resen map (below right) is of the same type.

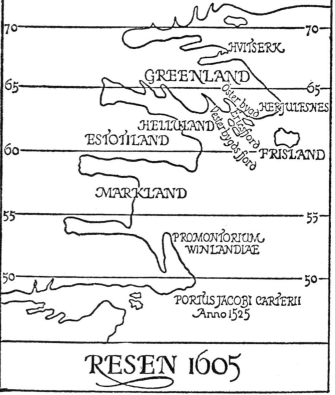

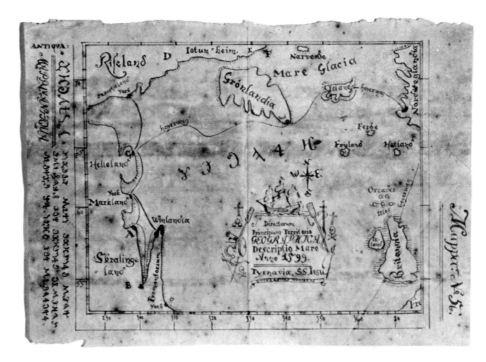

on Greenland's west coast. This is significant because, in the course of time, the location of Austerbygden was forgotten and for a long time it was thought to have been on the east coast of Greenland.

The long peninsula with the label 'Promontorium Winlandiæ' has in addition, a striking similarity to the most northerly part of Newfoundland. It is true that to the west of the peninsula a deep fjord has been indicated, but it did take a considerable time after the discovery of these regions before it was ascertained that what separated Newfoundland and Labrador was a narrow stretch of water—the Strait of Belle Isle.

*Ill. 81*    A map of a similar type was drawn by Hans Poulsen Resen in 1605. This map cannot be a copy of the Skálholt map because it has a Latin text which strongly suggests that it was based on a map several centuries old.

*Ill. 82*    In addition, I have discovered a formerly unknown map of the same type which in various aspects is of great interest. Remarkably enough, it was found in Hungary in the old archbishop's residence in the town of Esztergom on the Danube. During the Second World War, the Germans made the archbishop's residence their headquarters and it became the scene of fighting. When the town was liberated, ancient books, documents and maps from the library came to light, as well as copper engravings and other valuable antiquities which had been strewn around. Among these things the map was found.

The Hungarian map was probably copied by Jesuits in the former university town of Nagyszombat in the northern part of Hungary.

The map is dated 1599. Strangely enough, part of the text is written in Hungarian runes: the name for the northern part of the Atlantic ocean, and a legend on the left of the map which says:

North Sea [route], so by [along] northern world/Europe[?] and northern new world, there on to York and Winlandiae.

An interesting feature of the map is the marked route which leads from Scotland to Norway and also the route which leads from a place in Norway, which corresponds to Bergen (the shipping port for Greenlanders) across the ocean to Iceland, Greenland, Helluland, Markland and Winlandiae. The most remarkable thing about the map, perhaps, is that at the very tip of the long peninsula where the word 'Promontorium' has been written and below the name Winlandiae (which is written right above the tip) there is a boundaried area marked in black. (The Norse settlement discovered and unearthed during my expeditions lies at the northern tip of Newfoundland—see Chapter 6.)

There is not sufficient space here to digress on other interesting details of this map, but when it is considered in relation to the two other maps of similar type, the Skálholt map and Resen's map, the general picture which emerges suggests that they were all based upon old geographical information and that northern Newfoundland corresponds to Vinland.

In 1965, Yale University Press published its sensational 'Vinland Map'; a publication which led to much discussion and controversy. It is related to the map of the Venetian, B. Andrea Bianco, published in 1436, but it has various features which do not apply to the Venetian one. It has a large island lying to the west and southwest of Greenland which is given the name of Vinland. Above the island there is a lengthy Latin legend. The authors came to the conclusion that the map could probably be dated to *circa* 1440. There are aspects of this map which, in my opinion, might indicate that it is genuine and of great antiquity, but it would be untenable at this juncture to take a definitive standpoint before various questions of scientific importance have been more fully examined.

One of the strongest objections to the map is that it portrays Greenland as an island. It is only relatively recently that Greenland has been found to be an island and the Vinland Map would presume that in those early days men had sailed around the northern tip—an event which is highly unlikely. This objection, however, seems to carry little weight. First, it was not unusual in early times to presume, without further exploration, a newly discovered or scarcely known land to be an island. Secondly, Greenland is portrayed as an island on several old maps without there being the least possibility that these cartographers knew it to be an island. Evidence of this latter point

*Ill. 84*

*Ill. 83.* The Vinland Map of Greenland, on the right, compared with a modern map of Greenland, left.

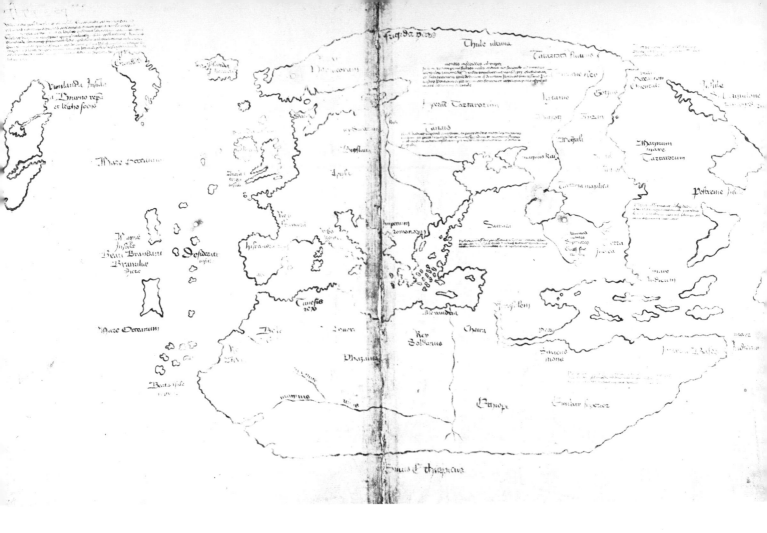

*Ill. 84.* The famous Vinland Map, the authenticity of which has been the subject of much discussion. It is related to the atlas of the Venetian, B. Andrea Bianco, issued in the year 1436, but contains features not found in his maps. The scientists who published the map consider it to be pre-Columbian, dating from *c.* AD 1440. The name *Vinlandia* appears on a large island west and southwest of Greenland.

*Ill. 83*

can be gained from the following maps: 'A Catalonian Compass Chart' from 1480–1500; the Italian 'King-Hamy Map' from *circa* 1502; 'Kunstmann No. 2'—a post-1502 map; 'Lorenz Friess' Ptolemæus Edition' of 1522; a Portuguese sea-map of *circa* 1550; Mercator's Maps of 1554 and 1569; 'F. Bertelis' Map' of 1565; 'Sir Humphrey Gilbert's World Atlas' of 1576 and in addition the above-mentioned Hungarian map of 1599.

Another objection has been that the lines of the Vinland Map correspond too accurately with the actual coastlines of Greenland and the conclusion has therefore been drawn that the map was made in our time. To this, one must reply that those contours which are most like those of modern charts cover chiefly those areas of the coast along which the Greenlanders, according to our evidence, sailed most often. This applies to large regions of the west coast, quite far north to the hunting areas, and to the east coast probably as far as Angmagssalik and possibly a little further north. In the course of nearly five centuries the native sailors must have come to have an intimate knowledge of these coasts. When we look at the northernmost part of Greenland as shown on the map, it is difficult to discern any similarity with modern charts which is worth naming.

It is also important to remember that in the course of those centuries there was a succession of priests and bishops on Greenland and a number of these would have been learned men. Norse ecclesiastics often received their education abroad—in England, France and Germany. Those who returned to Europe would have taken back a knowledge of Greenland with them. It also seems reasonable to assume that the Catholic Church would be very interested in more details of a land where it held a bishopric and many churches and where both tithes and crusade taxes were collected. It is further of interest to note that from the year 1360 we hear of a Minorite from Oxford, probably the mathematician, Nicholas of Lynn, who undertook a voyage to the Greenlandic settlements and further north. He presented an astrolabe to a Norwegian, probably Ivar Bardarson, who was the bishop's representative on Greenland. An astrolabe greatly increased the potentiality for more accurate cartography than would otherwise have been possible.

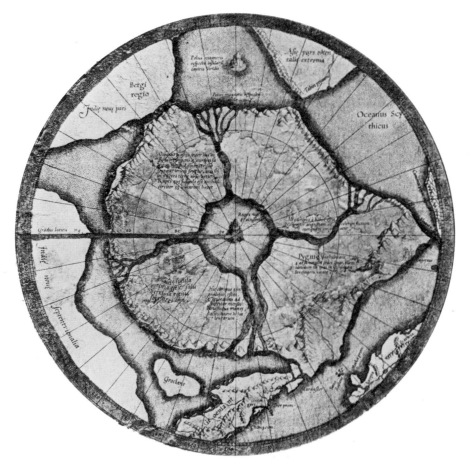

*Ill. 85.* The Arctic region as shown on Mercator's map of 1569. Mercator partly based his map on information relating to a polar expedition made by an English monk and astronomer (probably Nicholas of Lynn) from the Eastern Norse settlement in Greenland.

*Ill. 86.* Arrowhead made from quartzite found near a Norse farm, which is probably Sandnes, in the Western Settlement. It is assumed to be of Indian origin and might have been brought to Greenland by the Vinland voyagers.

Last but not least in the series of sources of evidence being presented comes one of a rather unusual nature. Near a Norse farm, at Vesterbygden on Greenland, the name of which was probably Sandnes and which probably belonged to Torfinn Karlsefni and his wife Gudrid, an arrowhead of quartzite was found which is assumed to be of Indian origin. This provides concrete evidence that the Norsemen had been in North America.

We now come to a consideration of the two sagas, *The Greenlanders' Saga* and *Eirik the Red's Saga,* as direct sources of information about various voyages undertaken by the Norse settlers to new lands west and southwest of Greenland around the year 1000. They were written about the fourteenth and fifteenth centuries and are based on earlier manuscripts.

*The Greenlanders' Saga* mentions first Bjarni Herjolfsson, who sailed from Iceland in 986 to visit his father who lived on the farm named Herjolfsnes on Greenland. En route he encountered bad weather and fog and, driven to the southwest, he came across the coastlines of several unknown lands of which the last had glaciers, but he never ventured on land. Eventually he reached Greenland.

Thereafter followed the planned journey of exploration of Leif Eiriksson, who wished to find those lands sighted by Bjarni. He sailed from Greenland with thirty-five men and came first to the most northerly land which Bjarni had seen last. It was a barren land, as flat as a flagstone and with great glaciers in the background. He named it Helluland (land as flat as a flagstone). He sailed further south and arrived at a forest-clad land which he called Markland (wood or forest land). Continuing his journey for another two days (døgr) he came to a third land which seemed to offer favourable possibilities and he named it Vinland. Here he constructed 'large houses' and remained for a year before returning to Greenland.

The next expedition was undertaken by his brother Thorvald. He reached Leif's houses on Vinland and settled there. During an exploratory journey he came across the natives (Skraelings) and in the course of a violent confrontation he was killed. Two years later the expedition returned to Greenland. The third brother, Thorstein, also set out on a Vinland voyage but, encountering bad weather, he returned.

Thereafter came the voyage of Thorfinn Karlsefni whose objective was to set up a Norse colony in this new land. He took with him sixty men and five women and all sorts of livestock. He reached Vinland and, like previous voyagers, settled in Leif's houses. While there, his wife, the beautiful Gudrid, gave birth to a child. He was called Snorre and so far as is known was the first European to be born in America. Thorfinn met the natives, traded with them and also fought them. After two years, the expedition returned to Greenland.

Finally we hear of the expedition of Freydis to Vinland. It comprised two ships and about sixty-five persons including women. She was a true 'Valkyrie', and cold-bloodedly had half the party killed to gain possession of their ship. After a year she returned to Greenland.

The information from *Eirik the Red's Saga* is different in various aspects: it concentrates on the Icelander Thorfinn Karlsefni; the discovery of the Greenlander Leif is covered in only a few lines. The latter incident takes place during a voyage from Norway to Greenland. Christendom plays a significant role in this narrative, in that the Norwegian King Olav Trygvasson had commissioned Leif to Christianize Greenland. The account of Thorstein and his unfortunate voyage is related but in a somewhat different way. The independent expeditions of Bjarni, Thorvald and Freydis are not related; the two latter are described as participants in Thorfinn Karlsefni's expedition. The saga relates that Karlsefni sailed from Greenland with three ships, 160 persons including women, and livestock. He discovered, like Leif, Helluland and Markland and eventually set up his headquarters at a place called Straumfjord. From there, he undertook a journey southwards to the so-called 'Hop'* where he came across the natives with whom he fought. After three years, the expedition returned to Greenland.

*A landlocked bay or estuary.

The two sagas thus contain different and conflicting information and for a long time there has been much discussion as to which is the more reliable. There is much to suggest that *The Greenlanders' Saga* is both the more reliable and originally the older.* The Icelandic historian, Jón Jóhánnessen, has in recent times demonstrated this conclusively and he has also shown that the author of *Eirik's Saga* not only knew *The Greenlanders' Saga* but used material from it at his own discretion.

*The existing version is inserted in the famous Icelandic codex, *Flateyarbók,* written in the last part of the fourteenth century.

The interpretation of these sagas offers many problems: the original versions were written about two hundred years after the events and probably on the basis of oral tradition. It is easy enough to find inconsistencies and parts that can only be legend, but the most significant point is that the sagas reveal a knowledge of sea travel, geography, ethnology and astronomy which makes it clear that the Norsemen reached the shores of North America about the year 1000. This corresponds to the evidence from the other sources already mentioned.

# The Evidence of the New World

*Ill. 87.* Central and South American legends tell of fair-skinned, fair-haired, bearded culture-bearers who came from the east and then, having taught the native populations the arts and crafts of civilization, departed, promising to return. In the highlands of Peru and around Lake Titicaca, the culture-bearer's name was Viracocha Con-Tici. A statue of him —one of the few not destroyed by the invading Spaniards—still stands in the ruins of the great pre-Inca temple complex of Tiahuanaco. It is because Viracocha and the parallel, bearded culture-hero, Quetzalcoatl in Mexico, had promised to return that Pizarro and Cortés were mistaken for their reincarnations and allowed to proceed unopposed to the heart of the Inca and Aztec empires.

# 4 Isolationist or Diffusionist?

**Thor Heyerdahl**

THE SPECULATIONS AS TO CONTACTS between the Old World and the New before the voyages of Columbus have never ended. In scientific terms, they have gradually hardened into two opposed schools of thought: Isolationism and Diffusionism. The Isolationists believe that the two main oceans surrounding the Americas completely isolated the New World from Old World contact until AD 1492; this school of thought allows only for primitive food-gatherers to have passed from the Asiatic tundra to Alaska in the Arctic north. The Diffusionists, in contrast, believe in a single common cradle of all civilizations; they postulate various hypothetical voyages to aboriginal America from Asia, Europe, or Africa in pre-Columbian times. Extremists in both schools have one marked characteristic in common: little or no appreciation of such oceanographic factors as prevailing winds and currents. To them, the oceans are dead, immobile lakes. The difference between them is that the extreme Isolationist believes that these dead expanses of water represent barriers to human movement in any direction, whereas the extreme Diffusionist considers them rather as open 'skating rinks' upon which aboriginal voyagers could travel in any direction as they pleased. This disregard for geographical reality has led Diffusionists to postulate frequently ill-founded migration theories, which have had no other effect than to harden the attitude of the Isolationists. At the same time, the dogmatic manner in which the Isolationists have defended their case—solely by passing the burden of proof to the Diffusionists—has caused equal resentment among the latter. Indeed, the Isolationists have never attempted to adduce direct proof for their case, considering their position to be sufficiently vindicated by the absence of proof for the Diffusionist position: lack of proof of contact, they regard as proof of no contact.

Everyone agrees that there are many—and often remarkable—similarities between the civilizations of pre-Columbian America and those of the Mediterranean world. The Isolationists believe that these parallels and occasional identities can be ascribed to independent evolution along parallel lines. This is based on the knowledge that the human mind is apt to react inventively in a similar way to similar environmental challenges on either side of a geographical barrier—in this case, the Atlantic and Pacific Oceans.

The identity or parallel occurrence, therefore, of certain tools, ornamental design, customs, or other cultural traits might obviously be the result of independent evolution and is, accordingly, invalid as proof of contact or oversea migration. A great majority of modern scholars have accepted the logic of this reasoning, and with its acceptance fell a whole series of formerly convincing arguments for global migration produced by the Diffusionists. Ideas and inventions, such as pyramid building, sun worship, marriage between brothers and sisters in royal families, mummification, the wearing of false beards among priest-kings, trepanning, script, calendar systems, the use of zero, irrigation and terrace agriculture, cotton cultivation, spinning and weaving, pottery, fitted megalithic masonry, the sling, birdman deities, musical wind-instruments, reed boats, fish hooks, necropolises, mural painting and relief carving, adobe-brick manufacture, hierarchic society, paper manufacture, ceramic stamps, and wheeled toys, were all elements that could have been thought of twice and are therefore considered inconclusive as evidence of trans-oceanic influence. Consequently, whenever Diffusionists emerged with a new case of Old and New World cultural parallels to indicate trans-Atlantic or trans-Pacific contact, the argument was predestined to be labelled 'non-proven'.

*Ills. 100–103, 173*
*Ills. 112, 174, 175, 182, 209*
*Ills. 97–99*
*Ills. 110, 111*
*Ills. 89–91*
*Ills. 116, 179, 188; Ills. 115, 187*
*Ill. 206*
*Ill. 114*

In spite of the setbacks that the Diffusionist movement suffered from the Isolationist doctrines, attempts to muster arguments in favour of cultural contacts across the sea never quite disappeared, and in recent years they have even gained momentum, not least in America, where resistance had for many years been strongest.

There can be but two reasons for this return of the pendulum towards Diffusionism. Either the Diffusionists' arguments are beginning to convince an increasing number of scholars, or else the arguments of the Isolationists are falling short of being generally thought conclusive. It seems that the latter is the case, for since the Diffusionists' evidence is sometimes vague, the comeback of their doctrine can only be due to the failure of the Isolationists to demonstrate the watertight validity of their own views. In a paper on 'Theoretical Issues in the Trans-Pacific Diffusion Controversy', D. Fraser clearly demonstrates how the available evidence can be interpreted either way and that what stands as valid evidence of diffusion for one scholar is interpreted in precisely the opposite way by another. He shows how the Asian game of *parcheesi* and the closely analogous Mexican one of *patolli* are used by both Diffusionist and Isolationist to bolster his own respective case. One camp argues that

*Ill. 88. Patolli* is a game of chance, widespread in ancient America, played with dice and using beans as counters. It has an exact counterpart in the Asiatic *parcheesi* game, and has been used by both Isolationists and Diffusionists as 'proof' that their theories were right!

*Ills. 89–91.* Megalithic masonry is one of the many cultural traits common to the Old and New Worlds. The examples from Gizeh, Egypt (above left), and from Lixus, Morocco (above right), bear astonishing resemblances to the walls of the pre-Inca fortification at Saccsahuamán in Peru (below).

because of the similarity of these two games, links must exist, and it proceeds to search for such links; the other camp says that distance and other factors preclude relationship, and thus the existence of the game perfectly demonstrates the validity of the independent-invention doctrine. In the light of this example, one can see that the difference in opinion calls for cautious and fully unbiased attitudes from both sides and that the Isolationist should divide his efforts equally between the rebutting of the Diffusionist's case and a search for positive evidence in support of his own views. Although it is often claimed that the burden of proof falls heaviest on the Diffusionist, it certainly does not fall on him alone, and until either side has conclusively proved the validity of its case, controversy is bound to continue.

An ever growing number of scholars, however, perhaps now even the majority, seems recently to have adopted a cautious middle course, not siding with either of the two extreme doctrines but admitting that ocean currents *may* have carried individual craft with surviving aboriginal crews to or from America, without this necessarily representing a population movement on a major scale. I will therefore use the term Diffusionist for one who *generally* favours human contact as an explanation wherever cultural parallels occur and Isolationist for one who dogmatically believes that the oceans surrounding the Americas were impassable before AD 1492.

Let us then look impartially at this impenetrable barrier that the Isolationists erect around America before Columbus. Without

*Ills. 92, 93.* The tendency to think that the shortest distance between two geographical points is a straight line—even when considering distances on a globe—and the usual representation of the equator as a straight line on maps often misleads us into thinking that the equator remains the shortest crossing of the Pacific Ocean from Asia to America (below left). The second illustration shows the same globe orientated so that the route which had seemed to be longest in the first illustration now appears as a straight line. As both are great circles between the same points, they are in fact the same length. The North Pacific route—called the Urdaneta route—is, actually, the only practicable Asia–America crossing (*cf. Ills. 94, 212*).

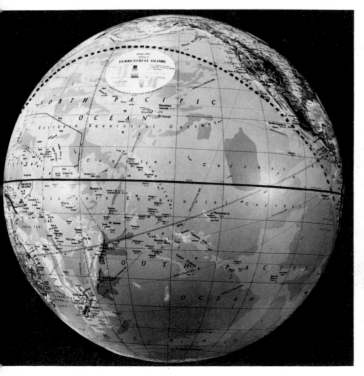
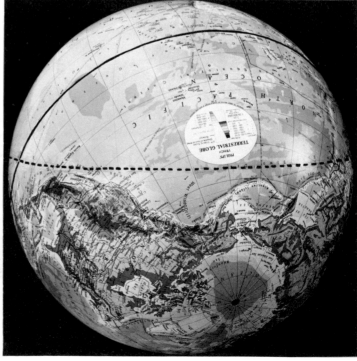

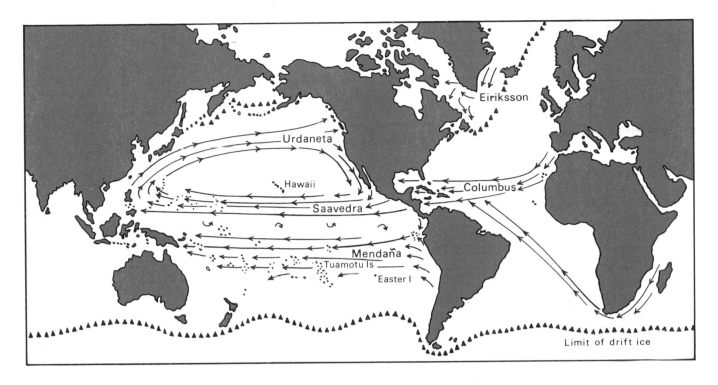

question, an ocean is normally more effective than a desert, swamp, jungle, or tundra when it comes to stopping the geographic progress of aboriginal man. But an ocean nevertheless has pathways of currents and winds that facilitate its crossing.

*Ills. 92, 93*

There are two basic observations that must constantly be remembered when long trans-oceanic voyages are considered. The first is that the distance between two antipodal points is never shorter along the Equator than along the great circles curving by way of the northern or southern hemispheres. Our minds are so used to map projections showing the Equator as a straight line that we forget that it is, in fact, a circle. The second is that the voyaging distance of a surface craft travelling straight from one geographical point to another is not equal to the measurable distance between these points (dead distance), nor is it equally long in both directions. The dead distance between two points may be measured in miles, but this has very little relation to the actual water span to be traversed between them. This is a ratio between the speed of the current and the speed of the vessel in question. Take, for instance, the dead distance between Peru and the Tuamotu Islands. It is approximately 4,000 miles, yet the raft *Kon-Tiki* reached the islands from Peru after crossing only about 1,000 miles of surface water. The reason for this is that the ocean surface itself was displaced about 3,000 miles from east to west during the time needed for the crossing. Had we been able to sail back along the same route at the same speed, we would have had to cover about

*Ill. 96*

7,000 miles of surface water before reaching Peru.* This means that for *Kon-Tiki* the Tuamotus are only 1,000 sailing miles from Peru, whereas Peru is 7,000 sailing miles from the Tuamotus. This factor must be taken into consideration whenever one thinks in terms of any ocean crossing in primitive craft.

There are three main natural oceanic routes to the New World—two on the Atlantic side and one on the Pacific—and three routes away from it—two on the Pacific and one on the Atlantic. These routes are so well defined that they may be named after their historically recorded discoverers.

In the Atlantic, the approach routes are, first, the Leif Eiriksson Route, from Norway to Greenland and Newfoundland by way of the Faeroes and Iceland. This route is favoured by very short oversea distances and a fast, south-sweeping current along the east and south coasts of Greenland to Labrador and Newfoundland. The second, the Columbus Route, is longer, but offers gentle climatic conditions and extremely favourable currents and prevailing winds. It originates along the northwest African coast and runs with the Canary Current straight to the West Indies and the Gulf of Mexico. It receives a strong southern feeder from Madagascar and South Africa, which enters the West Indies by way of the Brazilian coast. Although born as two separate African units, these pathways must be considered as sub-divisions of one sea route pulling tropical America close to Africa, yet conversely setting Africa farther from the New World.

*The idea behind this is clarified by analogy with an escalator: think of going *up* and then *down* the 'up' staircase.

*Ill. 94*

*Ill. 95.* Map of the raft voyages across the Pacific since *Kon-Tiki* in 1947. This shows how the prevailing winds and currents form a conveyor belt from South America to Polynesia. *Tahiti Nui I* attempted the eastward journey from Tahiti but was unable to sail against the winds and currents.

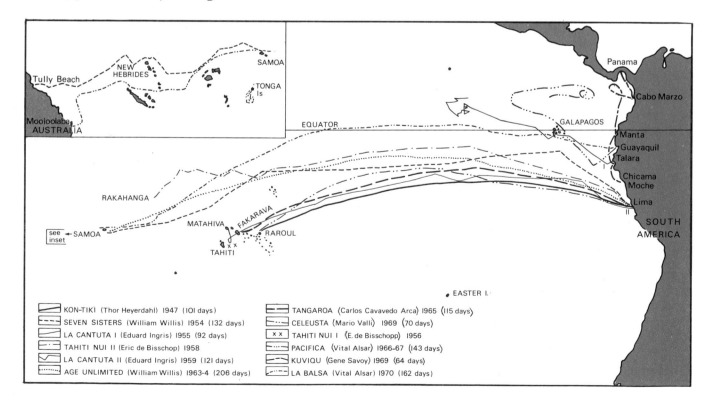

KON-TIKI (Thor Heyerdahl) 1947 (101 days)
SEVEN SISTERS (William Willis) 1954 (132 days)
LA CANTUTA I (Eduard Ingris) 1955 (92 days)
TAHITI NUI II (Eric de Bisschop) 1958
LA CANTUTA II (Eduard Ingris) 1959 (121 days)
AGE UNLIMITED (William Willis) 1963-4 (206 days)
TANGAROA (Carlos Cavavedo Arca) 1965 (115 days)
CELEUSTA (Mario Valli) 1969 (70 days)
TAHITI NUI I (E. de Bisschopp) 1956
PACIFICA (Vital Alsar) 1966-67 (143 days)
KUVIQU (Gene Savoy) 1969 (64 days)
LA BALSA (Vital Alsar) 1970 (162 days)

*Ill. 96.* The raft, *Kon-Tiki*, was a medium-sized balsa craft measuring 45 ft. × 18 ft. It was set adrift in the coastal current off Callao and entered the Tuamotu Archipelago ninety-two days later, landing on Raroia eight days after that, and thus proving the possibility of trans-Pacific navigation in Inca vessels and of cultural contact between South America and Polynesia.

The departure route from America on the Atlantic side is the Gulf Stream, which starts from the Gulf of Mexico, sweeping northeastwards across the North Atlantic and up the west coast of Britain; but its importance is not very great in as much as it would be inhospitable to tropically acclimatized natives of Central America who would be little prepared to survive the long northbound drift into the cold North Atlantic.

On the Pacific side, the principal sea routes are, first, the Mendaña Route, named after the first European who set sail from the New World in search of the inhabited Pacific islands reported by Inca merchants. For this reason, it might also be called the Inca Route. Its potential for aboriginal craft was demonstrated by the raft *Kon-Tiki* in 1947 and subsequently by seven other raft expeditions from Peru. The second route, from Mexico to Indonesia, may be named the Saavedra Route in reference to the first crossing made in this area by Saavedra in 1527 and subsequently consistently followed by the Spanish galleons for two hundred years. At first sight, this route seems very long, but it is considerably reduced by the powerful North Equatorial Current and is aided by favourable local trade winds.

The only marine conveyor from the Orient to the New World, as discovered in 1565, is the Urdaneta Route, named after the navigator whose written records revealed it to subsequent voyagers—although Arellano completed the same crossing three months before Urdaneta. This route is drastically shortened by the eastbound Kuroshiwo Current, which brings warm water and a mild climate directly from the Philippine Sea to the northwest American coast and then down the west coast of the continent to Mexico. The belt of contrary trade winds is avoided and the 'loop' north of Hawaii is, as we have seen, entirely illusive even in dead miles—as this is a great circle route. This is the only natural Asia–America route.

*Ills. 95, 96*

*Ills. 92, 93*

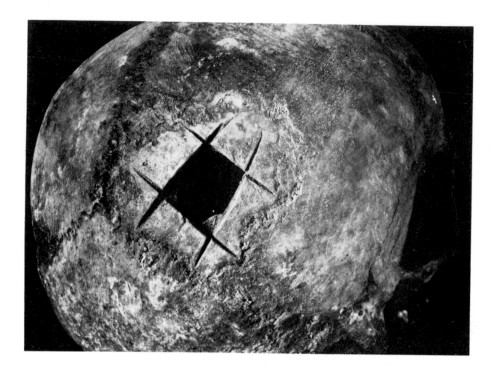

The Equatorial counter-current that figures prominently on most maps as running eastbound towards America between the westbound north and south Equatorial currents is nothing but an interrupted series of eddies and is of scant use to trans-Pacific voyagers, as Eric de Bisschop and Eduardo Ingris, on separate voyages, have found out to their cost in recent years. In conclusion, therefore, one could say that rather than acting as a barrier, the oceans are crossed by gigantic conveyor belts that will transport from one region to another anything remaining afloat on them.

Clearly, the value of currents and winds to the Diffusionists' case depends on the nature and the chronology of contact evidence found at either end of such a conveyor belt. Without adequate regard for both the nature and the chronology of the contact evidence, the Diffusionist can readily misinterpret available data—even if the geographic conveyor belt is in his favour. The nature of contact evidence means the particular manifestation of a given phenomenon that renders it identifiable and specific: a surgical procedure, religious practice, building technique, or social organization, for example. That any one of these—say, trepanning—could evolve independently on both sides of the Atlantic is possible. The same can be said for pyramid building. A single culture element found to appear at both ends of a natural sea route may very well be the result of coincidence or independent evolution along parallel lines. To become a reasonable indicator of contact, a whole array of identities or similarities of

*Ills. 97–99*

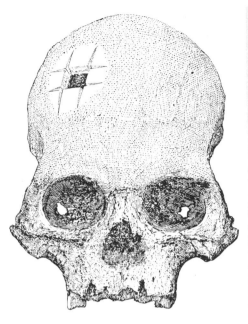

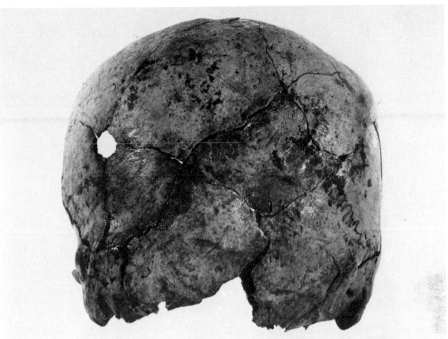

extraordinary nature must be found concentrated in the two areas linked by a land bridge or marine conveyor. Far too often, a Diffusionist will find, say, a particular petroglyphic symbol, artifact, or funeral custom repeated in two areas, and from such a single case of parallelism, he will postulate theories of human migration. This tendency on the part of too many Diffusionists, to draw far-reaching conclusions on the basis of detached, individual pieces of evidence, has been justifiably criticized by the Isolationists, who thus gain something of an upper hand in the debate merely through the default of their opponents. The Diffusionist case, however, could be rendered considerably stronger, not necessarily by the adducing of new evidence, but merely by the presentation of evidence already at hand in a statistically convincing manner. It must be borne in mind that the cultural phenomena mentioned earlier as characterizing the civilizations of the Mediterranean area and pre-Columbian America are not isolated, individual factors existing outside any larger context. Quite the contrary: on both sides of the Atlantic, they are profoundly intermeshed and integral elements of complex and sophisticated social systems. It is no more meaningful to treat them separately as unconnected cultural phenomena than it would be to treat unconnected words without regard to their parent language.

What confront us, then, on both sides of the Atlantic are arrays of cultural parallels. And when these are dealt with as complexes, we are *Ills. 100–103* faced by amazing statistical indications. True pyramids, for example,

123

have a limited distribution on both sides of the Atlantic (Mesopotamia, Egypt—Mexico, Peru) and, as stated, might well have been developed independently. The same can be said of mummification. But when both pyramids and mummification appear in the same two restricted areas, then the likelihood of coincidence is considerably decreased. Trepanation can also have been developed independently, but when this difficult art—with its very restricted distribution—appears together with pyramids and mummification, then the strength of the Diffusionist argument is not only tripled but, according to statistical rules, increases in an ever-steepening mathematical curve. When, further, the use of false beards among priest-kings, intermarriage among royal siblings, sun worship, reed boats, fitted megalithic masonry, bird-man deities, and the whole list of Mediterranean-American parallels are considered together as an entity then the probability of Diffusion rather than independent development does not increase arithmetically but exponentially; for instance, a cluster of twelve parallels grouped together, say, in Mesopotamia and Mexico does not weigh twelve times heavier in the discussion than a single parallel, but rather, according to the laws of probability, has increased its significance by a truly astronomical amount. Among other things, this means that the Isolationist's technique of negating these parallels one by one by labelling them 'coincidence' is mathematically invalid. The Isolationist may choose any one—or even two—perhaps three—of the culture traits he wants to eliminate, but no matter which he chooses, the rest will remain on the Diffusionist's side of the scales.

Turning next to the problem of chronology, we find that the failure of the Diffusionists to give due consideration to chronology has

*Ills. 112, 174, 175, 182, 209*

*Ills. 97–99*

*Ills. 115, 187; Ills. 89–91*
*Ills. 116, 179, 188*

Bateau du port de Sⁿ Francisco

*Ill. 104.* Lithograph showing a reed boat in San Francisco Bay.

*Ills. 105, 106,* Reed boats—existing from the highest antiquity both in the Old World and the New (*Ills. 104, 115–119, 187*)—continue to be used today. Thor Heyerdahl is seen (left) in a reed boat inspecting papyrus plants on Lake Chad prior to building *Ra I*. In Sardinia (right) these craft are still used by local fishermen, as they are by the Marsh Arabs of the lower Euphrates River.

*Ills. 107–109.* The totora-reed boat is used both on the northern coast of Peru (below left), as is its larger counterpart on Lake Titicaca (*Ill. 117*), and, until recently, on Easter Island (below right). Although no longer extant in Mexico, the reed boat was at one time used in eight different states; Thor Heyerdahl photographed one of the last to be built by the Seris Indians in the Gulf of California in the early 1960s (bottom).

pyramid building, etc. fully developed—on the unfavourable jungle coast of the Gulf of Mexico, precisely where the marine conveyor from Africa ends.

Why, ask the Diffusionists, are the Isolationists unable to show us a single geographical area in America where the local evolution they champion can be verified? And why was there no corresponding evolution among the aboriginal inhabitants of the climatically more stimulating areas that are now the United States, Chile, and Argentina, all of which were originally peopled by the same migrant stock that arrived via Alaska? Here, it is the Isolationists who are lost for a satisfactory answer.

To sum up, the Isolationist position rests on searching out flaws in the Diffusionists' argument—and on a peculiar approach to geographical factors. The Isolationists base their school of thought on recognition of the fact that men are physically and mentally so alike that they will normally duplicate each other's actions and achievements irrespective of time or geography. Nevertheless, the Isolationists deviate enormously from this attitude in attributing totally different abilities and inclinations to trans-Atlantic travellers before and after 1492. A typical example of this inclination to consider 1492 a turning point in anthropology, with a clear break in all former rules of human behaviour, is found in a paper on 'Diffusionism and Archaeology' by J. H. Rowe (*American Antiquity*, January 1966). The author compiles a most impressive array of no less than 60 remarkable parallels between two restricted areas within the Old and the New Worlds. He himself describes this assembly as 'a substantial list of specific cultural features of limited distribution which were shared by cultures of the ancient Andean area and the ancient Mediterranean prior to the Middle Ages'. His list ranges from reed boats to sandals of hide or coiled rope, of which he says that: 'Very specific resemblances in design and manufacture can be traced.' One might think that this thought-provoking list had been compiled to bolster the case for Diffusion. But this is not so by any means, as the author lets us know in no uncertain terms. He starts his paper by stating: 'Doctrinaire diffusionism is a menace to the development of sound archaeological theory . . . . In the science-fiction world of the diffusionists . . . time, distance, and the difficulties of navigation are assumed to be irrelevant. Archaeology has too long and honourable a tradition to be surrendered without a protest to fantasies which require us to start with our conclusions and use them to deform the evidence.' But Dr Rowe is basing his own entire argument on just such a method of starting with conclusions. In fact, he presents his list of parallels to argue that areas he tacitly assumes are too far apart for any pre-Columbian contact to have occurred—like the Andean area and the Mediterranean world—still possess an array of very specific culture features in common. Ergo, he concludes, even the most impressive array of parallelism can arise through independent evolution. In other words, he assumes as a basis for his entire argument that Peru and the Mediterranean world are too far apart for contact and uses this assumption to discredit cultural identities as evidence of Diffusion.

On what basis can it be regarded as axiomatic that Peru is 'too far' from the Mediterranean world for contact to have taken place prior to 1492? In Columbus's own lifetime, with a crew of no more than normally endowed men, Francisco Pizarro travelled straight from the Mediterranean world to Peru by way of Central America. Like Columbus shortly before him, he managed the oceanic voyage entirely without navigational charts of the waters around the Americas. He then succeeded in traversing the jungle-covered Isthmus of Panama to the Pacific side, whence he sailed onwards in new vessels, past the impenetrable coastal swamplands, until he reached the favourable, open terrain of Peru, where he established a settlement. His compatriot, Cortés, on the other hand, had already landed on the jungle coast of the Gulf of Mexico, making his way up into the open Mexican high-plateau country far from his landing site and establishing a settlement there.

We of European extraction are surely not so blindfolded by our own history that we consider ourselves a line of supermen, able to do four centuries ago what the great civilizations of Asia Minor and North Africa could not have done earlier. It must not be forgotten that these people of antiquity had skills and capacities that far surpassed anything imitated in Europe during the Middle Ages. The Egyptians and their neighbours in Mesopotamia and Phoenicia knew more about astronomy, the key to ocean navigation, than any Europeans contemporary with Columbus, Cortés, and Pizarro. And the Phoenicians, in collaboration with the Egyptians, were circumnavigating Africa as early as the time of the Pharaoh Necho, twenty centuries before Columbus set sail in an ocean Europeans believed was filled with dragons and ended in a precipice at the horizon.

*Ill. 63*

We marvel at the abilities and capacities of the ancients as embodied in their titanic pyramids and obelisks, sophisticated mathematics and calendar systems, profound literature and philosophy, perfect mastery of maritime architecture as evidenced by the functional form and complex rigging of their ships of planks and reeds 3,000 years BC, and their spirit and skill in exploration and colonization as revealed by the numerous archaeological vestiges of Phoenician settlement all the way down the Atlantic coast of Morocco dating back 3,000 years. But is it realistic to stand in awe of these achievements only to deny the ancients the intellectual and mechanical ability to do what Pizarro did with a handful of men in an age beset by ignorance and superstition?

One of the 60 parallels cited by Dr Rowe as being shared by the ancient civilizations of Peru and the Mediterranean world was the reed boat. Is it the boats of the ancients that we do not trust? The seaworthiness of these craft has been empirically demonstrated quite recently. In fact, in 1969, the entire coastal voyage between Peru and Panama was successfully undertaken by a Peruvian totora-reed boat. The experimental voyage, by an untrained crew with no sea-going experience led by Gene Savoy, took two months, from 15 April to 17 June. At about the same time, from 25 May to 18 July, my own *Ill. 130* papyrus-reed boat, *Ra I*, built according to African design, sailed *Ill. 129* from the Old World to the vicinity of Barbados. This experimental voyage was repeated on *Ra II* the following year, and in 57 days, our reed boat, manned by an inexperienced crew, crossed safely from Africa to tropical America. These three reed-boat voyages all took place within a period of 16 months. Neither Gene Savoy with his companions nor I with mine would have had any greater trouble walking across the Isthmus of Panama than had Pizarro—or any other voyagers who might have reached the Isthmus before him. The swampy jungle country of the Isthmus area did not tempt Pizarro and his men to found a colony upon arrival there; instead, they pushed on across land and water until they reached the hospitable coastal terrain of Peru. Why should other people have acted differently if they preceded Pizarro across the Atlantic? By attributing motivations and accomplishments to Pizarro's little group of medieval voyagers—and rejecting the very idea that other Mediterranean voyagers might independently have benefited from the same winds and currents and thus ended up with a similar itinerary—the Isolationist does violence to the very basic law of Isolationism: that people are apt to duplicate each other's feats, given the same environmental conditions.

Too many anthropologists, of both schools, have an unrealistic conception of what constitutes a geographical barrier to jungle hunters and coastal fishermen. Inexperience with jungle life or with the effects of natural marine conveyors can lead even prominent anthropologists to draw seemingly reasonable conclusions, which nevertheless all too often arise from misinterpretations of physical geography. Such anthropological conclusions have often penetrated associated literature as supporting evidence supposedly having different origins. Striking examples of such circuitous reasoning are to be found in the field of ethnobotany, the study of cultivated plants. As we have seen, both Isolationists and Diffusionists have used the same cultural parallels to support opposite points of view. Botanical evidence, however, is subject to far fewer subjective variables, almost none of which is available to human manipulation, and the evidence of genetic factors is therefore accorded considerably more respect in objective scientific circles.

The history of the common garden bean, *Phaseolus vulgaris,* clearly illustrates how preconceived opinions on aboriginal navigational possibilities have biased the reciprocal conclusions of botanists and anthropologists. In 1885, Körnicke pointed out that this important crop plant was formerly generally accepted as having been cultivated by the Greeks and Romans under the names of *Dolickos, Phaseolos,* etc. (Aristophanes and Hippocrates wrote about it in about 400 BC.) When it was discovered that the same bean was cultivated among the aborigines of the New World, it was thought that it must have been introduced by the early Spaniards. This was accepted until Wittmack, in 1880, discovered the common bean at the prehistoric cemetery of Ancon, on the coast of central Peru, where it had been buried as grave food. These burials long antedated the European discovery of America. *Phaseolus vulgaris* was later encountered in pre-Inca sites along the entire coast of Peru, and botanists were confronted with ample evidence of its pre-European cultivation in America. A theoretical introduction by the Spaniards thus became untenable as an explanation. At this time, however, pre-Columbian specimens of the bean were no longer available. The theory was therefore reversed and the view taken that *Phaseolus* had originated in aboriginal *America,* from whence it had been carried to *Europe* by the Spaniards. A re-examination of this confused botanical issue by Hutchinson, Silow, and Stephens in 1947 convinced them, however, that *Phaseolus* was not indigenous to the New World and that its peregrinations represented a piece of botanical evidence for contact from the Old World to the New World before Columbus.

The bottle gourd, *Lagenaria vulgaris,* represents another piece of *Ill. 110* botanical contact evidence. This important culture plant was widely cultivated in Africa before Columbus. Although the gourd itself is of only moderate food value, its rind was fire-dried and used as a water-tight container from Mesopotamia and Egypt to Morocco. When botanists came to study plants in the New World, they found it cultivated and used for the same purpose in all the American high-culture areas, including Mexico and Peru. It was supposed, as it had been for the bean, that the Spaniards had brought it over; again, however, this theory was gradually abandoned when the bottle gourd was found by archaeologists in pre-Columbian culture sites in both Mexico and Peru. It was one of the most consistent culture elements within the American high-culture areas. A second theory was then advanced: the bottle gourd could have floated across the Atlantic from Africa, been washed ashore in tropic America with live seeds, and grown. The Indians would have noticed that the rind, when dried over a fire, made an excellent container, and the original African use of the gourd would thus have been rediscovered. This, of course, is a deliberate attempt to dispose of a piece of undesirable

*Ill. 110*. Eight bottle gourd floats, dating from at least 1500 BC, embedded in the remains of a long cotton fishnet, were found at Huaca Prieta in the Chicama Valley of Peru. This shows the antiquity of the utilization of the bottle gourd in the New World.

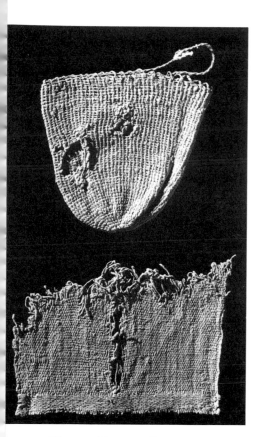

*Ill. 111*. Top, small pouch made of cotton, dating *c.* 1700 BC, and, bottom, part of a plain-weave cotton fabric, showing characteristic compact twining at warp ends, made *c.* 1500 BC. These pieces of cotton fabric, together with the net (*Ill. 110*) show the earliest known use of cotton in the New World.

hybridiz
about th
America,
question
The w.
New Wo
of Mexic
some spe
absent in
World co
ing in A1
being des
the gourd
one, we
when the
recognize
American
hybrid w.
which to
then inve
loin-cloth:
clothing v
however,
then it wo
into existe
natural fo1
stock with
chromoso1
Mexico to
and stone
World, an
type of clo
whence the
Experim
months in
Atlantic O
seen a cott
is hardly t
currently b
who, tryin
matter how
A similai
*disiaca*) in A
and for thi
have taken

*Ill. 111*

evidence. The Isolationists, with the intention of being cautious, are, in effect, throwing the baby out with the bath-water. They attempt to wipe away an important African fingerprint in America: solid genetic evidence. As anyone who has drifted across oceans will be well aware, small, edible objects—like gourds—will immediately become the prey of both sharks and boring organisms such as the shipworm. The four months needed for an African gourd to drift alone across the Atlantic would subject it a thousand times over to being gulped down by scavenging sharks or penetrated and quickly rendered unviable by the ever-present shipworm, *teredo*. To a raft voyager, it sounds paradoxical to hear it claimed that of two African culture elements—the terrestrial gourd and the maritime boat—the gourd can drift successfully by sea to America but not the boat!

The cotton plant, *Gossypium*, provides even more intriguing evidence. Wild cotton is short-linted, unspinnable, and unsuggestive of any practical use to man. Yet, when the Europeans came to America, they found the Indians all through the high-culture area from Mexico to Peru wearing sophisticated cotton clothes of outstanding quality. In fact, subsequent archaeological excavations in the mummy tombs of Peru have uncovered cotton cloth from the earliest pre-Inca period exhibiting a fineness of mesh and decorative patterns unsurpassed anywhere. Obviously, then, the very founders of Peruvian civilization had somehow come into possession of a cultivated, long-linted species of cotton, as well as the spindle whorl

and the loom. The progress from useles
wild, via spindle whorl and loom, to finis
all self-evident until it has already been co
a declared Isolationist as Dr Rowe in his
parallels, the method and the results of c
the same as those in the Old World. He s
loom with two warp beams used by the
used in Egypt in the New Kingdom,
Mesopotamia. He adds that the second of
looms, the horizontal loom staked out on
Titicaca Basin, was also the same as tha
observers have noted remarkable similarit
loin-cloths produced on these looms in A
likewise in the ancient Mediterranean area
so far as to use the word 'identical' in li
dress, consisting of a rectangular piece of
body under the arms and pinned on both
waist with a girdle . . .'.

In 1947, Hutchinson, Silow, and Stephe
of the genetics of cotton from all over th
that cotton could be differentiated into thr
number and size of its chromosomes. A
World, both wild and domestic species, h
somes. In the New World, however, there
between the wild and the cultivated cotto
America have thirteen small chromosome
species—and there were three of them fro
twenty-six chromosomes, thirteen small
there was no large-chromosome cotton a
species, and since the cultivated American
some unaccounted-for species must have b
American cotton cultivators at the rise of l
them to produce what was obviously a ma
seem very reasonable, since it is the thirtee
have been added, that they somehow obtai
cultivated species from the Old World, a
spinnable lint developed and spread wit
Mexico and Peru.

Wherever one finds aboriginal civilizatio
also finds twenty-six-chromosome cultivate
from the Pacific coast into Polynesia as Am
into this adjacent island area. From the weste
all the way into Southeast Asia, however, c
was unknown. The Polynesian cotton at
before the Europeans arrived proved to be

134

oceanic expedition, but the concept of the wheel could be carried in the mind, and the wheel could be used on hand-drawn vehicles, even if the Mexican jungle, almost impenetrable with its dense timber and muddy soil, did not favour the elaborate development of extensive wheeled traffic. It was not until the recent discovery of wheeled figurines in early Olmec tombs that we learned that the wheel was, in fact, known in early America. We would not have known it if the small wheels discovered had not been made of enduring ceramic. Paved roads of pre-Columbian origin have been found in the jungles of Mexico, where wheeled transport might have been used. But since ceramic was unsuitable for full-scale vehicles, and iron was unknown, wheels could only have been made of wood, and such perishable material from the Olmec period would not have come down to us. Why the wheel never survived in America once it was known by the founders of local civilization remains a mystery. What is noteworthy, however, is that even today, the Indians of the Peruvian highlands, like their cousins in the Mexican jungle, completely ignore the existence of the wheel, despite centuries of intimate contact with Europeans.

It is a long way from the eastern Mediterranean to the Gulf of Mexico, yet Columbus was born in Italy and sailed to America three times. At least twenty-seven centuries before Columbus, Phoenicians, sailing from the innermost corner of the Mediterranean, were engaged in large-scale exploration, with colonization on the open Atlantic coasts north and south of Gibraltar. Of course, one cannot imagine ordinary marooned sailors shipwrecked or blown off course founding the high cultures of Mexico and Peru. A handful of uneducated eastern Mediterranean seamen cast ashore among small, unorganized, family groups of primitive people—although probably given the same friendly reception as Columbus—would hardly be able to transmit their limited knowledge of their own civilization to the scattered natives who met them. The transmission of concepts such as hieroglyphic writing, the zero, or the techniques of mummification and trepanation needs more than just a knowledge of their existence, or even a cursory knowledge of their working, on the part of the teacher. A group of ocean voyagers capable of founding a culture like that of the Olmecs must have been large enough to include representatives of the intellectual élite of its own homeland: something like a premeditated and fully equipped colonization voyage that went off course. Both archaeology and written history witness how large organized groups of colonists left the Mediterranean to found major settlements and trading posts along the coast of west Africa. The earliest written record is the stele in Carthage, which records how the Phoenician king, Hanno, in about 450 BC, sailed with sixty ships crowded with men and women to establish colonies all down the Atlantic coast of Morocco. And archaeology shows that

138

*Ills. 112–114.* The domesticated dogs of America were not only of the spitz or husky types: in Mexico and Peru, they resembled the dogs of the Old World. They were often mummified—a practice also current among the Egyptians (opposite, above left). The bridge and spout jar from Nazca, Peru (left) and the wheeled toy from Vera Cruz, Mexico (above), show two examples of these dogs from pre-Columbian America. The wheels on the Mexican toy further confuse the Isolationist case, as it was long thought that the wheel had not been introduced into America before Columbus.

Hanno was not a pioneer. When he arrived, other organized expeditions from the inner Mediterranean had long since founded the large megalithic city of Lixus far south of Gibraltar, just where the ocean current sweeps past directly towards the Gulf of Mexico.

The history of Lixus has vanished into the dawn of history. The Romans called it 'The Eternal City' and said it was the burial place of Herakles. It was built by unknown sun-worshippers who oriented the gigantic megalithic walls according to the sun. Its oldest known name, in fact, is 'Sun City'. Whoever founded and built Lixus, it is clear that astronomers, masons, scribes, and expert potters were among them. Around 1000 BC, just before Olmec culture suddenly began to flourish in America, organized colonists from the eastern Mediterranean, with ample knowledge of both Mesopotamian and Egyptian civilizations, had penetrated as far as the Atlantic area where eternal winds and currents constitute a marine conveyor to the Gulf of Mexico. Such boatloads of colonists as might have been blown off course here would certainly not be the founders of the vast Inca, Maya, and Aztec cultures. Traditional history, supported by archaeology, clearly shows that these great historic and proto-historic nations of the Andean area and Mexico were purely local products—amalgamations of indigenous peoples. These, however, owe their inspiration to more obscure predecessors. Thus, in Mexico, for instance, culture seems to have originated from what was origin-ally a restricted group which has been given the name of Olmecs, whose early activity began in a limited area around the Gulf of Mexico.

*Ill. 90*

*Ill. 115.* An early Chimu ceramic pot in the shape of a reed boat with two paddlers.

*Ill. 116.* Mythical birdman ready to board his reed boat (*cf. also Ills. 179, 188*). This scene from a pre-Inca pot shows the birdman which often accompanies the god or culture-bearer in high-culture areas of the Americas and Polynesia, as well as in Egypt and Mesopotamia.

*Ill. 114; Ills. 97–99*
*Ills. 206–208*
*Ills. 116, 179, 188;*
*Ill. 206*

*Ill. 104*

*Ill. 109*

All that is left to consider is the missing link, the water craft that might have carried to Mexico the gourd, the cotton seed, the banana, the knowledge of the wheel, the loom, the customs of trepanning and circumcision, the ideas of human deities with hook-beaked birds' heads, adobe manufacture, megalithic carving, paper making for written hieroglyphic texts, mural paintings, mummification, terrace agriculture, metalwork, and the countless other ideas and inventions that never reached the Indians much above the Mexican border because they were unknown to the original immigrants from Siberia. Indeed, the Vikings and Phoenicians had excellent wooden ships with frames of ribs and planked hulls that could sail across any sea provided they were navigated by a trained crew and provided they were not filled by breaking seas. Planked ships, however, were not known in pre-Columbian America, and the Isolationists are certainly right in their logical claim that the mariners who came and built pyramids would hardly have forgotten how to build the type of water craft in which they arrived. Prior to Columbus, the only types of water craft known in America were rafts, canoes and kayaks of birchbark, hide, or dugout log—the latter sometimes heightened by a sewn-on plank gunwale—and a peculiar type of boat-shaped raft-ship made of bundles of reeds bound together in a highly sophisticated manner. This type was undoubtedly the most highly developed vessel found by the Conquistadores in the New World. It constituted a basic element in the culture of the Incas and their civilized predecessors, both on the coast and in the highlands. In Mexico, it was formerly used in seven different states. The last reed boats in Mexico were abandoned by the Seris Indians of the Gulf of California in the early 1960s, while they are still in common

*Ill. 117.* A reed boat on Lake Titicaca (*cf. caption to Ills. 107–109*).

*Ill. 118.* Right, the reed boats of the ▶ troops of Sennacherib, shown in pitched battle with the inhabitants of the sea-marshes of the delta of the Tigris and Euphrates, naturally enough resemble very closely those of the Marsh Arabs of today, but more surprisingly are also very similar to those of the Mexican and Peruvian Indians (*cf. Ills. 107, 109*).

use on Lake Titicaca in Peru and sporadically occur on Peru's north coast.

The sail was known in pre-Columbian America, where it was sometimes made of cotton canvas and sometimes of reed mats. In both cases, it was hoisted on a peculiarly straddled bipod mast. The very same type of reed boat, with the same type of mast, was characteristic of ancient Egypt—a fact that would not have been known to us were it not for the realistic reliefs and paintings in old Egyptian tombs. Reliefs from old Nineveh, however, show naval battles on the same kind of reed boats navigated on the ocean, with double rows of warriors chasing the crew overboard to waiting crabs and fish, while other reed boats crammed with men and women escape across the sea. Reed is a perishable material, and were it not for these illustrations in stone from Mesopotamia and Egypt, combined with still earlier petroglyphs from the Sahara, we would not have known how extremely important such water craft were to the ancient Mediterranean cultures. Smaller versions of these reed boats, used by poor fishermen, have survived into the present century from the Mesopotamian rivers and the source of the Nile in the east, by way of such Mediterranean islands as Corfu and Sardinia, to the Atlantic

*Ills. 107, 117, 120*

*Ills. 119, 125*
*Ill. 118*

*Ill. 106*

coast of Morocco, where reed boats of amazing buoyancy were built precisely at the site of the megalithic city of Lixus until shortly before World War II.

Wherever reed boats were used in the ancient Old and New Worlds, stupendous megalithic ruins show the vigour and competence of local cultures in antiquity, whereas modern dwellers in the same areas live in humble huts. It can well be imagined, then, by seeing the reed boats of present-day fishermen, what large reed ships the rulers of antiquity could have made with the labour and materials they had available. Their sun-oriented, megalithic walls, fitted together with a highly specialized masonry technique, have come to our knowledge through direct survival, whereas the reed boats, made as they were of perishable plant stalks, have survived only through traditional skills passed on from father to son.

Both these cultural phenomena are of very limited distribution, and yet they are found side by side from the eastern Mediterranean to Lixus on the Atlantic coast of Morocco, and thence in Mexico and Peru, as well as on Easter Island. These modest boats have at best *Ills. 107, 108* been seen by few modern scientists, but they have not been ocean tested for their true capabilities. Laboratory tests made with loose sections of papyrus reed have shown that this material becomes waterlogged and loses all carrying capacity in less than two weeks. Tank experiments with the same reed in still seawater have also shown that the cellular core of the reed quickly starts to deteriorate. For this reason, anthropologists, papyrus specialists, and maritime experts have all agreed that the ancient papyrus raft-ships could only have been used on rivers and lakes, where they could be hauled ashore and sun-dried at short intervals. It was unanimously deemed impossible for such reed craft to cross the ocean span from Africa to America. To judge the qualities of a papyrus ship by testing a piece of papyrus reed, however, seems as meaningless as to drop a piece of iron into a tank and conclude that the *Queen Mary* would not float. There is, of course, a tremendous difference between testing a material and testing a completed boat. Nor does the constantly changing water encountered by a moving boat encourage rotting as does the stagnant water in a tank. My own testing of reed boats on Easter Island, Peru, and Mexico on one side of the Atlantic, and in Lake Chad and at the *Ill. 105* source of the Nile on the other, had impressed me immensely. No other vessel of corresponding size could muster the carrying capacity, stability, and safety of a reed-bundle boat. Still, it was probably the study of ancient Egyptian boat designs that, more than anything else, *Ills. 119, 125* convinced me of the probable invalidity of contemporary scientific opinions on the seaworthiness of such vessels.

In 1954, the dismantled pieces of a ship made of Lebanon cedar were discovered in a megalithic chamber at the foot of the Cheops *Ill. 124*

Ills. *119–121*. When Thor Heyerdahl decided to build a modern papyrus boat, all he had to go on were the reliefs on Egyptian tombs (above) and the practical experience of the few reed-boat builders of today. *Ra I* was built by Buduma tribesmen from Lake Chad in the shadow of the pyramids (below), while *Ra II*, its successor, was built by Aymara Indians from Lake Titicaca with an altogether different technique (right). Curiously enough it was the boat built by the South American Indians which resembled the Egyptian prototypes more closely than the boat built by contemporary Africans.

*Ill. 124*

*Ill. 125*

◄ *Ill. 122*. Left, *Ra II,* ten feet shorter than *Ra I,* was launched at Safi like its predecessor. Fifty-seven days later she sailed into Bridgetown harbour, Barbados, without a reed out of place, in spite of the battering of the seas and repeated difficulties with her steering gear. The experts who had predicted that a papyrus boat would become waterlogged in two weeks were confounded, and proof of the feasibility of long ocean voyages in this sort of craft—the missing link and possible means of conveyance of the many cultural traits common to the Old and New Worlds—was established.

pyramid in Egypt. The largest of the well-preserved planks, which weighed nearly a ton each, were over 75 feet long, about 20 inches wide, and nearly $4\frac{1}{2}$ inches thick. Egypt's Chief Curator of Antiquities, Ahmed Joseph, and his staff worked for years before they succeeded in reassembling the pharaonic vessel, which proved to be $146\frac{1}{2}$ feet long and nearly 20 feet wide. This ship, the oldest preserved vessel in the world, was built in Egypt about 2700 BC. Reassembled, the ship immediately exhibited two striking features: it was consistently papyriform in design, and it had the characteristic lines of an ocean-going vessel rather than a riverboat. The papyriform features include a longitudinal crescent shape with highly raised bow and stern each ending in a trumpet shape, clearly suggesting a papyrus prototype. Even the stern of the Cheops boat was curved inward, as is typical of a papyrus boat. There is no reason for a wooden ship to have this extremely complicated form, natural to pliable papyrus but hard to imitate in rigid wood. The sole reason the tradition-bound pharaoh could have had for imitating the papyrus form was his desire to respect the vessel design used by his own earliest ancestors, the gods. In all Egyptian funeral art, the sun god himself and his bird-headed human attendants are shown voyaging on papyrus boats. It was only natural that papyrus preceded wood as ship-building material in ancient Egypt, where papyrus reed grew in abundance, while the cedar used by the pharaoh had to be imported from the forests of Phoenicia, in present-day Lebanon. Even before it was reassembled, Pharaoh Cheops' boat was generally referred to as a 'solar' boat, as it was assumed that it had been built for the exclusive purpose of conveying the dead pharaoh to his eternal resting place with his ancestor, Ra, the sun.

Ahmed Joseph had already discovered that the Cheops ship was no mere funeral vessel when we carefully studied the construction together in his laboratory during the early months of 1969. The wood showed clear evidence of wear from considerable use: grooves had been worn in the hard planks through the chafing action of the rope lashings binding them together. The ship, then, had clearly been a utilitarian vessel and not merely used for the pharaoh's funeral. Like the few others permitted to examine the ship at the final stage of reassembly, I was tremendously impressed by the vessel, whose lines were perfectly designed for deep-sea waves and whose dimensions were more than twice those of the largest preserved Viking ship. A boat designed for the Nile, where waves can be measured in inches, would not have a longitudinal curve and tremendously high, curved bow and stern—features evolved by ancient deep-sea navigators, such as the Vikings and Polynesians, whose boats had to negotiate surf and ocean waves. The cross-sections of the Cheops boat were those of a vessel intended to roll and pitch with big waves, not with the current of the Nile. The design has absolutely no functional relevance for a riverboat.

Having duly absorbed the spectacular, ocean-going lines, I was the more surprised to be shown that the heavy woodwork of the ribless vessel was simply fitted together like the pieces of a jigsaw puzzle, end-to-end, with no overlaps, and was held in place by glue and rope seams. Even equipped with a longitudinal hawser, the beautiful craft would disintegrate in its first encounter with ocean swells. I knew enough about boats to see that there was no correspondence between the overall shape of the boat and its intrinsic construction.

Impressed by the seemingly eternal durability of the Phoenician cedar ships, the Egyptian ship-builders of 2700 BC began to import wood from Phoenicia, although they strove to maintain the traditional papyriform design of their own local ancestors. This, more than anything else, gave me confidence in the seagoing capabilities of papyrus, since the original lines of the pharaoh's ship had been developed for compact vessels of papyrus bundles. The papyrus boat, then, antedated the wooden ship in Egypt, yet it gave the wooden ship its spectacular, ocean-going shape. How could this be if papyrus as a material would sink or dissolve? I decided to make a practical experiment.

In 1969, I organized the building of a papyrus boat near the Cheops ship at Gizeh in Egypt, using local funerary-art depictions as models. Since wild papyrus, for unknown reasons, has become extinct in Egypt—and the papyrus boat-building craft accordingly forgotten— I brought 12 tons of sun-dried papyrus reeds about 10 to 12 feet long from Lake Tana in Ethiopia and two experienced boat-builders, with interpreter, from Lake Chad in central Africa. The latter area seemed to be the closest one to Egypt where large-sized papyrus boats of apparently robust construction are still in common use.

The feasibility of a coastal voyage along North Africa was not disputed by anyone, since it would allow the periodic beaching and drying out of the papyrus vessel, and we therefore decided to launch our boat directly into the ocean from the ancient Phoenician port of Safi on the Atlantic coast of Morocco—in the midst of an area rich in archaeological evidence of extensive colonization and settlement from Asia Minor. The papyrus boat, named Ra (the word for sun in ancient Egypt as well as on all the islands of Polynesia), was launched on 17 May 1969 and set sail eight days thereafter, manned by a crew of seven men from seven nations.* Food and water were stored in 160 ceramic jars copied from an ancient prototype in the Cairo Museum, as well as in several goatskin containers, wooden chests, and wickerwork baskets. All food on board was either fresh, dried, smoked, salted, or otherwise preserved as customary among ancient peoples. The several tons of superstructure and cargo, including bipod

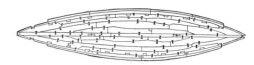

Ills. 123–125. The Cheops boat (reconstructed, right) was found in a pit at the foot of the pyramid of Cheops. Though built of wood in the traditional Egyptian manner whereby relatively thick timbers were pegged and 'sewn' together (above), it has the shape of its prototype, the papyrus boat (below opposite), and its structure at once suggested great ocean-going stability. The size of the Cheops boat—140½ ft. long, with a beam of 20 ft.—and its means of construction would not have allowed it to sail on anything but the wavelets of the Nile; its lines, however, confirmed in Thor Heyerdahl's mind the thought that papyrus boats of this size were built for ocean navigation. Pliny, quoting Eratosthenes (VI, XXIII, 82) speaks of papyrus ships sailing to Ceylon from the Ganges in twenty days, but this had always been thought an exaggeration.

Ill. 105

*Norman Baker (USA), navigator; Yuri Senkevitch (USSR), ship's doctor; Abdullah Djibrine (Chad), papyrus expert; Santiago Genovés (Mexico), anthropologist; Carlo Mauri (Italy), expedition photographer; Georges Sourial (Egypt), skin-diver; Thor Heyerdahl (Norway), expedition leader.

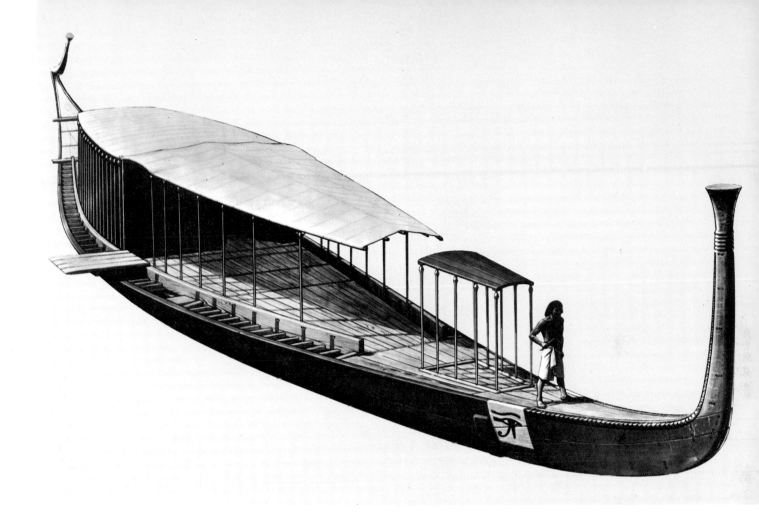

*Ill. 130*

mast, wickerwork cabin, steering platform, and heavy double rudder-oars, made remarkably little impression on the degree of buoyancy, and the reed vessel did not heel when its 500-square-foot trapezoidal sail filled with strong lateral winds. Just beyond the Safi breakwater, *Ra* was immediately caught by the powerful current and trade wind that together constitute the eternal 'Columbus conveyor' to tropical America.

The first day out, through inexperience, we broke both our rudder-oars, and on the second day, the yard supporting our Egyptian sail broke. Although repaired with rope splicings, the wooden oars kept repeatedly breaking in rough weather, thus converting the whole experiment to a scientifically more valuable drift voyage. Within three weeks, the reed boat had rounded the entire northwest coast of Africa from Safi to the Cape Verde Islands off Dakar, a distance equivalent to a voyage from Egypt to France, before the elements took us on the actual trans-Atlantic leg of the journey. By now, the papyrus bundles of the *Ra* had been floating in sea water for a month and demonstrated a spectacular ability to ride ocean waves even in a

gale with crew and cargo dry. The ocean swells and rollers, following the current and prevailing winds, caught *Ra* astern, but the extremely high, arched stern tipped upward and caused *Ra* to ride each crest without shipping water. When the ocean swells passed underneath amidships, the sagging bow and stern of the wooden Cheops ship would have caused it to break in half, whereas the springiness of the papyrus bundles allowed *Ra* to undulate without damage. Our first major discovery during the experiment was that the characteristic ancient Egyptian rigging copied on *Ra* proved conclusively that the original papyrus ship was not designed for use on the ripples of a river, but was intended for riding ocean swells. On the calm Nile, a bipod mast could have been held erect by one stay running forward and another running aft. As the hull would be floating on an even surface, no other stays would be needed. However, the complicated original rigging copied by us showed one rope running from the top of the mast forward to the bow and six parallel stays running aft from each leg of the mast to each side of the vessel shortly behind midships. No stay at all ran from the mast all the way to the stern. However, the ancient Egyptian illustrations depicted a rope running from the elegantly in-curved tip of the stern diagonally down like a harpstring to the afterdeck—as though intended to preserve the attractive curved shape of the papyrus boat's scorpion tail. I was sure that the in-curved tail must have had some obscure practical function, whereas general opinion was that it was purely an aesthetic detail. However, like everyone else, I and my Chad boat-builders were convinced that, whatever the function of the curved tail, that of the 'harpstring' was solely to retain the tail's curvature. It never occurred to us that the tail curve was to tension the rope, and not vice versa.

*Ills. 126–128.* The Buduma tribesmen who built *Ra I* were finally persuaded to give her an upturned stern (left) rather than the cut-off one of their own reed boats. The rope which they had used to hold the scorpion tail during construction—shown on Egyptian and Mesopotamian prototypes (below left)—was thought not to have any practical purpose, as the stern kept its shape without it; it was only halfway across the Atlantic that its use became apparent: it supported not the tail, but instead the deck aft of the mast stays. Without this 'harpstring', the stern deck buckled and was soon submerged (right).

*Ill. 126*

*Ill. 128*

So the Chad boat-builders removed the 'harpstring', showing us that they had curved the tail so durably that it would never straighten out. And as they proved correct, we never reattached that rope till it was too late. By then, *Ra* had buckled transversely at a marked angle just where the rearmost of the parallel stays from the mast reached the deck. And although the tail retained its beautiful curvature, the afterdeck, now hinged at the buckling line, sagged into the sea. Now, instead of lifting to ride over the waves coming from behind, the sloping afterdeck acted as a beach, inviting the breakers to hammer aboard like surf. We now realized that the in-curved tail was there to act as a giant spring, which, by means of the 'harpstring', would hold the otherwise unsupported afterdeck on a level with the rest of the boat, which, in the manner of a suspension bridge, was hung by the stays running fore and aft from the mast. The ancient boat designers had wisely hinged, so to say, their pliant afterdeck to the mid-deck by making a complex rig, allowing the necessary flexibility in riding deep-sea waves without the taut stays breaking the mast.

Repair proved impossible once the afterdeck had sagged; it now both acted as a brake and prevented straight steering. Moreover, the waves, having direct access to the rear cabin-wall, caused constant abrasion between the lashed-on wicker cabin and the papyrus deck, severing the ropes holding the papyrus bundles together on the windward side. In the final storm before reaching the West Indies, we therefore began to lose alarming quantities of papyrus on the starboard side. The individual papyrus reeds left in the wake behind *Ra* still floated, and instead of having deteriorated they had become rubbery and strong, like rope, rather than brittle and fragile as they were when dry before being launched into the sea. However, after the last storm, the starboard bundles had lost so many papyrus reeds that the vessel listed steeply, and this, rather than an overall loss of buoyancy, posed a threat to life in the event of another storm. The port two-thirds of *Ra* were undamaged and floated so high that we could, if necessary, have completed the last leg of our drift voyage to the islands ahead—and, in fact, the entire crew wanted to do so. But, as expedition leader, I saw no reason to risk human life in a scientific experiment, virtually all of the questions of which had by this stage been answered.

It was now clearly established that papyrus was a first-class boat-building material. Instead of rotting in seawater, it became stronger and more sinewy through immersion; and rather than sinking after two weeks, the intact reed bundles were still carrying all of us and our tons of provisions and superstructure after one week in port and eight weeks in the roughest ocean waves. The papyrus boat itself proved to be astonishingly buoyant, stable, and seaworthy, capable of riding out any storm—as we learned during our first weeks in the ocean, before our own complete lack of experience in building and handling such a vessel reduced it from sailing ship to drifting raft of reeds. Finally, we learned that the weak points in such a vessel are not at all the flexible reeds, but rather the rigid wood and the friction of wood against ropes. Any mariners breaking their rudder-oars as we did in an encounter with the heavy rollers of the Canary Current off the Moroccan coast would be gripped by the 'Columbus conveyor' as we had been and transmitted with great speed in the direction of the Gulf of Mexico. Unlike us, however, ancient mariners would have been forced to hold on to the bitter end, whereas we had the opportunity of terminating our voyage at will once its scientific purpose had been achieved. When we transferred ourselves, our pet animals, and our

*Ill. 129.* Map of the courses of *Ra I* and *Ra II* across the Atlantic.

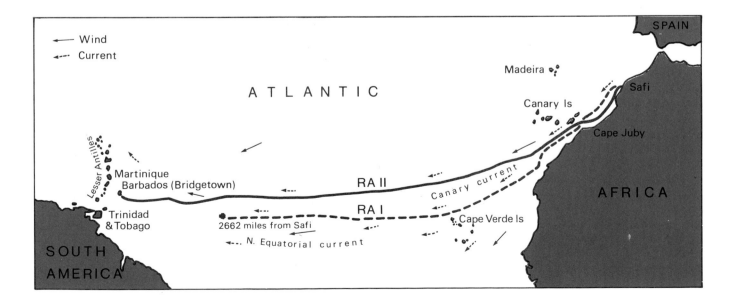

*Ill. 130.* The departure of *Ra I* at Safi. Within twenty-four hours the rudder oars had been broken by the seas; thus there began a drifting voyage which was to prove conclusively that—provided it stayed afloat—a primitive craft would be automatically carried by the currents from the well-colonized Moroccan shore to the Americas.

*Ill. 129*

*Ill. 122*

*Baker, Senkevitch, Genovés, Mauri, Sourial, Heyerdahl, and new participants: Kei Ohara (Japan), cameraman; and Madani Ait Ouhanni (Morocco), responsible for ocean-pollution studies.

*Ills. 117, 120*

cargo to a yacht that had come out to film us, we had covered 2,700 nautical miles in eight weeks—or the same distance as from Safi in Morocco to Quebec in Canada. Had we begun our voyage in Senegal on the west coast of Africa instead of in Safi, this same distance would have carried us straight across the Atlantic and more than 1,000 miles up the Amazon.

On 17 May 1970, ten months after the termination of the first papyrus-ship experiment, the second reed ship, *Ra II*, set sail from the same Moroccan harbour with six tons of cargo and superstructure and an eight-man crew, six of whom had sailed on *Ra I*.* The papyrus was brought once more from the source of the Nile, but whereas *Ra I* had been built in Egypt by Buduma fishermen from Lake Chad in central Africa, *Ra II* was built in Morocco by four Aymara Indians and their Bolivian interpreter brought from Lake Titicaca in South America. Strangely enough, although the former boat-builders came from within the same continent as Egypt—while the latter came from the New World—it was the Lake Titicaca reed boat that followed the main building principles once typical of ancient Egypt, *i.e.,* with both bow and stern pointed and raised high above water and with rope lashings running uninterruptedly around the large-bundled vessel from deck to bottom. The Chad boat-builders, in contrast to those of ancient Egypt, were used to cutting the sterns of their boats abruptly off at water level and constructing their vessels of superimposed layers of slender reed bundles bound together with vulnerable chains of interlocking rope rings. The Chad system was perfectly adapted to lake transport, whereas the overdesigned and strikingly ingenious Titicaca type yielded a solid block capable of surviving far more violent conditions than would ever be encountered on Lake Titicaca. Basically, this vessel consisted of two huge cigar-shaped bundles squeezed together by a continuous and tightly drawn spiral rope encircling a smaller, central bundle, which, as the ropes were tightened, disappeared between the larger two. Once the pointed bow and stern were turned upward and two smaller bundles added along the upper edges to increase the width of the deck, an almost incredibly robust and seaworthy water craft resulted, which concurred remarkably with the designs of ancient Mesopotamia and Egypt.

So set on returning home within a two-month building period were our South American boat-builders, that fully one third of the 12 tons of papyrus lay unused when *Ra II* was ready for launching. Whereas *Ra I* had been 15 metres (almost 50 feet) long, *Ra II* was only 12 metres (not quite 40 feet), and with its rounder cross-section, *Ra II* had far less volume. We had become so impressed with the fantastic carrying capacity of a papyrus raft-ship that we yielded to the temptation to load *Ra II* with far more cargo tonnage than a conventional vessel of her modest dimensions could ever have accommodated without going straight to the bottom. Although burdened down, with her deck almost to water level, *Ra II* rode out a full gale in mid-Atlantic when the now-colossal shaft of one of her rudder-oars broke and turned the vessel helplessly broadside to breaking seas until the papyrus above the water line was thoroughly soaked. Yet *Ra II* accomplished the complete crossing of 3,270 nautical miles from Safi in Morocco to Barbados in the West Indies in 57 days—an average speed of 65 statute miles per day. The papyrus vessel had crossed the entire Atlantic at its widest part without loss of, or damage to, a single reed—although one of the thick, rigid, wooden rudder-oars had broken, even on this trip.

*Ill. 122*

The experimental voyages of *Ra I* and *Ra II* had conclusively proved that the reed boat, which is one of the culture elements common to the Old World and the New World in pre-Columbian times, was perfectly capable of a trans-Atlantic voyage. It is thus needless to resort to fantastic theories of gourds and cotton seeds drifting haphazardly into the hands of food-gathering tribes among the jungle trees of the Gulf of Mexico. The discovery of the true merits of the reed boat does not prove pre-Columbian contact, but it does make such a theory more realistic than any other hypothesis so far offered in explanation of the impulse behind the American high cultures.

# 5  Some Points of Controversy

## Birgitta L. Wallace

*For the more far-fetched claims of pre-Columbian penetration in the New World, see: Charles Boland, *They All Discovered America*.

*Ill. 131*

A VAST BODY OF MATERIAL purports to be tangible evidence of pre-Columbian European penetration into the western hemisphere: in Canada and the United States there are no less than twenty-four inscriptions, sixty-nine artifacts, and fifty-two sites. By and large, this material is attributed to the Norse Vinland voyages.*

The evidence is concentrated into two major areas: the Atlantic seaboard and the Great Lakes region. The evidence from the Atlantic coast allegedly dates from the Viking Age and is specifically associated with the voyages of Leif Eiriksson and his contemporaries. The Great Lakes evidence, on the other hand, is commonly associated with the later Middle Ages in general and with one Swedish-Norwegian expedition of the 1360s in particular. Both are areas in which people have searched actively for archaeological proofs of the Norse ventures.

## Inscriptions

*Ill. 133*

The best known supposedly pre-Columbian document in America is the Kensington stone inscription. Found on a farm in Kensington in Douglas County, Minnesota, in 1898, it is a runic inscription spelling out the misfortunes of a thirty-man strong expedition of Norwegians and 'Goths' travelling westwards from Vinland on a 'journey of discovery'. It professes to have been written in 1362 as a desperate message and a memorial to ten of the expedition members who met with violent death. The inscription ends by stating that ten other members have stayed behind in Vinland 'fourteen days' journey from this island' to guard the expedition's ships.

The finder of the inscription was a Swedish immigrant, a carpenter turned farmer by the name of Olof Ohman who arrived in Douglas County in 1879. In 1891 he bought a farm near Kensington and it was while clearing a knoll on this farm that he came upon the inscribed stone. The story is that Ohman was felling a small aspen and, pulling up its stump, he noticed the stone lying entangled in the roots with a corner protruding slightly. Evidently the stone had been in this position for some time for the roots had partially formed round it. It is not clear whether Ohman was alone at the time, or if not, who else observed the stone; one report states that he was accompanied by his son Edward, others that a neighbour was with him. Nor is it clear exactly when the inscription was first observed.

The finding of the inscribed stone was reported to the news media about two months later, and simultaneously the stone itself with drawings and photographs of the inscription was submitted to scholars in the fields of philology and runology, both in the United States and abroad. Their unanimous opinion was that the inscription was not a document from 1362 as it purported to be, but a nineteenth-century fabrication.

There matters rested until 1907 when a young Norwegian-born writer and lecturer, Hjalmar Rued Holand, began taking an interest in the stone. Declaring war on expert opinion and claiming the stone to be an authentic fourteenth-century document, Holand began an active campaign in support of his claim which lasted until his death in 1963. Holand gained much popular support in spite of the fact that experts in the fields of runology and Scandinavian philology consistently and continuously found the inscription a typical nineteenth-century product.

Just how modern the Kensington inscription is will be seen from the illustrations. Rune and grammatical forms unknown to the fourteenth century have been circled. Notice that the circling covers the major portion of the inscription.

The language alone furnishes a valuable clue to the identity of the carver: it is colloquial nineteenth-century 'Scandinavian' of a kind that developed in Minnesota wherever Swedes and Norwegians lived close together. This kind of 'Scandinavian' which is neither pure Swedish nor pure Norwegian is still a striking characteristic among the old inhabitants of Douglas County. It bears no resemblance to medieval versions of the same languages. The carver was probably Swedish, for Swedish predominates in his 'Scandinavian', and he uses the word 'Goths' (see below).

Hjalmar Holand cited a wealth of material in support of the claim that runes as well as text were genuinely medieval. None can stand scrutiny, however, and the references given are without exception misleading or false. Additional arguments of a historical character have, on the other hand, been repeated so often that they have become accepted almost as established truths. It might therefore be of interest to examine them further.

The great influx of Scandinavians into Douglas County began in 1857, forty-one years before the Kensington inscription was discovered. Originally the knoll on which the stone was found was

*Ill. 131.* Right, map of alleged pre-Columbian Norse sites in America. ▶

*Ills. 133, 134*

156

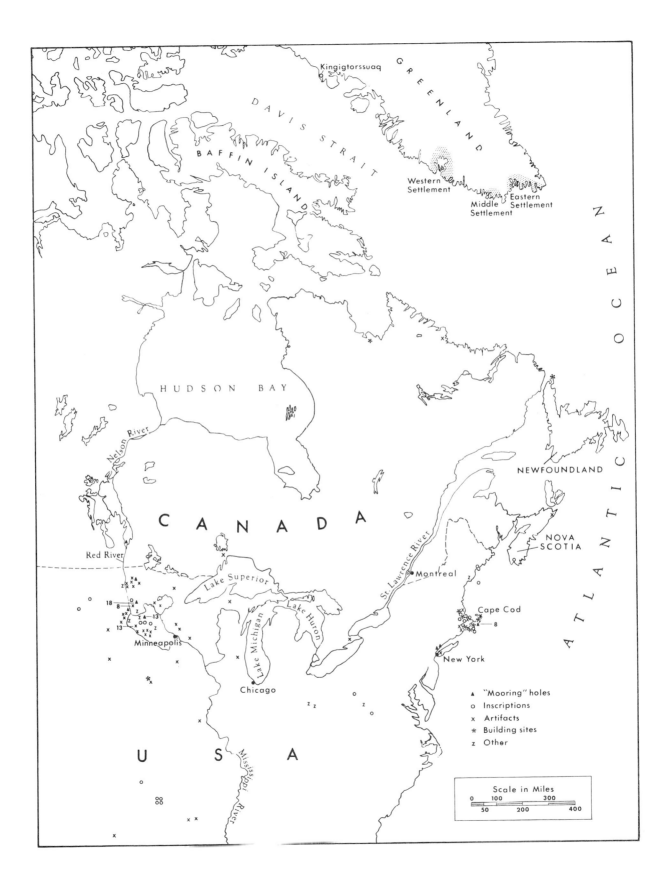

GREENLAND

Kingigtorssuaq

DAVIS STRAIT

BAFFIN ISLAND

Western
Settlement

Middle
Settlement

Eastern
Settlement

HUDSON BAY

Nelson River

NEWFOUNDLAND

C A N A D A

Red River

Lake Superior

St. Lawrence River

Montreal

NOVA
SCOTIA

18
8

Lake Huron

Lake Michigan

13
8

13

Cape Cod

8

Minneapolis

New York

Chicago

z  z

z

z

U S A

Mississippi River

▲ "Mooring" holes
o Inscriptions
x Artifacts
∗ Building sites
z Other

A T L A N T I C   O C E A N

Scale in Miles

0    100         300
  50       200        400

*Ill. 132.* The Kensington stone, found in 1898 near the village of Kensington, Minnesota, is a small, naturally shaped block of gray-wacke with a runic inscription chiselled on two of its four sides. The inscription begins in the upper left corner of the broad side and continues perpendicularly on the narrow face of the stone. The inscription bears the date AD 1362, but both runes and language are a product of nineteenth-century historical romanticism. The stone is about 2½ ft. high, 15 ins. wide and 3–6 ins. thick. The runes are about one in. high and appear to have been cut with an ordinary one-inch chisel. The cuts are fresh and sharp and lack the patina of the stone. They have darkened slightly during the seventy years that have elapsed since the stone was discovered but no more than the 'H' near the bottom of the narrow side which was cut in 1908 by Hjalmar Holand.

*Ills. 133, 134.* The text of the Kensington inscription bears vivid ▶ testimony to its recent origin. Left hand panel, shaded are runes, unknown in 1362 or conflicting with fourteenth-century usage. Right hand panel, shaded are grammatically and syntactically recent words. The type of 'Scandinavian' language portrayed in the inscription in fact shows that the stone was carved by a Scandinavian settler in the American Middle West. This particular dialect developed in that region and is still spoken by the old-timers in the Kensington area but is unknown in other parts of the world. It is also obvious that the inscription was carved by someone with an embryonic knowledge of runes, but who lacked familiarity with medieval Scandinavian languages. The carver could have been almost any one of the early Scandinavian settlers in Minnesota, all of whom knew something about runes but who generally had no philological education.

wooded, and the first settlers used to go there to help themselves to timber and firewood. Eventually the land was homesteaded by a Norwegian, who cleared it. Ohman bought the land from the Norwegian, and by this time, the knoll was already covered with secondary deciduous timber growth. Since eye-witnesses established that the tree growing over the stone was no more than thirty and possibly as little as ten years old, there was ample time for the stone to have been inscribed after the Scandinavians arrived on the scene.

Accounts of when the inscription was first observed are conflicting and incomplete (there is even some confusion over the month in which the stone was found). They leave room for the possibility that the inscription could have been carved *after* the finding of the stone and it could be that the finding of the stone in its peculiar position planted the idea of carving the text.

There is practically no weathering at all of the inscription. The runes are remarkably fresh and sharp. The cuts are angular and keen. They were made with chisels and awls, a fact in itself remarkable for runes were rarely chisel-cut in the Middle Ages. More remarkable yet, they

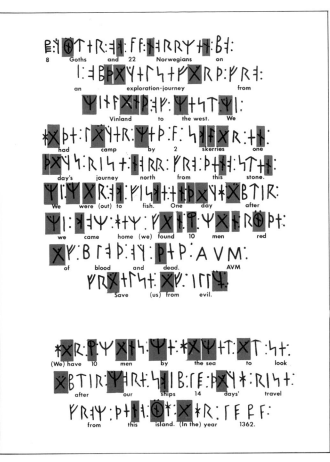

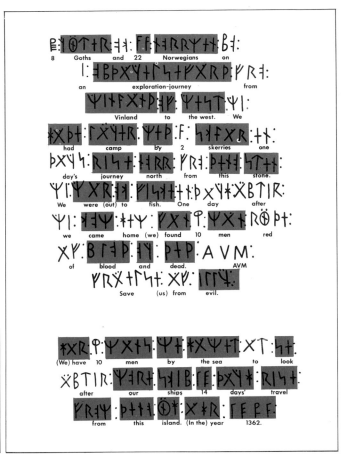

were cut with a chisel with a regular one-inch bit, a variety commonly sold in American hardware stores.

The term 'island' for the knoll where the runestone was found, although incorrect in English, is the correct term in Swedish, even if the 'island' is surrounded by fields rather than water. In the case of the runestone knoll, this term is doubly appropriate since it rises out of swamps which in the nineteenth century were often flooded, making the knoll a real 'island'.

A historical document cited in support of the inscription's veracity is an order by King Magnus Ericson of Norway-Sweden dated 1354 for a vessel of armed and spiritual support to the Greenland Norse colonies. However, the order concerns Greenland, not Vinland or countries west of Greenland. It is adventuresome to speculate that after a 3,000-mile long journey from Norway, the ship ventured another 1,000 miles into Hudson Bay and from there followed an erratic course for an additional 1,000 miles into Minnesota. After all, these Norsemen were not searching for the Northwest Passage but their own settlements.

King Magnus, the hapless ruler of a united Norway and Sweden from 1319 to 1356 and of Sweden alone from 1356 to 1363, is a legendary figure in Swedish history, and even today children sing nursery rhymes about his fair queen, Blanche of Namur. To the nineteenth century, the era of Magnus Ericson offered special attractions: romance, chivalry, and grandeur as well as incomparable tragedy with the hardships of the Black Death, the dissolution of the union, and bloody family feuds, all events which singled out this epoch for special attention in schools and in popular romance.

Sweden and Norway were again under joint rule in the nineteenth century, with Sweden as the dominating nation. By the 1890s the political situation was tense, with Norway demanding her independence one way or the other. It is tempting to see this political situation reflected in the Kensington inscription which rather contemptuously gives '8 Goths' precedence over '22 Norwegians'.

Other historical sources cited in support for the authenticity of the inscription concern Nicholas of Lynn, an English monk who made several exploratory voyages northwards. The theory is that Nicholas sailed with the Norwegian expedition and that together they reached Hudson Bay. But the evidence at hand shows that on the contrary, Nicholas's expedition was an English enterprise, originating in and returning to northern England in 1360, and that it aimed for Iceland from where it continued *northwards*. Here Nicholas observed the magnetic influence of the pole and whirlpools in the Greenland Sea, the same phenomena that had been described a hundred and fifty years earlier by Giraldus Cambrensis. There is nothing to show that Nicholas ever saw Hudson Bay.

Because no one has ever confessed to carving it, the authenticity of the Kensington stone still has its fervent protagonists. The person most often suspected to have carved the inscription is the finder, Olof Ohman. Ohman has unfairly been portrayed as a dull-witted farmer, honest but poor, uneducated and simple-minded. Contemporary records do not confirm this simplicity. He was on the contrary said to be a 'queer genius', a man who 'talked little but thought much'. He was reasonably successful financially and could afford to return to Sweden for two years, 1884–1886, in itself an unusual feat for a farmer in Douglas County in the late nineteenth century. He knew something about runes. He had little formal schooling, but like so many of his countrymen he possessed a keen interest in history, of which he read a great deal. In this he was a typical product of nineteenth-century Sweden. The chief subjects taught in the little country schools were religion and Swedish history, and history was studied in minute detail, although from a provincial point of view, with heavy emphasis on the royal rulers and the past glories of the nation.

Two other Swedish immigrants to Douglas County have been mentioned as possible collaborators: Andrew Anderson and Sven Fogelblad. Anderson was a farmer, whose wife was a cousin of Mrs. Ohman; Fogelblad was academically educated and held a divinity degree from the University of Uppsala in Sweden. He served as a clergyman for a few years before resigning from the church because of conflicting religious beliefs. Ohman, Anderson, and Fogelblad were close friends and were interested in ancient history and mysticism, as is shown by their reading matter and Fogelblad's writings.

The Sweden that Ohman, Fogelblad, and Anderson grew up in was Tegner's and Geijer's Sweden, the era of National Romanticism and 'Gothicism' when Tegner's *Fritiofs' Saga* and Geijer's *The Viking* were the favoured readings in the farmsteads, alongside the Bible and Luther's Family Sermons. It was a time when runic writing was still used by the peasantry in remote provinces in northern Sweden such as Dalecarlia and Ångermanland (and Ohman was born in Dalecarlia and raised in northern Sweden). In other parts of the country, interest in runes was being revived under the influence of 'Gothicism' and increasing archaeological activities.

So for nineteenth-century Swedes to celebrate in runes the daring voyages of the old 'Goths' was quite in character. For Swedes, emigrants to distant America, it must have been natural to include 'Vinland' in the tale, especially since in their new homeland there was a widespread popular interest in the ancient Norse mariners. Whoever the carver may have been, Douglas County in Minnesota constituted the perfect setting for a carving such as the Kensington inscription, and the Kensington stone is indeed no more enigmatic than a Viking Age runestone in eleventh-century Sweden.

The Heavener inscription is an inscription eight symbols long on a large sandstone slab tipped into vertical position by nature, situated halfway up the slope of Poteau mountain near Heavener in southeastern Oklahoma. According to some sources it has been known since the late nineteenth century, but has not received widespread attention until recent years. Reading from left to right the runes spell out GAOMEDAT or GNOMEDAL, depending on whether the ᚺ and ᛏ runes are read as reversed symbols or not. GAOMEDAT has no meaning in any language commonly associated with runes; GNOMEDAL on the other hand does. In a quasi English-Old Saxon it could mean 'Gnome Valley', a gnome being an earth spirit which guards treasures. It could also be Norwegian if the inscription is read G NOMEDAL, Nomedal being a known Norwegian family and homestead name. As representing the recent development from an older form of the same name ending in -r, Nomedal as well as 'Gnome Valley' would indicate that the inscription is post-Columbian.

*Ill. 135.* The Heavener runic inscription in southeastern Oklahoma. Read from left to right it can be transliterated G N O M E D A L or G A O M E D A T.

Such a reading seems tempting since the runes also indicate a recent date for the inscription. They are runes from the Old Germanic runerow which ceased to be used as functional writing symbols some time around AD 900, not to be revived again until antiquarian interest in runes was initiated in the seventeenth and notably the nineteenth century. At least one of the runes, however, ᛆ, N or A, is not from the Old Germanic but from one of the late Viking Age runerows, the so-called Swedish-Norwegian futhark (ᛐ could be from the Swedish-Norwegian as well as the Old Germanic runerow). Such mixtures of runes are common in post-Columbian rune writing but practically unknown from earlier times, another indicator of a relatively modern date for the inscription.

By way of summary then, the runes as well as the text point to a recent date for the Heavener inscription. It is not necessarily an intentional fraud, or even a hoax; as we have seen above, familiarity with runes was widespread in Sweden a century ago. The same situation existed in Norway and the other Scandinavian countries. Moreover, in the nineteenth century, runes were used outside Scandinavia; for instance, the son of an English immigrant to Ohio told a few years ago how he learnt runes as a small boy from his father, who in turn had learnt them from his uncle, an uneducated farmer in Warwickshire.

The slab on the Poteau mountainside almost invites an inscription of one kind or another. The Poteau region was settled by Europeans in 1720, and early documents indicate that there were Scandinavians among them. Reminded of a runestone from his home country, one of them could have decided to leave his mark on the stone in a manner befitting the handsome slab, namely in bold and clear runes.

*Ill. 136.* The Yarmouth stone. The stone is on display in the Yarmouth Public Library, Yarmouth, Nova Scotia. Its upper part has been touched so often by visitors that it has become smooth and shiny. Some years ago the alleged date of the inscription, 1007, was painted on the side of the stone. Simultaneously, its symbols were outlined with white oil paint. The paint changes their appearance in a photograph. The symbols, therefore, are shown below in the text.

*Ill. 136*

The Yarmouth stone is a 30 × 29 × 18 inch sandstone boulder split to reveal a large smooth surface, with an uneven part remaining as a rough border. Small drilled holes and grooves lined up in a band across the smooth surface form what appear to be the following symbols:

The stone was first encountered in the late eighteenth century on the shore of Yarmouth Bay, Nova Scotia. Little attention was paid to it at first and it was not until some seventy years later that interest focused on it, when people began to consider the possibility that the stone could represent a runic inscription from the Vinland Norse. One Henry Phillips claimed the signs read 'Harkussen men varu' which supposedly, according to Phillips, was the Old Norse for 'Harko's

*Ills. 137, 138.* Right, the controversial Beardmore find, allegedly discovered in the early 1930s on a mining claim near Beardmore, Ontario. The implements are Norwegian and from the Viking Age but were probably brought to Canada in 1923. ▶

son addressed the men', a reading as fanciful as it is imaginative. Another interpretation, offered by a Norwegian-descended school teacher many years later, was 'Leif to Eirik raises', which is equally fanciful. As it is, the symbols do not bear the faintest similarity to any known alphabet, and the provenance of the Yarmouth stone inscription remains an enigma.

Other inscriptions often considered in the debate of archaeological evidence of Norse voyages are those from Manana Island in Maine, at Hampton, New Hampshire, and at Bourne and Byfield, Massachusetts. However, the Manana, Hampton, and Byfield symbols are erosion phenomena; and the Bourne inscription, now in the Aptucxet Trading Post Museum near Bourne, appears to be a much eroded American Indian petroglyph.

Recently, accounts have been published which attempt to establish that the above 'inscriptions' are not only legitimate runes but that they contain, in cryptographic form, the dates of their manufacture within pre-Columbian times. However, the cryptographic readings are arbitrary and the published accounts fanciful.

## Artifacts

Purported evidence of the eleventh-century Norse voyages in the shape of artifacts is sparse. Most comes from the Atlantic seaboard. One piece is an axe from Tor Bay, Nova Scotia. Described as a typical Viking Age flared axe, it is in fact of a kind used in the trade with Indians by Russians, English, and French in the nineteenth century. Another axe from East Orleans, Cape Cod, is likewise of recent manufacture, and dates from the eighteenth or nineteenth century.

A rather puzzling find came to light in Ontario about forty years ago. It consisted of a rusty sword, broken in two, an axehead, a fragmentary horse rattle, and three small fragments, all of iron. The objects date from the latter part of the Viking Age, the axe and the

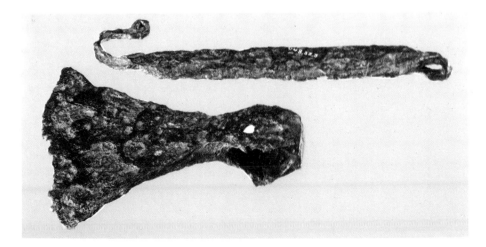

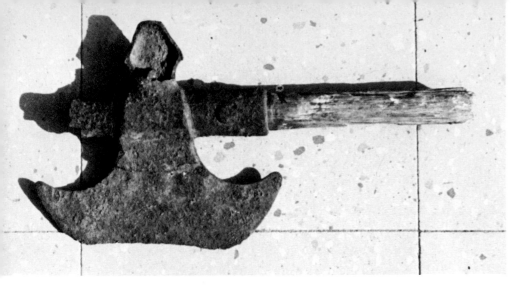

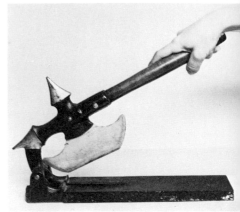

Ills. 139, 140. Left, 'halberd' found in the 1920s at Lake Darling, Douglas County, Minnesota, now in the collection of the Runestone Museum, Alexandria, Minnesota. This 'halberd' is in reality nothing more than a plug tobacco cutter from the latter half of the nineteenth century (above).

rattle being of eleventh-century type and the sword from the tenth century. Although there has never been any doubt about the authenticity of the implements, the find has become highly controversial because of conflicting stories about the circumstances of its discovery. One report states that the objects were found while dynamiting on a mining claim near Beardmore, Ontario; another that they lay in the basement of a private house in Port Arthur, Ontario. Both reports are substantiated with witnesses and circumstantial evidence, and both reports contain conflicting evidence within themselves to some degree. Seen in retrospect, however, the most substantial evidence favours the contention that the objects were retrieved from the Port Arthur basement. There are for instance bank records confirming a loan against which Viking Age weapons were supposedly deposited as a guarantee. The loan was made by the owner of the house to a young Norwegian named Jens Bloch (later changed to John Block) who arrived in Canada in 1923. Bloch's father, Andreas Bloch, was a well known artist and collector of ancient weapons in Norway. If the Bloch weapons are not identical to those said to come from Beardmore, there must have been two practically identical sets of Viking Age weapons in Ontario at this time, an unlikely situation.

It is also a matter for suspicion that the person who allegedly found the weapons on his mining claim had high financial stakes in the find: he had been paid $500 by the Royal Ontario Museum for the artifacts, which represented a considerable amount of money in 1938 when the deal was concluded. There is evidence, too, that the alleged finder enjoyed a reputation for tall stories in everything concerned with his mining claim. When the Royal Ontario Museum opened an investigation of the case in 1956, the finder's adopted son volunteered a sworn statement that he had seen his father come across the implements in the Port Arthur basement and had later taken them to his mining claim.

On the other hand, the person who reported that the weapons came from the basement and were rightfully his, not those of the alleged finder, never attempted to obtain a financial or other reward for the objects. It seems he had nothing to gain by his story, except adverse publicity—of which he received a considerable amount. As it turned out, he was practically ostracized by the entire Norwegian community in Port Arthur.

Thus, although genuine Viking implements, the Beardmore—or Port Arthur—weapons were, more likely than not, brought to America in 1923 rather than in the eleventh century.

Another group of artifacts associated with pre-Columbian Norsemen consists of forty-three implements found in the Great Lakes area. These include twenty-four axes or halberds, four swords, eight spearheads, and five firesteels. All have turned up as the direct or indirect result of the search for evidence in support of the authenticity of the Kensington stone. Consequently, they purport to date from the fourteenth century.

Detailed examination will show, however, that the oldest artifacts in the group, such as the axeheads from Erdahl and Brandon, date from the eighteenth century and are of French provenance, rather than pre-Columbian Norse. Others, such as axeheads from Mora and Harris, are goose-winged broadaxes of a type used throughout the nineteenth century.

*Ill. 139* The halberds are an interesting study on their own. There are six which are purportedly Norse or medieval. They are small and light with a crescent-shaped blade riveted into a socket with symmetrical, triangle-shaped blunted projections from both poll and socket. Because they are obviously unusable as weapons, these halberds have been termed 'ceremonial'.

Medieval halberds differ considerably in both design and construction. Although the American halberds display superficial resemblances to some Renaissance examples, they are closer in form to Oriental axes. This brings us to ask what possible purpose these halberds could have served in the Great Lakes zone in America.

*Ill. 140* A little research will show that these are not halberds at all but plug tobacco cutters, designed for the American Tobacco Company and used as a stunt in an advertising campaign for 'Battle-Ax' tobacco. Equipped with a short handle, the 'halberds' were hinged to a cutting board by a curved part extending from one spike. A large number of these tobacco cutters were distributed throughout the United States in the nineteenth century. Because of their interesting shape, many were detached from their cutting boards and kept as souvenirs or light axes after the hinge part had been sawn off. All the purported 'Norse halberds' show signs of such a removal. The only ceremony for which they were ever intended was cutting tobacco!

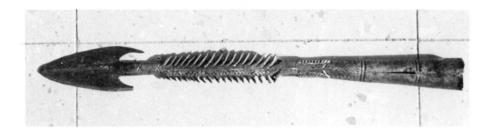

Spears were found in Trempealeau County, Wisconsin, in Alberta, and Chokio, Minnesota, Mustinka River and Hankinson, North Dakota. The Trempealeau spear, also called the Windjue spear after its finder, has a lanceolate, elongated point and was attached to the shaft via a socket and two long iron straps. Unknown in fourteenth-century Scandinavia, this kind of spear was common in the seventeenth century and later. It was also used by the British and French in America, and undoubtedly the Windjue spear stems from the time of the colonial troops. The Alberta spear is likewise colonial. The Chokio and Mustinka spears are of native copper, examples of the American Indian Old Copper Culture. The Hankinson spears— *Ill. 141* there are two—found in the 1930s in an Indian grave are interesting examples of cultural diffusion and archaeological confusion. They are nothing less than African! Spears of this kind could be purchased by *Ill. 142* mail order from establishments such as Bannerman's in New York around the turn of the century.

Of the swords, one, the so-called Brooten sword found near *Ill. 145* Willmar, Minnesota, which has a hilt of cast brass, decorated in a feather-like pattern, is a characteristic American-made naval cutlass of US model, 1841. Two others, one from Hibbing, Minnesota, and *Ill. 144* another from Cherokee, Iowa, are French swords designed by the *Ill. 143* distinguished French artist Jacques-Louis David for the École de Mars in Paris. They date from 1794. The fourth sword, found in 1911

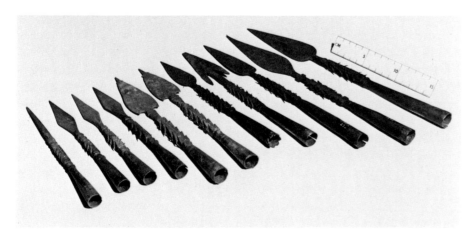

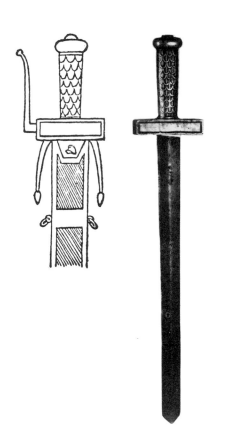

*Ill. 146*

*Ills. 143–145.* Far left, French sword designed by Jacques-Louis David for the École de Mars of 1794, a Revolutionary military academy. The sword was later issued in several variations. One variant was theatrical and used by actors playing Roman soldiers in Revolutionary pageants; others were intended for military purposes and used by the Frankish guards. It is very similar in design to the alleged Norse sword found near Sutherland, Iowa (left). The so-called Brooten sword (above), termed medieval Norse by Hjalmar Holand, is an American cutlass of the 1841 model.

near Ulen, Minnesota, is very similar to the two French swords but seems to have been made in Philadelphia around 1809.

Of the other artifacts, none are pre-Columbian and most are of nineteenth-century American provenance.

Common to all the finds is the fact that they were discovered accidentally, generally during farming operations. Most had deeply corroded surfaces and some were encountered under considerable deposits of earth, one or two even among the roots of a very old tree. However, neither corrosion nor heavy soil deposits are necessarily a criterion of considerable age.

## Mooring Holes

About forty rock drillings termed 'mooring holes' have been reported from the Great Lakes region, chiefly Minnesota; there are a couple from the Cape Cod and Long Island Sound area. The holes occur in boulders strewn along present or past waterways. Generally, they measure about one inch in diameter and are between five and seven inches deep. Many are triangular. The theory is that ancient Norse ship crews drilled such a hole whenever they needed temporary mooring and assurance of a quick get-away. The hole was said to be intended for the insertion of a hawser pin of iron or wood, tight enough to hold the ship securely, but loose enough to allow the line to be flipped loose instantly when danger threatened. Thus the occurrence of such holes supposedly indicates routes travelled by Norse naval expeditions.

Aside from the fact that such a method would be cumbersome and unreliable (it would necessitate nightly drilling in rocks, and changes in temperature and humidity could affect the fit of the pin), the method is unknown in Norse seamanship, medieval or modern. In fact, the entire concept of 'mooring holes' is built on a misunderstanding.

The theory was developed by Hjalmar Holand after he observed Norwegian fishermen tying their boats to iron rings fastened in boulders and cliffs on the shore. These were permanently installed ring bolts, however, needed wherever ships sought port repeatedly. Such ring bolts are known the world over and are quite common in twentieth-century America.

Temporary mooring, on the other hand, is another matter. In Scandinavia, as in most other parts of the world, the procedure involves nothing more elaborate than a line thrown around a tree or a stone. If security was a factor, the ship simply anchored at a safe distance from the shore.

Other stones with identical drillings in the immediate vicinity of the 'mooring holes' provide a clue as to what they really are: they are blasting holes drilled by the early settlers to split stone for foundations, and no hole has been proved to be older than 1860. Many of the stones were never dynamited for one reason or another. The holes are triangular because they were drilled with a hand-held, dull or straight-edged drill bit which invariably produces a triangular hole. On the farms in nineteenth-century Minnesota blasting holes were commonly drilled with regular one-inch bits, hence the one-inch diameter of the holes. The 'mooring holes' are indeed in more aspects than one the most unbelievable archaeological evidence ever presented for Norse penetration into the American continent.

*Ill. 146.* Alleged mooring stone from Lake Jesse, Douglas County, Minnesota.

## Building Sites

The Newport tower is a small stone structure in the centre of the town of Newport, Rhode Island. It is circular, and about 24 feet high with two-foot thick walls. Only the stone shell remains, all perishable wooden components having disappeared before the end of the eighteenth century. Originally covered with a thick coat of stucco, the masonry consists of a jumble of stones, most of which are un-shaped and laid in haphazard fashion without regard to size or fit, held together with thick layers of mortar.

*Ill. 147*

Known from historical records since 1677, the tower became the centre of a heated debate concerning its origin after the Danish antiquarian C. A. Rafn in 1839 published his belief that the tower represented the ruin of a Norse baptistery or round church and that it was built by Vinland voyagers in the eleventh or twelfth century. Since then a large number of books and articles have appeared for and against this theory. Some have proposed that the tower is a Norse church of the fourteenth century; others again that it is a watch tower built in the sixteenth century by Portuguese or English explorers.

Arguments raised in favour of a medieval origin for the tower are that segmental arches, double-splayed casement windows, and low entrance ways are medieval, not colonial characteristics. Besides, the fireplace, equipped as it is with flues but no chimney, would posit a fourteenth-century date for the construction. But both flues and chimneys were used long before the fourteenth century, and neither were always present in post-medieval buildings. In a circular tower such as the Newport structure, the building of a chimney stack poses a structural problem, so there was reason to leave it out altogether. Low doorways and double-splayed casement windows are very much a characteristic of early colonial New England architecture, which perpetuated the medieval building traditions of rural England. The use of the segmental arch was, on the other hand, undoubtedly a continuation of a Renaissance theme.

An often used argument in favour of a Norse medieval origin of the tower is that supposedly the Rhineland foot was the unit of measurement employed in the construction. The argument is spurious. First, a Rhineland foot unit is not demonstrable in the diameter of the construction trench, which is the only measurement that can be made with any degree of certainty (the extreme irregularity of the masonry and stucco coat precluding others); secondly, colonial builders used dimensions of fractions of feet and inches in their buildings; thirdly, the Rhineland foot was *not* a standard unit of measure in medieval Scandinavia, where units varied from province to province and village to village; and fourthly, the Rhineland foot was, as its name implies, employed in the Rhinelands, not only in the Middle Ages but throughout the nineteenth century. Furthermore, a unit equal in length to the Rhineland foot was used in England in colonial times. Whatever the merits of the Rhineland foot unit, this argument cannot therefore be used as proof that the tower is of pre-Columbian origin.

In order to obtain further clues to the origin of the tower, archaeological excavations within and outside the tower were carried out in 1948–49 by William S. Godfrey, Jr., of the Peabody Museum. The excavations established the following facts:

1 Treasure hunters had dug several pits inside the tower. From the rubble used to fill up these pits, it was concluded that the earliest pit had been dug before 1750, the latest before 1840. None of the pits had been deep enough to reach the foundation of the tower.

2 The foundations of the tower consist of eight piles of random stone rubble, mixed with loam and set at even intervals in an annular trench, the outer diameter of which was 30 feet 6 inches. Probably because of their random composition, the foundation piles were larger than was actually needed to support the weight of the tower. The upper parts of the rubble heaps were solidified with loam and over this a thick cap of mortar was poured. The foundations rested on a firm layer of blue glacial clay (not on bedrock as earlier reports had it).

3 The tower had been burnt, probably in the late eighteenth century.

4 The tower had never been surrounded by any additional structure such as for instance an ambulatory.

5 The earliest finds associated with the building were no older than the mid-seventeenth century. Occurring on the construction level, these finds were sparse, as was to be expected in the case of a building of such a modest size which required neither a great length of time nor a large labour force to construct. Sparse as they were, the finds were conclusive, for they consisted of fragments of clay pipe, datable pottery, glass, a gun-flint, and nails together with chips and pieces of mortar. In one or two instances the foundation mortar caps had begun to crumble through the eroding effect of seeping rainwater and frost action. When a small amount of underlying loam was carefully spooned out, the loam was found to contain a piece of a clay pipe and a gun-flint, both of seventeenth-century date.

6 Near the bottom of the foundation trench the excavator found the heel imprint of a square-heeled boot. Under the imprint was the mark of a pick stroke which had cut through the floor of the trench and which therefore had been refilled. The fill had been tamped into the slit by the wearer of the boot, hence the heel mark. The significant part of all this is that in the fill were found two small fragments of clay pipes of early colonial type which must have been deposited there while the tower was under construction, for the overlying layers were demonstratively undisturbed.

All told, the construction and the archaeological finds as well as historical sources point to a date of building well within the seventeenth century. The position of the tower on one of the highest spots in Newport, facing a main street and overlooking the harbour and water approaches, gives the distinct impression that it was erected for observation purposes. Founded in 1639, Newport rapidly developed a far-reaching maritime trade, so there would certainly have been a need for a watch tower to overlook the waterways.

The construction of the tower on columns or 'stilts' reinforces the impression that the tower was a look-out point, for they give effective height to the tower with as little labour and material as possible. The off-sets of the columns, making the total circumference of the columns greater than that of the tower itself, increase the stability of the whole.

The presence of the fireplace and fixtures indicate that the tower was intended for more than cursory use. It was built of stone because stone was the preferred building material in Newport, where it needed to be cleared from the fields anyway and where there were good supplies of materials for the production of mortar. Stone towers commonly doubled as warehouses for the Indian trade, and this could have been an additional function.

*Ill. 147.* Right, the Newport tower. ▶ Originally the uneven stonework was covered with a heavy coat of plaster, a patch of which remains on one pillar. Archaeological excavations made in 1948–49 by William S. Godfrey Jr. showed that the tower was erected from an annular construction trench. The presence of distinctly colonial artifacts such as a gun flint, and pieces of colonial pottery and clay pipes in undisturbed parts of this construction trench demonstrate that the tower was built in the seventeenth century. This agrees with the date suggested by the architectural details.

In 1677 the Newport tower was owned by a Benedict Arnold (not the traitor) who had settled there in 1651 and served as President of the Rhode Island Colony from 1657 to 1663 and as its Governor from 1663 to 1678; he was also the richest man in the community. In 1677 the tower was used as a windmill, probably converted to this use after Newport's only mill burnt in 1675. Before antiquarian interest in the tower began, there was a strong oral tradition confirmed by Benedict's great-grandson Sanford Arnold that the tower was built by Benedict Arnold some time between 1653 and 1660. However, because of the lack of written records—many records concerning Newport must have perished in the great fire during King Philip's War in 1675—we will perhaps never know for certain who built the tower. Whoever it was, the tower is an interesting structure and probably one of the oldest buildings still standing in continental North America.

Mystery Hill is the name of a cluster of twenty-two small dry-walled structures, some with roofs formed by large boulders, others with corbelled vaults. They are situated in North Salem, New Hampshire, near the Massachusetts border. Of unknown origin, they have been associated in turn with Vikings, Irish monks, and the Megalith builders of the Old World. In popular parlance the site is also known as 'Pattee's Caves' after a former owner of the site, Jonathan Pattee, who lived there from 1826 to 1855. Although Pattee might have built some of the structures, there are indications that others might date from at least as early as the seventeenth century. The site is under current investigation by an interested amateur group who have found evidence that the site might have been used in illegal mining and fur trading, kept under cover to circumvent the Royal English monopolies in the early days of the colonies.

The site has been under repeated excavation, most of which has been unscientific and yielded little information. The most extensive scientific excavation was undertaken, in 1955, under the supervision of Dr Junius Bird of the American Museum of Natural History by G. Vescelius. Over 7,000 artifacts, practically all post-Columbian except a few which are native Indian, were found. An Old World, more precisely Mediterranean, provenance has been suggested for the latter, but American archaeologists familiar with pottery and tool forms of the Eastern United States are positive that the North Salem pottery belongs to the Point Peninsula or Owasco cultures (from 1000 BC to late pre-Columbian) and that the stone hoe is also from one of these cultures or even from the Archaic Period as this tool form was used for thousands of years in the New World.

Additional excavations in 1969 revealed an old turf level which was dated by the carbon-14 method to 2995 BP ± 180.* There is no archaeological proof, however, that this turf level is directly associated with the structures.

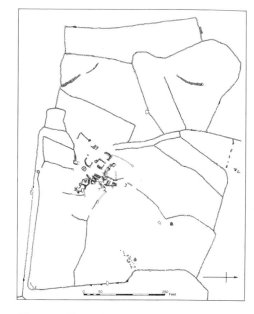

*Ill. 148.* Plan of the site at Mystery Hill.

*Ill. 149*

*Dates BP (before present) are calculated on the base year 1950. BC dates are therefore obtained from them by subtracting 1950 from the BP date. In this case, 1045 BC ± 180.

*Ill. 148*

Structures similar to those at Mystery Hill, consisting of small corbelled chambers dug into hillsides and mounds, occur in many localities in the New England region. One of these, situated at Newton, New Hampshire, yielded the carbon-14 date 850 BP ± 140. The dated sample stems, however, from the surrounding mound, and is probably irrelevant since it appears that the chamber was cut *into* the mound, thus post-dating it. Many of these chambers are known for a fact to be of early colonial date. Some represent provisional shelters built by the early settlers before they had time to construct a regular house, others are storage structures or sheep shelters. Others again seem to have been built as slave quarters for Negro slaves working on New England farms in the middle of the seventeenth century.

The site at Mystery Hill is criss-crossed with low stone walls and it has been stated that they are unique in New England in that they consist of a mixture of large slabs or boulders, 'megaliths', and small stones packed between them. New England fences were not built that way according to some local students of the site. Yet I have personally seen, throughout New England, regular stone fences built in exactly the same way as the North Salem walls; in fact, they occur wherever large boulders are particularly plentiful, which makes their occurrence at North Salem entirely logical.

Thus, both artifacts and radiocarbon dating suggest, independently of each other, that the North Salem site contains two levels of occupation, one representing Indian occupation from perhaps *c.* 1000 BC and the other, post-Columbian covering possibly the seventeenth, parts of the eighteenth and the nineteenth centuries. That such an interpretation is reasonable is furthermore suggested by the fact that Indian sites with pottery and tools such as those at North Salem are

*Ill. 149.* Stone huts at Mystery Hill, North Salem, New Hampshire, showing details of their construction and the so-called altar stone.

abundant in the area, and that, rather than being unique, the North Salem stonework fits into a regular colonial and later New England context.

Both archaeological and theoretical evidence has been presented that Leif Eiriksson's and Karlsefni's Vinland lay on the shores of Follins Pond on Cape Cod. The archaeological evidence consists of a post alignment thought to stem from the beach supports of a Viking ship; rectangular depressions, supposedly house sites; and post moulds forming an oval enclosure, believed to be Karlsefni's palisade. Since no colonial artifacts were associated with the features, a Norse origin was suggested. However, no Norse artifacts were found either. The theoretical evidence advanced in support for a Norse provenance is based on misunderstandings of Norse material culture and erroneous translation of the Vinland sagas. To date, there is no tangible evidence for Norse settlements on Cape Cod.

Sites discovered a few years ago on Ungava Bay in northern Labrador show intriguing possibilities of being Norse, if nothing else because of their close proximity to the Norse settlements in western Greenland. The sites contain buildings, dams, artifacts, and trail markers in the form of cairns. However, none of the evidence is of unequivocal Norse character and at least a share of the evidence is Eskimo as well as post-Columbian European.

In reviewing the evidence for Norse occupation in America, the result has been negative. One site remains: L'Anse aux Meadows in northern Newfoundland. The site furnishes the first incontrovertible archaeological proof that Europeans set foot in America centuries before 1492. L'Anse aux Meadows is of such significance that it will be discussed in a chapter of its own (Chapter 6).

More sites will probably be discovered in the future. Norsemen lived for five centuries in western Greenland, managing to keep in contact with distant Europe. It is inconceivable that they did not attempt to extend their sphere of interest westward to include America. America had valuable commodities to offer: timber, fur, and bog-iron with firewood nearby for smelting it. Where one should look for settlements is a matter of conjecture, although a northern location seems to be the reasonable place to begin. A small quartzite arrowhead of Indian manufacture found in a Norse grave at Sandnes *Ill. 86* in Greenland might point in the right direction: it seems to be of a kind found in the Lake Melville area of Hamilton Inlet. What we can expect to uncover are the nearly demolished remains of humble turf house complexes and simple everyday household articles, the kind of material which testifies to the Norse presence in Greenland. Although neither elaborate nor spectacular they will clearly demonstrate man's quest for new horizons.

# 6        Norse Sites at L'Anse aux Meadows

## Helge Ingstad

*'The Good' is probably a later addition.

*Ills. 132, 137, 138*
*Ill. 147*

*The theory is set out in *Landet Under Leidarstjernen,* Oslo 1959; *Land Under the Pole Star,* London and New York 1966.

EVEN IF IT IS PLAIN from a historical point of view that Norsemen sailed to North America *circa* 1000, the question of where they landed has still to be answered. Where is Vinland the Good* where Leif built his 'big houses'?

For about 250 years this problem has been vigorously discussed in an extensive literature. The location of Vinland has been presumed in the most widely varying regions from Virginia in the south to Hudson's Bay in the north. Most scholars have accepted the sagas' words regarding grapes and consequently concluded that Vinland would be situated relatively far south; they have thus suggested such places as Massachusetts, New York, Rhode Island and Virginia to name but a few. Not a single trace, however, of the Norsemen was found in North America to back up these suggestions. It is true that from time to time claims have been made that such things as the Kensington Stone in Minnesota, the Beardmore Find in Ontario and the Newport Tower in Rhode Island represent Norse traces, but they do not bear up to scientific investigation (see pp. 155 ff).

After a research journey to the Norse settlements on Greenland with my wife, during which I received a vivid impression of conditions there, I came to a conclusion at variance with the others about the location of Vinland. It was my opinion, on the basis of various factors, that Vinland would have to be located rather further north than was generally supposed—probably in Newfoundland and relatively far north there.* A few scholars, A. W. Munn, V. Tanner and Jφrgen Meldgård have come to a similar conclusion. My reasoning is, in essence, set out below.

The sagas' mention of grapes, wine and wild wheat should be regarded as a legendary addition. The partly meaningless talk of grapes and wheat supports this point. The Swedish linguistic expert, Sven Sφderberg, probably clinches the matter when he demonstrates that these terms have been taken over by the Icelandic saga writers from Adam of Bremen's widely circulated work (see p. 104). It is a work, as we have seen, which is in many instances unreliable. For a German, it might have been very natural to think that 'Vinland' means a land with grapes and consequently he made reference to them. It is also possible that he had in mind Isidor's *Insulae Fortunatae* which mention 'those blessed isles with wild grapes and self-sown corn'. Søderberg, however, is probably correct when he asserts that the name Vinland has nothing to do with grapes or wine but that the syllable 'vin' is the old Norse word for grass fields, found in so many place names in Norway, Sweden and the Shetland Islands. According to Søderberg and another authority, Magnus Olsen, there is no basis for setting a time limit on the use of the word 'vin' for grass as has been suggested by some. In other words, Vinland means 'The Grassy Land' and it was precisely pastures for their cattle that the Vinland voyagers were in the first place interested in finding.

Some have suggested that on the basis of the astronomical information supplied in *The Greenlanders' Saga,* Vinland should lie well to the south. The calculations, however, which various scholars have produced on the basis of their observations have led to such widely varying suggestions for locations (from Virginia to northern Newfoundland) that little can be determined from this approach.

Some further reasons for the theory that Vinland was located in Newfoundland can also briefly be mentioned. The short sailing times listed in the sagas have probably been preserved approximately correctly in the tradition of this seafaring people. They seem to correspond to three lands, Baffin Island, Labrador and Newfoundland, which in turn correspond to the lands of the sagas, Helluland,* Markland and Vinland. The 'marvellous beaches' or 'marvel strands' (Furdustrandir) are probably identical with the long beaches near Cape Porcupine in Labrador. *The Greenlanders' Saga* states that Leif Eiriksson took two days' sailing time from the long beaches of Markland to Vinland and it would take this time to sail from the beaches of Cape Porcupine to the northern tip of Newfoundland. This backs up a fragmentary Icelandic source (p. 105) which allows that it is not far from Markland to Vinland. On the Skálholt, Resen and the Hungarian maps there is a long peninsula which resembles the northern tip of Newfoundland and is labelled 'Promontorium Winlandiæ'. The route from Greenland to the north coast of Newfoundland is such a simple one that after its discovery subsequent expeditions would have no difficulty retracing it. Furthermore it would seem natural that a people from a polar land would choose to settle in a relatively northern area where they felt themselves at home, *i.e.* in one where their old culture pattern could be easily accommodated.

On the basis of all of this, I felt that it should be possible, through a systematic search by both plane and ship, to find traces of dwelling-

*The location of Helluland is particularly important for the evaluation of the location of Vinland, as Helluland was the first area discovered by Leif Eiriksson and the point from which he sailed south. Outstanding experts have suggested that Helluland is part of Labrador or Newfoundland. In 1970 I made an expedition to Baffin Island to examine its east coast. At about 70° N I investigated some large peninsulas and found impressive formations corresponding extremely closely with the description of Helluland in *The Greenlanders' Saga*: a land flat as a flagstone (helle) running towards great glaciers. It may be added that there are no glaciers in Labrador or Newfoundland.

*Ill. 171*

*Ill. 150*

*Ills. 80, 81*
*Ill. 82*

176

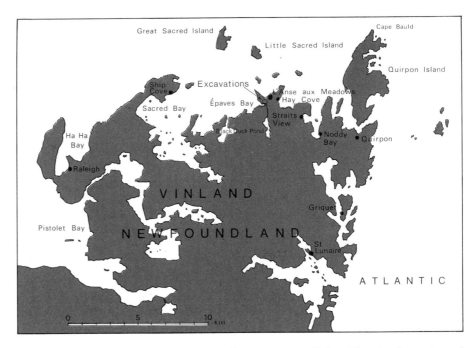

Ill. 147

places which the Norsemen had constructed in North America. I undertook such a study in 1960 with my daughter Benedicte. It became a long search along an apparently endless coast. During the journey I also wanted to examine some of the areas which others have suggested as the location of Vinland. I travelled northwards along the coasts of Rhode Island, Massachusetts and Nova Scotia, visiting the famous Newport Tower and a few other remains claimed to be Norse. There did not seem to be any acceptable foundation to these claims and I did not find anything pointing to Norsemen.

By midsummer I reached Newfoundland, where, according to my theory, Vinland should be. Newfoundland is a remarkable island which lies farther east than any other territory or island in North America. Its contours are odd, as if nature in a wilful moment had wanted to make an abstract work of art. To the south there is a large sprawling body of land, and from it, a long promontory, looking more like a horn than anything else, reaches out northwards. In the numerous fjords, small fishing villages are to be found in sheltered bays. Here I investigated those areas that seemed most likely, examined the landscape and questioned people about ruins. All I found, however, were traces of whaling stations and the overgrown dwellings of fishermen, which were not difficult to identify.

At length I came to the little village of St Anthony in the most northerly part of the island. This is the headquarters of the Grenfell Association which carries on impressive humanitarian work in Newfoundland and Labrador. I was just about to rent a boat which could take me round the whole of the northern tip—where I felt the most

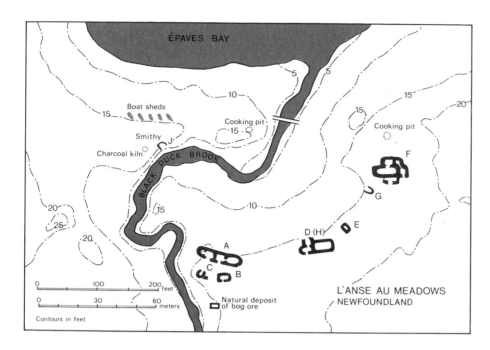

Ills. 151, 152

Ill. 151. Outline map of the L'Anse aux Meadows area showing the position of all the excavated sites. The sites marked with letters only are house sites. They are located on an old beach terrace.

Map labels: ÉPAVES BAY · Boat sheds · Cooking pit · Smithy · Charcoal kiln · BLACK DUCK BROOK · Cooking pit · F · G · D (H) · E · A · C · B · Natural deposit of bog ore · L'ANSE AU MEADOWS NEWFOUNDLAND · Contours in feet · 0 100 200 feet · 0 30 60 meters

Ill. 152. Right, aerial photograph of the Norse sites at L'Anse aux Meadows at the northern tip of Newfoundland. They were discovered by Helge Ingstad in 1960 and excavated during the following eight years. Sheds have been erected to protect some of the most important sites.

likely possibilities were—when I met Dr Gordon Thomas, who heads the Grenfell Association. He offered me a place on board one of the small hospital boats which was going north in the same direction and visiting all the little fishing ports. Nothing could have been more satisfactory.

We travelled northwards along the jagged coast and at each fishing village I continued my search of the land and my questioning of the people but met with disappointment after disappointment. Eventually we came to a very small fishing village called L'Anse aux Meadows. It was on the northern tip and faced north into the sea. There were about seventy inhabitants, living a very isolated existence, as there were no roads to the village and it was not visited by the coastal steamer.

George Decker, a dynamic fellow with a gleam of humour in his eye, was the first person I met. When I asked him about ruins, he swiftly retorted that there were indeed such things. He then led me a short distance to the west over a broad grass plateau to a small river with the name Black Duck Brook. A short space from the bay, Épaves Bay, there was an old beach terrace about four metres high and there I saw the faint contours in the grass of something that undoubtedly must be old dwelling places. It struck me that it was just at such a place that Norsemen would choose to settle: they had meadows about with food for their cattle and they had an outlook over both sea and land. Much reminded me of the locations of the Norse dwellings in Greenland. Only excavations, however, would give the true answer!

178

*Anne Stine Ingstad, 'The Norse Settlements at L'Anse Aux Meadows, A Preliminary Report of the Excavations', *Acta Archaelogica,* Vol. XLI, Copenhagen 1970. A popular account of these expeditions is given in Helge Ingstad, *Westward to Vinland,* Jonathan Cape, London, and St Martins Press, New York, 1969.

*Ill. 153*. Left, the largest of the house sites (F), comprising five or six rooms. The man is sitting where the long-fire was situated in the great hall. The dark, elevated areas are what remains of the turf walls where, in some places, a number of layers can be seen.

From 1961 to 1968, I undertook seven archaeological expeditions to L'Anse aux Meadows with the participation of experts from Norway, Iceland, Sweden, Canada and the USA. My wife, Anne Stine, led the archaeological work for the whole period.*

Our expedition ship, the *Halten,* was a Norwegian rescue ship made of oak. It was our plan that besides the excavations we would undertake some investigations of the far-flung coasts around us. *Halten* was shipped to Montreal and from there we travelled downstream on the St Lawrence River following the north bank of the Gulf of St Lawrence. Several researchers have suggested that the Vinland voyagers settled there and it was thus of interest to investigate this coastline on our way to L'Anse aux Meadows.

We disembarked at a number of places to find out what conditions were like and we visited small French villages where everything appeared the same as it had been for the past two hundred years. In addition we came across scattered Indian camps. The whole of this coast gave a bleak impression. There was much woodland but little grassland. When Jacques Cartier discovered this coast at the beginning of the sixteenth century, he called it, 'The Land which God gave to Cain'. It seems highly unlikely that the Norsemen would have settled there. We sailed through the Strait of Belle Isle, which was mostly ice-free, and so eastwards to the northern tip of Newfoundland until we anchored a little off from L'Anse aux Meadows.

L'Anse aux Meadows lies at a northern latitude of 51° 36′ and a western longitude of 55° 22′. It is, therefore, about the same latitude as London and in relation to Austerbygden on Greenland about 9° further south. The land inwards is undulating, with small hills, as the saga described the first unknown land Bjarni saw. The forests, at an earlier period, came much closer to the coast but are now quite some distance away because of the fishermen's need for building and firewood material. What is striking from a general survey is the great number of grassy stretches from L'Anse aux Meadows and along the coast. I have never seen such lushness in any corresponding place in the north.

Off the coast there are a number of islands dotted about, the furthest out, Great Sacred Island, acting as a superb landmark for those navigating their way to L'Anse aux Meadows. Further north can be seen Belle Isle and the blue coast of Labrador, along which the Vinland travellers must have sailed on their journey of exploration south.

The work of excavation began and tension was great. There were three possibilities: the sites might have originated with Indians or Eskimos; or with whalers and fishermen of the time following Cabot's rediscovery of Newfoundland in 1497; or with Norsemen at a time long before Columbus.

We began the excavations on one of the smaller house sites (B) on
the old beach terrace. It measured 2.75 × 2.75 metres in the interior.
Gradually the low remainders of the turf walls began to appear. As
we scraped down it became obvious we would find no flint pieces
indicating indigenous origin, nor were there any traces of whalers or
fishermen. Eventually we came across a small fireplace against the
west wall. It was nicely made of flat stones, with some of them
standing on end. Nearby we found a cooking pit containing masses
of charcoal and surprisingly enough a clump of slag. Elsewhere we
also found a slag clump and a very rusted nail.

Along one wall there was an elevation of the earth floor, and here
the inhabitants had probably sat or lain on twigs or skins. The most
fascinating find was a little four-cornered ember pit near a fireplace.
It measured 0.25 × 0.17 metres and it was made of thin, flat stones.
This type of ember pit is well-known from excavations of Norse
farms on Greenland. For people who used flint or jasper to ignite
their fires, this was a most useful appliance. In the evening the embers
(live coals) could be placed in the pit and covered with ashes, thus
avoiding the necessity of remaking the fire in the morning.

This was a promising beginning, and the continuing work revealed
that the turf covered many other similar types of secrets. In the
following pages only the most important excavations will be briefly
described and, for the sake of brevity, they will not be listed in order
of excavation.

Ill. 154. House site B. In the background is a fireplace made of stone,
with a cooking pit nearby. On the
left is an ember pit of Norse type,
made of flat stone. The embers
were placed in this and covered with
ashes and thus the inhabitants did
not have to make a new fire each
morning. Similar ember pits have
been found on Norse sites in Greenland and Iceland. To the right, in the
foreground of this picture of house
site B, is probably a post-hole.
Along the wall to the right, there is
an elevation where people probably
sat or slept.

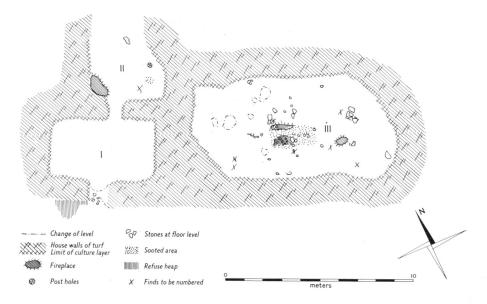

Change of level — · — · —
House walls of turf / Limit of culture layer
Fireplace
Post holes
Stones at floor level
Sooted area
Refuse heap
X  Finds to be numbered

N

0        meters        10

*Ill. 155*

One of the house sites (D(H)) was of considerable proportions. It was more or less of a rectangular shape and of the long-house type. It consisted of two rooms and had interior dimensions of 18.3 × 5 metres. It had a little annexe to the north. The walls were of turf and in many places the different layers could clearly be seen. In the central part of the largest room there was a long fireplace and near it an ember pit of the same type found in Greenland and Iceland. In the fireplace we found a small fragment of copper covered with cross stripings. It had possibly come from a belt. Analyses show that the copper had been smelted and contained various minerals. The copper cannot therefore have come from the indigenous inhabitants, who occasionally used native copper which is almost one hundred per cent pure, is worked by hammering and is not smelted. Here we also found a bone needle of Norse type.

A smaller dwelling (G) was different from the others. It was dug into the terrace and measured 3 × 2.75 metres. Here we found a fireplace, a rusty nail and a mass of fist-size stones which had been exposed to fire. There was much to indicate that this house could have been a steam bath, which is known from other Norse areas including Greenland.

Another interesting find was two large outside cooking pits which on the surface had a diameter of about 2 metres and a depth of about 0.7 metres. These contained ashes, charcoal and many beach stones about fist-size which had been exposed to fire. In the bottom of one a fragment of iron was found. Such large cooking pits must have been practical when food was being prepared for a large number of people. The soapstone or iron pots which the Norsemen had at that time would be presumably both too small and too few. In these fires,

*Ill. 157.* One of the large outdoor cooking pits at L'Anse aux Meadows. In this was found soot, charcoal and a great number of stones, each one about the size of a fist, which had been exposed to fire and, in the bottom, a piece of iron.

the stones would be heated and large pieces of whale meat, caribou meat or large quantities of fish placed on them and then covered.

The greatest surprise came to us on the most easterly part of the terrace. The terrain showed no evidence of there being a house there, but one evening, in the rays of the setting sun sloping over the grass and heather, we noticed an unusual shape which looked like a corner. We started digging there and came across a clearly defined culture layer, and so continued our search. Slowly a house site took shape, turf walls came into view, a large hall with a long fire, then more rooms with their fireplaces, cooking pits and other interesting features. We found rusted nails, slag clumps, a stone lamp, a whetstone for needles, and other such items. After several seasons' work, the old house site (F) was completely uncovered and it was the largest of them all. It had an interior of 14 × 21 metres and comprised six rooms. The walls were of turf and a number of layers could be seen.

*Ills. 166, 160*

*Ill. 153*

The largest room was of especial interest. It was a 'hall' of about 8 metres in length and 4 metres in breadth with curved walls. In the lengthwise direction there was a room at each side so that it took on the appearance of a long-house. The other rooms appeared as annexes to this. In the central area of the 'hall' there was a long fireplace which measured about 1.9 metres and it contained a flat stone, a cooking pit and a stone ember pit—three elements which are well known from Icelandic and Greenlandic long fireplaces. On both sides of the fireplace, and in against the foundation walls, the earth level was higher and here presumably were benches where the occupants sat and slept. In the other rooms there were also fireplaces and cooking pits. Near one stone fireplace which had been painstakingly made, there was a

*Ills. 160, 161.* Right, this stone lamp ▶ excavated in a house site at L'Anse aux Meadows is similar to two stone lamps which were found in Iceland (far right).

*Ills. 158, 159.* Above, a spindle whorl of soapstone excavated at L'Anse aux Meadows near a doorway of house site F. It is of the same type as the spindle whorl below, which was found at a Norse farm in Greenland.

circular impression on the earth floor, probably from a pot or a wooden tub which stood there.

A smaller room, which had no doors into the others, faced south and various circumstances suggest that this might have been occupied by women. Here a whetstone for needles was found and outside the house wall near the exit one of the most important finds was made: a spindle whorl of soapstone, about 3.5 centimetres in diameter. It was curved and sooty underneath and was probably made from the fragment of a lamp or a pot. This spindle whorl is of Norse type and it would have been difficult to have made a more interesting find, because it gives us information of a special kind. It indicates that there must have been women at L'Anse aux Meadows and that they must have had wool with which to spin; this wool, in turn, must probably have come from their own sheep.

These finds correspond to the details of the saga about Karlsefni's Vinland voyage in which we are told that on board his ships there were women and all kinds of livestock. Among the latter there must certainly have been such important animals as sheep. This also has another side to it, because if it is the case that the spindle whorl dates back to Karlsefni's expedition then we have to consider the express mention in *The Greenlanders' Saga* that Karlsefni settled in Leif's houses—and they were in Vinland. Thus it could have been that a Norse woman sat there spinning by a sunny wall of the large turf house at L'Anse aux Meadows, a thousand years ago.

Just how this large house was constructed we have no accurate knowledge. Presumably timber was used for posts, rafters and doors, but the walls and roof were of turf. In addition this was an unusual house in the sense that, although as in Iceland the rooms were built against each other, partly utilizing the same walls, here for the most part they must have had their own roofs. Finally, it is obvious that this house was burned, whether by accident or design we do not

know; but one day it went up in flames, like a huge bonfire over L'Anse aux Meadows.

Year by year the excavations proceeded and we got to know the land and conditions there well. The climate in that region is a maritime one and is influenced by both the cold Labrador current from the north and the Gulf Stream. It can vary greatly from year to year. Some summers were sunny and warm while others were rather chilly and windy. The winters are relatively mild. Some years there would be a little snow and it was often the case that the snow would be blown off the flat meadows by the sea and, in reasonable weather, cows and sheep could graze. In this connection *The Greenlanders' Saga* is of interest where it states: 'The nature of the land seemed so good that none of the cattle would require fodder for the winter.'

In 1961 the summer was especially fine with the sun shining constantly over the green fields and the blue sea. Flowers were everywhere and autumn produced more different kinds of berries than I have ever seen in such a confined area. There were blueberries, cranberries, whortleberries, cowberries, strawberries, gooseberries, raspberries, red currants and squash berries which the fishermen used to make wine. Behind the old house sites the marsh was golden with cloudberries.

Just beyond the houses, the Black Duck Brook splashed its way through the grass and the willows, with now and again a salmon heading upstream. It runs into Épaves Bay which is shallow for quite some way out. There are no landing spots about and this must be the reason why fishermen or whalers never settled in this bay but chose a place further to the east where their boats could dock. It was commonplace for the Norsemen to drag their shallow draught vessels on to land.

The bay teemed with small flounders and one day we did what Karlsefni had been described as doing in the saga: we dug large pits in the sand at low tide. The next morning we found a number of flounders in these pits. Driftwood was constantly being swept in so those earlier dwellers must have had a continuous supply of firewood just outside their doors. In those days there must have been big heaps of driftwood spread out along the beach.

On the whole, living conditions at L'Anse aux Meadows must have been pleasant in early times and especially when wild life would be so much richer than it is today. The sea abounded with cod, seals and whales. There were salmon in the stream and berries all around, and special mention should be made of the caribou, still to be found on Newfoundland but which in those days would have roamed in large herds.

A short distance to the west of the houses there was a small hill about 130 feet high running towards the sea. On it, we found the

*Ill. 162*

*Ill. 162.* Imaginary reconstruction of the houses at L'Anse aux Meadows.

*In *The Greenlanders' Saga* occurs this remarkable astronomical observation: 'the sun had there [in Vinland] *eyktarstad* ['eykt' place or 'none' place] and *dagmálastad* [breakfast place] on the shortest day'. This means that the sun was up over the known marks for 'none' and breakfast on the shortest day. A number of scholars believe that the latitude of Vinland might be determined if the meaning of *eyktarstad* is made clear. It is considered to be a point on the horizon (a bearing on the sun) between south and west, but the exact point of *eyktarstad* is still under discussion.

*Ill. 70*

remains of several cairns of moss-covered stones. The two largest stood side by side and were so placed as to be difficult to sight from the ocean. They could thus scarcely be landmarks for sailors. Who constructed these and what was their purpose? There is no certain answer, although it was an old Norse custom to build cairns near dwelling places. We also know that the Norsemen could build cairns in relation to the position of the sun and thus gauge the time of day. This reminds one of the sun observation recounted in *The Greenlanders' Saga* in connection with Leif Eiriksson's stay in Vinland, *i.e.* the much discussed 'Eyktarstad problem' which some believe is the key for determining the location of Vinland.* One has to be careful about drawing parallels here, but it is the case that—seen from the largest dwelling—the cairns lie directly on the horizon in the south-south-west direction and the sun is above them about 3 pm, the former time for 'eykt' in Norway and Iceland.

During our forays along the coasts we encountered traces of the Dorset Eskimos, of whom there must have been many on Newfoundland. Another people lived there also, the Beotuk Indians. Both peoples have long since disappeared. The fate of the Eskimos is unknown; the Indians were shamelessly exterminated by the whites. At one time these natives must have been the neighbours of the Norsemen and the sagas relate trading and violent encounters between the natives (Skraelings) and the newcomers. The community at L'Anse aux Meadows would have had to be constantly on the watch.

For a more accurate evaluation of L'Anse aux Meadows, it was important to become acquainted with the Vinland voyagers' route north of the settlement, *i.e.* their route southward from Greenland. As has been mentioned above, a number of factors suggest that they first sailed over to Baffin Island, which was probably Helluland, and so south along the coast of Labrador, which was probably Markland. In considering this route several questions come up. Would it be a natural continuation of their journey along Labrador to hold course for the northern tip of Newfoundland? Where were those long beaches in Markland accounted for in both sagas and described in

*Ills. 164, 165.* The excavation of five boatsheds at Épaves Bay, L'Anse aux Meadows (left), which might have looked like those from the Faeroe Islands (right). A row of boat-sheds was a typical west Nordic feature.

but below that of the iron. A good smith in Viking times was a much respected man and when it came to settling down in a strange land he would be considered indispensable.

If iron had been produced at L'Anse aux Meadows, where were the deposits of natural bog-iron, where was the kiln which produced charcoal for the smelting and where were the smelting pit and smithy? By chance a considerable deposit of bog-iron was found not far from the house sites. When we lifted the turf, we found underneath closely packed clumps of bog-iron which were rust-red in colour. We had also noticed that on the west side of the brook and uppermost on the terrace there was a depression which must have been man-made. Excavations here brought interesting results. We discovered a room about 3.75 × 2.75 metres large which had been dug into the terrace (J). The sandy floor had large black patches made by soot and charcoal. Here we found several hundred slag clumps, fragments of iron and a little bog-iron. In the centre there was a rather large, somewhat cracked stone with a flat top and it was firmly lodged in the ground. Nearby there were traces of a fireplace. There was no doubt that this was the smithy: the stone was the anvil and the fireplace the forge.

*Ill. 163*

Seven metres from the smithy there was a depression in the ground, which upon excavation showed it had had a rim with a diameter of about 2 metres. There were layers of charcoal down to a depth of about 70 centimetres. This must have been the kiln where charcoal was produced for work in the smithy or for smelting. No smelting hole was found and it would be difficult to find. There was much to suggest that it, together with part of the terrace, had slid downhill into the river.

A short way down from the smithy and near Épaves Bay, the grass-covered field had an irregular wavy shape. We dug here and soon found layers in the earth and sand which must have been the work of man. Further excavation revealed that here there had been four, or *Ills. 164, 165* perhaps five, boatsheds in a row. This was of considerable interest, not only because it enlarged our picture of all the settlement, but also because to build boatsheds in a row was a typical west Nordic custom.

Our last find, and one of our most important, was made by the side of Black Duck Brook where excavation conditions were very difficult. *Ills. 168, 169* We discovered here a large long-house (A) with curved turf walls. The layers in many sections were clearly distinct. The interior measured $24 \times 4$ metres and it had four rooms. We found fireplaces, *Ill. 166* large cooking pits, post holes, nails, slag and so on. The most

*Ill. 166.* Helge Ingstad showing a nail excavated at L'Anse aux Meadows. It was so rusty that hardly any iron was left.

important find, however, was a ring-headed pin of bronze, 10 centimetres long, which was discovered by the cooking pit in the centre of the house. This ring-headed pin is typical of Viking times and is well known from Norse areas such as the west coast of Norway, the Faeroe Islands, Iceland and the Isle of Man. It was probably used by men to fasten their capes on their right shoulder so that their sword arm would be free.

Summing up the total of finds from the excavations, we have eight house-sites including a smithy and possibly a bath-house, four (or five) boatsheds, a kiln and two large outdoor cooking pits. In assessing this archaeological material, the house type is of great significance. The usual dwelling of the Vikings in Scandinavia was a long-house which was roughly rectangular and often had curved walls and only one room. Some could, however, have several rooms in a lengthwise formation and also various annexes, although we do not know exactly when this type became common. The construction material varied according to local conditions. In Greenland turf and stones were used, whereas in Iceland turf was the most important material in construction just as it was at L'Anse aux Meadows where it was difficult to find utilizable stones.

The turf houses at L'Anse aux Meadows are of the long-house type and house A is the most distinct example. Parallels to the house type *Ills. 168, 169* here have been found in Norway, Iceland and Greenland. In Greenland, for example, a long-house has been unearthed at Narsaq in Austerbygden. From a runic inscription found there, it can be dated to about the year 1000. In Iceland, house sites of similar type have been excavated at Tjorsadalur which was a settlement buried by a volcanic eruption from Hekla, probably in the year 1104. In this connection, the Støng farmhouse, a long-house with annexes, is of particular interest. The L'Anse aux Meadows fireplaces also have Norse characteristics. A good example is the long fireplace in the largest house (F). The same is also true of the ember pits, the smithy *Ills. 153, 154, 163, 164* and the boathouses.

The finds are not many. On the acidiferous terrace, conservation conditions were as poor as they could be. Even the bones for the most part have decomposed and the nails were mostly rust. With the passage of time, the natives, as in Greenland, would take those things for which they had a use. Important finds were made, however, such as nails, iron fragments, a piece of copper, jasper, a whetstone for *Ills. 156, 166* needles, a stone lamp of old Icelandic type and a Norse type bone *Ill. 160* needle. In addition, there are the two most important finds: a Norse type spindle whorl of soapstone and a Viking era type bronze ring-headed pin. *Ill. 167*

*Ills. 167–169.* Right, the excavated house site A at L'Anse aux Meadows, which is 88½ ft. × 19½ ft. (outside measurements). The excavated part in the background to the left is outside the walls. Several sections have been cut in the walls of turf, revealing a number of layers. The plan (below right) clearly shows the four rooms, several fireplaces and cooking pits. It is a typical Norse long house with parallels in Norway, Iceland and Greenland. The ring-headed pin of bronze, *in situ* (left), was found close to the cooking pit in the central part. It is of a type well known from Viking times, and similar examples have been found in Norway, Iceland, the Shetland Islands and the Isle of Man.

*Ill. 170*

An archaeological assessment of the collected material leads one to the conclusion that the houses are Norse and date probably from the eleventh century. This corresponds to sixteen radiocarbon datings (carbon-14), from the different house sites, which on the average point to the year 1000. The earliest dating is 1080 plus or minus 70 years. When these dates are looked at in conjunction with the archaeological evidence, the conclusion is reinforced that the houses at L'Anse aux Meadows are indeed Norse and stem from *circa* 1000. The archaeological material precludes the houses belonging to Indians, Eskimos, whalers or fishermen. It should be further stated that all the excavations revealed not the slightest evidence of the presence of

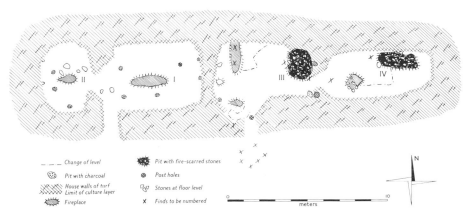

193

whalers or fishermen. No fish hooks, tackle or clay pipes were found. In fact there was a total lack of any find of that nature.

A number of questions are raised by the discovery of this settlement at L'Anse aux Meadows and many of them can have no certain answers. When we survey the whole complex of the houses and other buildings, we are struck by the hard labour which their very existence evinces. The variety of constructions which were built to satisfy various needs is also a feature of great interest. There are not only surprisingly large dwelling houses, but also a probable bath-house, a smithy, a kiln and boatsheds. Together they give a fairly complete picture of a small, compact community.

It is difficult to assess how many people lived at L'Anse aux Meadows. It could have been a sizeable number to judge from the houses themselves. On the other hand, it must be remembered that we do not know with certainty whether they were all occupied simultaneously. As was stated previously, living conditions must have been good. The settlers could hunt and fish in a virgin area and around the settlement there were excellent grazing pastures for cattle. There has been much discussion about the nature of the climate, a thousand years ago, in those northerly stretches. I shall limit myself to saying that the research carried out by the pollen analyst, Dr Kari Henningsmoen, during my expeditions reveals that the climate at L'Anse aux Meadows when the Norsemen built their turf houses seems to have been about the same as today.

It is reasonable to assume that the people living at L'Anse aux Meadows made various exploratory and hunting expeditions along the coasts, and the sagas also give some information in this connection. We have, however, no knowledge of how far south they journeyed.

Who were these Norse people who lived on Newfoundland's northern tip such a long time ago? To answer this question one must look at the historical background. I would refer back to my interpretations of the sagas and the other sources, not least to the geographical information and the short sailing times. Among other things, there are the ancient maps, and those long beaches by Cape Porcupine in Labrador, which must be seen to correspond with the *Ill. 171* saga's mention of long beaches in Markland, from which it took Leif Eiriksson two days' sailing time to reach Vinland. All these different pieces of information lead on to an assumption that the Vinland travellers settled in northern Newfoundland which is presumably Vinland. Then there is the fact that the houses at L'Anse aux Meadows, according to radiocarbon dating techniques and archae- *Ill. 170* ological evidence, were occupied about the year 1000 and that was the period when the Vinland voyages took place. As in so many other archaeological cases, however, it is impossible to provide sufficient scientific proof linking these houses to known historical personages.

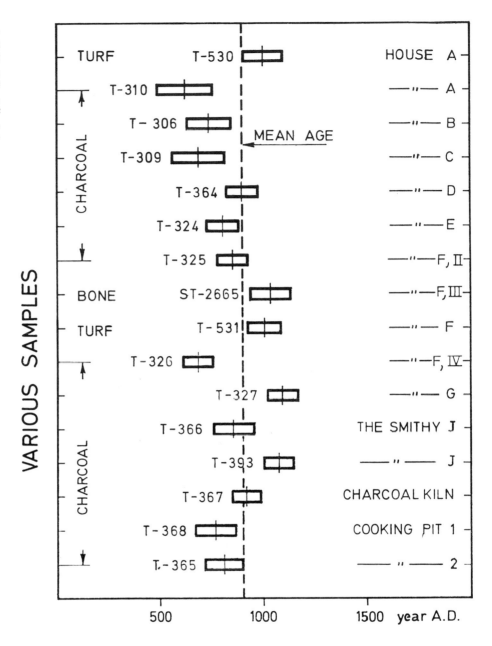

*Ill. 170.* Table showing the radiocarbon dates from L'Anse aux Meadows, obtained by analyses at the Radiological Dating Laboratory, Trondheim, Norway and at the Radioactive Dating Laboratory, Stockholm, Sweden. These were prepared by Dr Reider Nydal, Director of the Laboratory at Trondheim.

But whether this was the house of Leif Eiriksson or not is of less importance. The important thing is that Norsemen, one thousand years ago, lived at L'Anse aux Meadows.

When we consider the comprehensive settlement that existed at L'Anse aux Meadows, and also that the route to this new land was known in Greenland where there was a Norse community for nearly five centuries, it seems natural to ask why permanent colonization of L'Anse aux Meadows did not come into being, especially when it offered better living conditions than the polar island of Greenland.

There is the possibility that Greenland emigrants may have inter-married with the natives, but the most obvious explanation for the lack of viability of a Norse colonization is that Eskimos and Indians constituted too much of a danger. The Norsemen were daring enough but they attempted colonization of North America several hundred years too early, at a time when people from Europe were unable to carry it through. The most decisive factor was that, unlike Columbus, they had no firearms. They had to face the natives with more or less similar weapons such as bows and arrows, spears, axes and swords. Furthermore, the natives had an overwhelming advantage in that they were massively superior in number.

During the years of our excavations we did our best to ensure that these remarkable testimonies of the Norsemen would be preserved for posterity. We co-operated with the Newfoundland government which has had buildings put over the most important of the house sites to protect them from the wind, rain and snow. A road now goes to L'Anse aux Meadows and year by year it is being visited by an increasing number of tourists. This sudden break in the isolated peace of this remote northern area came as a shock to both the fisher-folk and ourselves. L'Anse aux Meadows has now been made into a national park and plans for a museum and other facilities are being made.

A thousand years ago L'Anse aux Meadows was a different place. *Ill. 162* Then the turf houses stretched along the old beach terrace and smoke swirled into the sky from the roofs. Men returned home weighed down by loads of bloody caribou meat and others were out in their small boats fishing. The steady blows from the smithy on the other *Ill. 163* side of the brook indicated that the smith was at work. In the large house by the long fire people sat and chatted about the new, strange *Ill. 153* land to which they had come and about small everyday matters.

These Norsemen, sometimes accompanied by their women, who sailed the ocean in ships without compasses and with the most rudimentary facilities, must have been daring and skilled men. They had drive and a thirst for adventure, but foremost in their thoughts was the hope of finding a new and good land where their families could settle. Thus it was that young sailors once stood under a square sail, gazing wonderingly across the water to where a strange shore rose above the sea—a New World. *Ill. 1*

*Ill. 171.* Right, the extensive beach north of Cape Porcupine in Labrador. It is about forty miles long and up to two hundred feet wide. It may be seen from a long way out to sea, and the Vinland voyagers sailing south along the coast of Labrador could not have avoided seeing it. This must be the *Furdustrandir* ('marvel strands') of the sagas.

# 7    The Bearded Gods Speak

## Thor Heyerdahl

*Ills. 89–91*
*Ills. 173, 227, 228, 238*

◀ *Ill. 172.* Left, Early Chimu effigy jar, depicting Viracocha. This is one of a number of similar jars from pre-Inca Peru showing a bearded, hook-nosed figure. The style of the beard and the features varies from the rather high-cheekboned and some-what drawn faces to fuller-faced, round-bearded types. In some examples the headdress shows two rounded ears or even a feline head, which indicate a connection with the ubiquitous jaguar cult.

IT WAS RESEARCH IN THE PACIFIC that led to my own curiosity as to whether or not men could have sailed across the Atlantic before Columbus. This seeming paradox arose from my readings into the existing literature on the obscure provenance of the Polynesians and their culture. Early writers, such as A. Fornander, S. P. Smith, W. J. Perry, and E. Best, writing around the beginning of this century, all strongly argued that there was ample evidence that Polynesia—and especially Easter Island—had been originally settled by migrants from Egypt, Mesopotamia, or some other centre within the ancient high-culture area of the eastern Mediterranean. These early Polynesianists pointed out that striking correspondences were concentrated within these two antipodal areas, such as fitted megalithic masonry, stepped temple pyramids, monolithic statues, mummification, trepanation, priest-kings, royal brother-sister marriage, a calendar system, genea-logies, gods of solar lineage, and hieroglyphic tablets. It was invariably stated that the hypothetical migration from the eastern Mediterranean to Polynesia had crossed India or the Indian Ocean, the Indonesian Archipelago, either Australia with Melanesia or Micronesia, and, finally, all of Polynesia, to settle ultimately on Easter Island. It is only on this last little island, off the coast of South America, that script and all the rest of the culture elements parallel to the eastern Mediterranean have been found. Since no traces could be found in the vast continental and oceanic territories purportedly traversed by these migrants, it was very easy for more cautious, subsequent scholars to dismiss these early Diffusionist theories as geographically and chronologically untenable. Yet, such early Diffusionist discoveries as the fact that certain im-portant gods and place names in ancient Egypt and Mesopotamia survive in Polynesia made a lasting impression on Polynesianist literature. For example, the sun and the sun god were known and worshipped as *Ra* in ancient Egypt, while *Ra* was the name of the sun on all the hundreds of islands of Polynesia. Another example is that consistent Polynesian traditions speak of *Uru* as an important tribal

*Ill. 173.* The pyramid of Papa Ra in Tahiti, after Dumont D'Urville, *Voyage autour du Monde,* 1854. This shows a step pyramid similar to those of the New World and possibly harking back to Old World prototypes (*cf. Ills. 100–103*).

and place name in their original, extra-Polynesian homeland, which was interpreted as a reference to the ancient Mesopotamian culture centre of Ur. Although the early theories of direct migrations from Ur and Egypt were dismissed by most scholars, the idea that the ancient cultures of the eastern Mediterranean or Arabian worlds figure indistinctly somewhere in the lost origins of the Polynesian people has never completely lost its grip on the Polynesianist subconscious.

A glance at a globe will show that Easter Island is closer to Mesopotamia by way of the Atlantic than by way of the Pacific and Indian Oceans. The only unavoidable way-station along the Atlantic route is tropical America—and here, in the high-culture area from Mexico to Peru, are to be found all the aforementioned Mediterranean-Polynesian culture elements of which no traces exist along the semi-global Indo–Pacific route. In fact, the legendary Polynesian name, *Uru,* is also the name of the ancient and important Indian tribe dwelling now on Peru's Lake Titicaca and assumed to have formerly inhabited the entire area from the megalithic ruins of Tiahuanaco down to the Pacific coast. At the time of the Spanish Conquest, the Uru were the principal reed-boat builders on Lake Titicaca, living, in fact, on floating islands of totora reed. The very same reed, a characteristic South American species, had been brought by man to Easter Island and planted in the local, fresh-water lakes for the purpose of building the same boats of the same material as those of the Uru Indians. And

*Ill. 120*

*Ill. 94*

according to Easter Island tradition, the god who brought this exotic fresh-water reed to the island was called *Uru*.

Two of the world's major marine conveyors, what we earlier termed the Columbus Route in the Atlantic and the Mendaña Route in the Pacific, lead straight from the Mediterranean world to Polynesia—with the Isthmus of Panama posing only modest terrestrial interference to downwind conveyor passengers. In fact, Mendaña, the first European to set foot in Polynesia, had sailed from the Mediterranean world and crossed the Isthmus of Panama on foot to reach Polynesia by way of Peru. As pointed out in the chapter on Isolationism and Diffusionism, there is no logical reason to assume that an itinerary possible for a medieval European should have been impossible for the bearers of the great civilizations of antiquity.

Although it was not until years later that I found out through experiments how easy it was to travel by aboriginal craft from Africa to America and from America deep into Polynesia, I began early in my research to suspect that the first bearers of culture had reached Easter Island and the adjacent Polynesian groups from South America—irrespective of whether or not tropical America had received any inspiration from the ancient Mediterranean world. Like the great majority of investigators of Polynesian cultural origins, I observed that Polynesian culture was a composite: that more than one group of migrants had ended up on the islands of the extreme East Pacific. With a background including geographical training, and with the practical experience of aboriginal life in Polynesia, I had come to the conclusion that the Southeast Asiatic elements in these islands had come from the Philippine Sea via the Japan Current and Northwest America, only to arrive at islands many of which had long since been reached by pre-Inca voyagers from South America.*

The racial composition of the Polynesians remained a puzzle, however, no matter to what shores of the Pacific their origins were ascribed. Although clearly of racially mixed stock, the Polynesians are among the tallest people in the world, frequently long-headed, and with a skin hue often as light as that of southern Europeans. Indeed, throughout Polynesia there runs a strain of Europoid or, rather, Arabo-Semitic type, with strongly hooked noses, narrow lips, marked beard growth, and, frequently, reddish-brown hair. This strain, often running through entire families, was observed all the way from Easter Island to New Zealand by the first Europeans to voyage there. The type, recognized by the Polynesians themselves under the name *Uru-Keu*, was said by them to be descended from an earlier race of blond-haired, white-skinned gods originally inhabiting the islands. These physical features of the Polynesians contrasted in all the aforementioned characteristics, as well as in blood type, with the Papua Melanesians, Negritos, Malays, and Indonesians inhabiting the area

*After years of debate, the fact that South America had been a source area for the peoples and cultures of the Pacific was finally unanimously accepted by resolution of the 3,000 scientists attending the Tenth Pacific Science Congress in Honolulu in 1961. The background evidence is treated at length for the general reader in my books, *American Indians in the Pacific*, Allen & Unwin, London, 1952, and *Sea Routes to Polynesia*, Allen & Unwin, London, 1968.

whence most modern scholars hypothesized the Polynesians had arrived. This physiological enigma helped keep alive the wild theories concerning the Arabo-Semitic component. The physical characteristics of the South American Indians tallied in general with those of the Malays and Indonesians, to whom they were related; and apart from their agreement with Polynesian blood types and nose shapes, the physical traits of the South American aboriginals differed as much from those of Polynesia as did those of Southeast Asia.

Tall, blond or red-haired people with beards were as non-existent in Mexico and Peru as in Indonesia and the rest of Southeast Asia. These short, slight, yellow-brown peoples on both sides of the Pacific simply were anatomically beardless. How, then, did the Polynesian islanders obtain their deviant physical characteristics, which they ascribed to an early, legendary race?

On Easter Island, the Polynesian outpost farthest from Asia and closest to the New World, detailed traditions insist that the islanders' earliest ancestors came from a vast desert land to the east—that is, from the direction of South America—and reached the island by sailing for sixty days in the direction of the setting sun. The clearly mixed Easter Islanders insist that some of their earliest ancestors had white skins and red hair, whereas others were dark-skinned and black-haired. This was confirmed by the first Europeans to reach the island. When the Dutch under Roggeveen discovered the island in 1722, they recorded that among the first natives to come aboard their ship was 'an entirely white man', and they recorded about the Easter Islanders in general, 'One finds some among them of a darker shade, and others quite white, and no less also a few of a reddish tint as if somewhat severely burned by the sun.'

All the early visitors noted, too, that some of the Easter Islanders were not only very fair and tall, but had soft, reddish hair as well. Could such people really have come from the east, from South America, where the Quechua, Aymara, and Uru Indians have the same physical characteristics as the black-haired, yellow-brown, very small people of Southeast Asia? Could it be that the pre-Inca culture people of Peru had physical features different from those of the small, round-headed, black-haired Indians living there in historic times?

It is remarkable that in the earliest traditions collected on Easter Island (Thomson, 1889, pp. 526–532) the Easter Islanders claimed that the land sixty days to the east, from which their ancestors came, was called the 'Burial Place'. They added directly:

> In this land, the climate was so intensely hot that the people sometimes died from the effects of the heat, and at certain seasons, plants and growing things were scorched and shrivelled up by the burning sun.

Westward from Easter Island, all the way to Southeast Asia, there is nothing that corresponds to this description, since all the coasts are verdant, if not covered by dense jungle. But to the east, in the direction and at the distance recalled by the Easter Islanders, lies the desert coast of Peru and northern Chile, and nowhere in the Pacific does there exist a territory more in keeping with the Easter Islanders' description —regarding both climate and name. All along this South American desert coast are abundant, almost contiguous necropolises, many of which grew to fill vast areas as a result of the accumulation of human remains and funeral objects that were preserved almost indefinitely in a climate without rain. In fact, that climate and these burial grounds provide us with the possibility of studying human remains from early periods, whereas organic remains rapidly decayed in adjacent territories with wetter climates, such as Central America, Mexico and the Pacific island world.

This means that modern archaeologists have direct evidence of the remarkable fact that true mummification was practised by the very founders of the earliest pre-Inca civilization in Peru. In fact, true mummification—with evisceration through the anus and rubbing with resinous and oily preservatives —was common both to Peru and adjacent Polynesia, while it was totally unknown in Indonesia. But whereas hundreds of actual mummies are still available from the desert region of Peru, we have mainly the written records of early voyagers to attest to the wide distribution of the practice of mummifying royal persons throughout the far-flung islands of Polynesia—

*Ill. 174*   from Easter Island in the east, to Hawaii in the north, to New Zealand in the southwest. The very widespread occurrence of this elaborate practice in a tropical island area whose damp climate prevents lasting success shows that it must have spread from a common cultural source outside the island area. Since mummification cannot have reached the islands from Southeast Asia, it is all the more noteworthy that two most elaborate royal mummy-bundles recently brought from a cave

*Ill. 175*   in Hawaii to the Bishop Museum in Honolulu correspond in striking detail with the sophisticated mummy-bundles of the pre-Inca Tiahuanaco culture.

In the tropical rain forests of Central America and Mexico, no human remains of corresponding antiquity have withstood the humid climate. Yet the jade mummy mask and decayed bits of red cloth wrapping attached to the eroded bones found in the giant stone-lidded sarcophagus inside the old Mexican burial pyramid at Palenque testify that it is only because of the unfavourable climate in Mexico and Central America that our access to pre-Columbian human bodies is restricted to the desert areas of Peru.

*Ills. 182–184*   Do the mummies of ancient Peru exhibit the same homogeneous characteristics of small stature, round-headedness, and stiff black hair as do the Indians inhabiting that area today? Or was there, in pre-Spanish times, a more heterogeneous population in Peru that included tall and fair ethnic types like the puzzling *Uru-keu* strain of neighbouring Polynesia?

When large-scale excavations of Peruvian necropolises in the middle of the nineteenth century began to provide science with abundant mummy heads for study, European anthropologists were startled to find that some of the heads—both in cranial shape and in colour and texture of hair—displayed physical traits thought to be alien to the aboriginal inhabitants of the Americas. Wilson (1862, vol. 2) had found that hair examined by him from Indian graves elsewhere 'retains its black colour and coarse texture, unchanged alike by time and inhumation'. From the ancient Peruvian cemeteries of Atacama, however, Wilson described some mummies with brown, soft, wavy hair, stating that these 'reveal important variations from one of the most persistent and universal characteristics of the modern American races'. He even speaks of 'essential diversity in cranial conformation'.

Wilson (*ibid.*, p. 228) was especially struck by the contents of one grave at Chacota Bay on the Pacific coast below Tiahuanaco. Here lay the mummies of a man, a woman, and a child—evidently persons of high rank. Their funerary effects included some perfectly preserved brightly coloured bags containing locks of human hair, probably from members of the same family. Of the male mummy, Wilson says:

> The hair has undergone little or no change and differs essentially from that most characteristic feature of the Indian of the northern continent. It is brown in colour and as fine in texture as the most delicate Anglo-Saxon's hair.

Wilson continues:

> The body of the female from the same tomb presents in general similar characteristics. The hair is shorter and somewhat coarser but fine when compared with that of the northern Indians. It is of light brown colour, smooth, and neatly braided . . . .

The scalp of the infant, he writes, 'is thickly covered with very fine, dark brown hair'. Most remarkable is Wilson's description of the various individual hair samples found in the coloured bags: 'All the hair is of fine texture, of various shades, from fine light brown to black, and to all appearance has undergone no change.' Describing the hair of a mummy found in another tomb in the same vicinity, Wilson observes that 'it is not only brown but remarkably fine, waved in short undulations, with a tendency to curl'.

Wilson was one of the first scholars to suspect, on the basis of these and similar observations, that Peru had supported a heterogeneous population in pre-Spanish times:

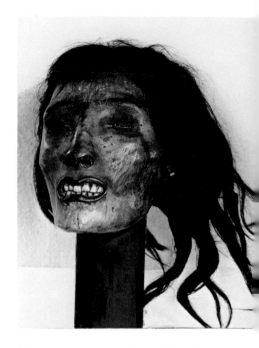

*Ills. 174, 175.* The Polynesians, like the South and Central American Indians, practised mummification, a culture trait which probably spread to the islands with pre-Inca colonists and which reminds one of similar Old World practices. Above, a mummified head from New Zealand. Right, a mummy casket of coconut sennit—as yet unopened—from Hawaii.

The colour and texture of the hair are facts of great importance to the ethnologist, as indicating essential differences from the modern Indians in one important respect; and therefore confirming the probability of equally important ethnic differences suggested by other evidence.

In conclusion, Wilson stressed that the finding of mummies with fine silky brown hair on the coast of Peru went far 'to disprove the assumed unity of physical type throughout the western hemisphere. No feature of the modern Indian is more universal, or yields more slowly even to the effacing influence of hybridity than the long, coarse, black hair. . . .'

*Ill. 182*

In 1925 the noted archaeologists Tello and Lothrop discovered two major necropolises on the Paracas peninsula of the south central coast of Peru, where several hundred carefully wrapped mummies of important personages were preserved in burial caverns and stone-walled tombs that have been carbon-14 dated to the centuries around 300 BC.

It is interesting to note that in the vicinity of these human remains, and dating from the same period, large quantities of hardwood *guara*, used as a kind of centreboard in the navigation of sail-carrying rafts, are constantly being found, attesting to extensive maritime activity there in early pre-Inca times.

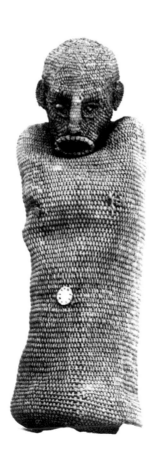

When the colourful and exquisitely designed and woven cotton funeral garments were removed from the more than 2,000-year-old Paracas mummies, it was discovered that the physical attributes of the bodies differed markedly from those of any known South American Indians. The physical anthropologist T. D. Stewart (1943), analysing the skeletal remains of these pre-Inca mummies, found a considerable discrepancy in body heights between the Paracas mummies and skeletal remains from known Peruvian Indians—the Paracas individuals being of notably taller stature. As it had previously been taken for granted that pre-Inca peoples were of the same ethnic stock as the historically known Indians of Peru, Stewart's discovery came as quite a surprise. And, at a loss for an anatomical explanation, he speculated: 'This may be a selected group of large males and not typical of the population as a whole.' Apart from the fact that mummification according to physical stature is unknown in America and elsewhere, this theory assumes that hundreds of tall individuals were available as candidates. Moreover, the elaborate burial and careful preparation of these bodies shows that the mummies had not been mere fishermen or peasants, but were persons of high rank.

Stewart also found that the skull shape of the Paracas mummies was different from that of known Indians in that it exhibited a marked narrowness of the facial features. Failing again to find an anatomical the Paracas mummies as such, everything pertaining to their physical appearance may be misleading, and, for those who wanted to know what these early people looked like, nothing is to be gained by seeing them.

If, on the other hand, we assume that these mummies are what they seem to be—the remains of individuals with physical traits alien to the historic aboriginal population of Peru and commonly associated with the Caucasoid type of the Old World—then we have found in pre-Inca Peru what we were looking for: a natural source of the *Uru-keu* strain on the adjacent islands of Polynesia and an explanation of the blond ancestors of the Easter Islanders, cited by them as having come from a desert land to the east known as the Burial Place.

We do not have to go to the opposite side of the world in search of a source of the Caucasoid element in Polynesia; there is ample archaeological evidence that such a physical type was present on the nearest coast east of Polynesia centuries before the first human arrivals there. Could such a people once have made its way across tropical America, leaving eastern Mediterranean culture elements in its wake?

One need not delve deeply into the literature on Peru before discovering that local records are filled with tales of white, bearded migrants, who first appeared from an unspecified region and departed into the Pacific long before the Spaniards arrived. When Francisco Pizarro discovered Peru, his cousin, the chronicler Pedro Pizarro, who accompanied him, recorded for posterity that some members of the local ruling classes were 'whiter than Spaniards' and that he saw among the Indians some who were white-skinned and blond. Pizarro added that the latter were held by the Incas to be descendants of their gods, the Viracochas. In fact, no sooner had the Spaniards landed on the coast than Inca messengers, running in relay, brought word to the emperor in the highlands that the Viracochas—or sea-foam people—had returned, as they had promised they would according to sacred Inca tradition. The people of Peru had no beards, but they had a word for beard (*sonkhasapa*) as well as a word for white foreigner (*viracocha*), which is still frequently applied by them to Europeans today. Because of their white skin and beards, Pizarro and a handful of men were allowed to march, unmolested, through the fortified mountain valleys of Peru and conquer the largest contemporary empire in the world, the vast army of which stood by in awed reverence of these returning Viracochas whose ancestors had played such an important role in Inca traditional history.

The false Viracochas under Pizarro took full advantage of the Inca mistake concerning their identity. They strangled the emperor with impunity in front of his own army and entered Cuzco's sacred temple, where they found realistic images in gold and marble of the ruler of the original Viracochas, Con-Tici Viracocha, whom the Incas

The colour and texture of the hair are facts of great importance to the ethnologist, as indicating essential differences from the modern Indians in one important respect; and therefore confirming the probability of equally important ethnic differences suggested by other evidence.

In conclusion, Wilson stressed that the finding of mummies with fine silky brown hair on the coast of Peru went far 'to disprove the assumed unity of physical type throughout the western hemisphere. No feature of the modern Indian is more universal, or yields more slowly even to the effacing influence of hybridity than the long, coarse, black hair. . . .'

Ill. 182

In 1925 the noted archaeologists Tello and Lothrop discovered two major necropolises on the Paracas peninsula of the south central coast of Peru, where several hundred carefully wrapped mummies of important personages were preserved in burial caverns and stone-walled tombs that have been carbon-14 dated to the centuries around 300 BC.

It is interesting to note that in the vicinity of these human remains, and dating from the same period, large quantities of hardwood *guara*, used as a kind of centreboard in the navigation of sail-carrying rafts, are constantly being found, attesting to extensive maritime activity there in early pre-Inca times.

When the colourful and exquisitely designed and woven cotton funeral garments were removed from the more than 2,000-year-old Paracas mummies, it was discovered that the physical attributes of the bodies differed markedly from those of any known South American Indians. The physical anthropologist T. D. Stewart (1943), analysing the skeletal remains of these pre-Inca mummies, found a considerable discrepancy in body heights between the Paracas mummies and skeletal remains from known Peruvian Indians the Paracas individuals being of notably taller stature. As it had previously been taken for granted that pre-Inca peoples were of the same ethnic stock as the historically known Indians of Peru, Stewart's discovery came as quite a surprise. And, at a loss for an anatomical explanation, he speculated: 'This may be a selected group of large males and not typical of the population as a whole.' Apart from the fact that mummification according to physical stature is unknown in America and elsewhere, this theory assumes that hundreds of tall individuals were available as candidates. Moreover, the elaborate burial and careful preparation of these bodies shows that the mummies had not been mere fishermen or peasants, but were persons of high rank.

Stewart also found that the skull shape of the Paracas mummies was different from that of known Indians in that it exhibited a marked narrowness of the facial features. Failing again to find an anatomical explanation for this difference, he suggested that the facial features might have been altered as a secondary result of the practice in Paracas of artificial deformation of the upper skull. This explanation seems less than plausible in view of the fact that corresponding deformation of the upper skull was widely practised on infants both in the Americas and in the Old World—without resulting in narrower facial features.

To avoid deriving erroneous conclusions based on upper-skull deformation, Stewart refrained from hypothesizing on the natural cephalic index of the Paracas mummies, which, like their facial form, differed from that of the round-headed American Indian norm. A year after Stewart's Paracas studies, however, A. L. Kroeber (1944), reporting on pre-Inca crania from further north on the same coast, stated that the majority of undeformed Early Chimu skulls were long. Thus, these earliest pyramid builders of Peru were not identical with their historic successors, all of whom are round-headed, like the people of Indonesia. Moreover, excavations at the principal pre-Inca site of Tiahuanaco (A. Chervin, 1908, vol. 3) show that there was a marked mixture of cranial types in this germinal centre of ancient South American civilization, the Tiahuanaco cranial indices ranging from 71·97 to 93·79—that is, from extreme long-headedness to ultra round-headedness. Thus, prior to Inca times, people with utterly different cranial forms co-existed in the principal culture centres of the Pacific slopes of South America.

While Stewart examined the bones of the Paracas mummies, a hair analysis on pieces of scalp from ten of them was simultaneously conducted by M. Trotter (1943). She reported that, in general, the colour was 'rusty brown' but that in most cases the sample was 'interspersed with very light, yellow hairs'. She furthermore remarked that the hair of two of the mummies 'was quite definitely wavy', whereas that of the others appeared to be straight. The degree of cross-sectional ovalness in human hair seems closely associated with the extent of waviness or curliness of the hair itself; thus, the Mongoloid hair of the common American Indian is circular in cross-section, while that of Europeans is commonly oval. Analysing the cross-sectional shape of Paracas mummy hair for classification according to the standard grading system, Trotter (*ibid.*, p. 72) states: 'The cross-section form shows so much divergency between the different mummies that they cover all divisions of hair form.'

Apart from the colour and degree of waviness/ovalness, the fineness of the cross-sectional area is an additional factor used for classifying hair types—the Mongoloid hair of American Indians being very large in cross-section compared to the hair of most Europeans. Trotter found that in cross-sectional area as well, the Paracas mummy hair showed wide variation. And yet, she found the average of all her samples to be approximately 30 per cent less than the average mean cross-sectional area of four other previously studied American Indian tribes. She therefore concluded: 'The size of the hair was much smaller than has been found for other Indians, but not so small as has been recorded for at least one white racial group [the Dutch].'

Dr Trotter, a hair expert misled by the current anthropological doctrine that only Mongoloid stock was indigenous to South America, attempted to account for these remarkably non-Mongoloid hair characteristics by suggesting that cross-sectional shape and area might have changed through post-mortem dehydration and the colour through 'fading'—the reddish-blond hair having faded from black and the blond hair having darkened from white.

In answer to queries from me in 1951, Dr Trotter re-examined all her evidence with her collaborator, O. H. Duggins, formerly of the Hair and Fibre Section of the Federal Bureau of Investigation, and wrote as follows (22 June 1951):

> The hair of the Paracas mummies, which I examined in 1943, may have changed colour and texture slightly. However, the amount of change in either colour or texture, from any evidence we have, would not deny that the original colour was a reddish brown and that the original texture was fine.

I also consulted a leading British authority, W. R. Dawson (1928, p. 127), who had examined a large number of mummies both from Egypt and from South America and had himself reported the discovery of a mummified pre-Inca woman with 'abundant, light brown hair'. He wrote as follows (21 May 1951):

> My opinion is that hair does not undergo any marked change post-mortem. The hair of a wavy or curly individual remains curly or wavy, and that of a straight-haired person remains straight. In mummies and desiccated bodies, the hair has a tendency to be crisp and brittle, but this is the natural result of the drying-up of the sebaceous glands . . . It seems to me very unlikely that any change in colour would take place in a body which had never been exposed to the light . . . To sum up, then, all the evidence I have indicates that the nature of hair does not alter after death except in becoming dry and brittle.

However one may choose to explain them, the Paracas mummies alone certainly do not suggest that the founders of Peruvian culture looked like the Indians of today.

As we have seen, it has been suggested that all the main physical traits of the mummies analysed misrepresent, in one way or another, the ethnic stock to which those mummified belonged: a result of selective burial, childhood skull-deformation, and post-mortem changes. If this be so, nothing has been learned from the discovery of the Paracas mummies as such, everything pertaining to their physical appearance may be misleading, and, for those who wanted to know what these early people looked like, nothing is to be gained by seeing them.

If, on the other hand, we assume that these mummies are what they seem to be—the remains of individuals with physical traits alien to the historic aboriginal population of Peru and commonly associated with the Caucasoid type of the Old World—then we have found in pre-Inca Peru what we were looking for: a natural source of the *Uru-keu* strain on the adjacent islands of Polynesia and an explanation of the blond ancestors of the Easter Islanders, cited by them as having come from a desert land to the east known as the Burial Place.

We do not have to go to the opposite side of the world in search of a source of the Caucasoid element in Polynesia; there is ample archaeological evidence that such a physical type was present on the nearest coast east of Polynesia centuries before the first human arrivals there. Could such a people once have made its way across tropical America, leaving eastern Mediterranean culture elements in its wake?

One need not delve deeply into the literature on Peru before discovering that local records are filled with tales of white, bearded migrants, who first appeared from an unspecified region and departed into the Pacific long before the Spaniards arrived. When Francisco Pizarro discovered Peru, his cousin, the chronicler Pedro Pizarro, who accompanied him, recorded for posterity that some members of the local ruling classes were 'whiter than Spaniards' and that he saw among the Indians some who were white-skinned and blond. Pizarro added that the latter were held by the Incas to be descendants of their gods, the Viracochas. In fact, no sooner had the Spaniards landed on the coast than Inca messengers, running in relay, brought word to the emperor in the highlands that the Viracochas—or sea-foam people—had returned, as they had promised they would according to sacred Inca tradition. The people of Peru had no beards, but they had a word for beard (*sonkhasapa*) as well as a word for white foreigner (*viracocha*), which is still frequently applied by them to Europeans today. Because of their white skin and beards, Pizarro and a handful of men were allowed to march, unmolested, through the fortified mountain valleys of Peru and conquer the largest contemporary empire in the world, the vast army of which stood by in awed reverence of these returning Viracochas whose ancestors had played such an important role in Inca traditional history.

The false Viracochas under Pizarro took full advantage of the Inca mistake concerning their identity. They strangled the emperor with impunity in front of his own army and entered Cuzco's sacred temple, where they found realistic images in gold and marble of the ruler of the original Viracochas, Con-Tici Viracocha, whom the Incas

*Ill. 177*

*Ill. 177.* Ruins of the temple of Viracocha at Cacha, Peru. It was in this temple that the Spaniards found a huge, bearded, stone statue of Con-Tici Viracocha, which they took to be St Bartholomew. Note the temple's megalithic foundations.

◀ *Ill. 176.* Left, this woodcut, published in 1534, only two years after the event it portrays, shows the Inca, Atahualpa, shaded by a parasol and carried on a litter, meeting Father Valverde and Pizarro in the great square at Cajamarca. Valverde, Pizarro's chaplain, tried to convert the Inca to Catholicism, but the latter seized the Bible proffered him and flung it to the earth. At this gesture, Pizarro's troops, who were in hiding, came out and attacked. Although outnumbered by the Inca's retinue of 4,000 men, the Spaniards —with the help of twenty-seven horsemen and a few cannons— massacred the Inca army and assassinated the Inca. After this the conquest of Peru was a relatively simple matter.

venerated as a god. The Spaniards melted down the gold image and smashed the marble statue to pieces, leaving only a written record in which they described the image as being '. . . both as to the hair, complexion, features, raiment, and sandals, just as painters represent the Apostle, St Bartholomew'. The Conquistadores continued southward along the high Andean plateau, looting and pillaging their way from Cuzco to the huge Inca temple at Cacha, devoted to the worship of Viracocha. Inside this architectural masterpiece, they found a huge stone statue of the divine priest-king Con-Tici Viracocha himself, represented as a long-robed man of regal bearing with a long beard. A contemporary, Inca Garcilasso, chronicling the encounter, wrote:

> The Spaniards, after seeing this temple and the statue with the form that has been described, wanted to make out that St Bartholomew might have travelled as far as Peru to preach to the Gentiles, and that the Indians had made this statue in memory of the event.

Indeed, the Spaniards were so impressed by this statue and Inca accounts of this wandering foreigner, who had visited Peru with his white and bearded entourage some time in the distant past, that the statue and the temple escaped destruction for many years. And the Spanish-Indian Mestizos of Cuzco formed a brotherhood, adopting this statue of 'St Bartholomew' as their guardian. Ultimately, however, the Spaniards realized their mistake, and the huge temple was destroyed; the statue, first disfigured, was later carried off and broken into pieces.

They also tell . . . that, on the Island of Titicaca, in the past centuries, there was a bearded people white like us, and that a chief by the name of Cari . . . passed over to the island with his men, and waged such war on the people of which I speak that he killed them all.

In a special chapter on what he calls the ancient buildings of Tiahuanaco, Cieza de Leon has this to say:

I asked the natives . . . if these buildings had been constructed in the time of the Incas. They laughed at this question, affirming what has been already stated, that they had been made long before they ruled . . . For this reason, and also because they say they have seen bearded men on the Island of Titicaca and that the building of Vinaque had been constructed by similar men, I say that perhaps it may be that before the Incas reigned there may have been some people of intelligence in these realms, come from some parts not known, who had done these things, and they being few in number and the natives many, they might have been killed in wars.

When Bandelier arrived to excavate among the ruins of the Island of Titicaca 350 years later, this version of local history still persisted. He was told that in very ancient times, the island was inhabited by gentlemen of unknown provenance similar to Europeans; they had cohabited with the local native women and the resulting children became the Incas, who 'drove out the gentlemen and held the island thereafter'.

All the chroniclers accompanying the Conquistadores and visiting Peru immediately after the conquest included in their reports references to the pre-Inca Viracochas. These reports, while differing in

*Ill. 180.* The sunken temple at Tiahuanaco. In the foreground, Stela 15 and two smaller stelae. In the background, the stairway to the main entrance of the Kalasasaya Temple, a monumental complex dating from the Inca occupation of the sacred city.

*Ill. 181.* Right, Peruvian Indian holding a *quipu*, shown in the *Chronicle* of Huamán Poma de Ayalá. Similar knotted string memory aids are also found in Polynesia and testify to the long trans-Pacific journeys of the early Peruvians.

minor details as a result of having been gathered from informants in widely scattered parts of the vast Inca empire, nevertheless agree in all essentials. The Spaniards' informants included professional Inca historians, who passed on their history from generation to generation, sometimes aided by a system of knotted strings—*quipu*—or painted boards. Common to all accounts of how culture reached Peru is the admission that the ancestors of the Incas lived more or less as savages till a light-skinned, bearded foreigner and his entourage came to their country, taught them the ways of civilization, and departed. Inca Garcilasso provides the following striking account, in which he interviewed his royal Inca uncle about the earliest history of Peru:

*Ill. 181*

> Nephew, I will tell you what you ask with great pleasure, and you should preserve what I have to say in your heart . . . . Know, then, that in ancient times, all this region which you see was covered with forests and thickets, and the people lived like wild beasts, without religion, or government, or town, or houses, without cultivating the land, or clothing their bodies, for they knew not how to weave cotton nor wool to make clothes. They lived two or three together in caves, or clefts in the rocks, or in caverns underground. They ate the herbs of the field and roots or fruit like wild animals, and also human flesh. They covered their bodies with leaves and the bark of trees, or with the skins of animals. In fine, they lived like deer or other game, and even in their intercourse with women, they were like brutes; for they knew nothing of living with separate wives.

Cieza de Leon, writing of the period 'before the rule of the Incas in these realms, and even before they were known', says the period of barbarism ended with the appearance of the personification of the sun on the Island of Titicaca:

> And immediately after this event, they tell that from the south [of Cuzco] there came and stayed a white man of tall stature, who, in his appearance and person, showed great authority and veneration. . . . In many places they tell how he gave rules to men how they should live, and that he spoke lovingly to them with much kindness, admonishing them that they should be good to each other and not do any harm or injury, but that instead they should love each other and show charity. In most places they generally call him Ticciviracocha . . . In many parts, temples were built to him, in which they placed stone statues in his likeness. . . .

The chronicler Betanzos, who took part in the discovery of Peru, recorded:

> . . . When I asked the Indians what shape this Viracocha had when their ancestors had thus seen him, they said that according to

the information they possessed, he was a tall man with a white vestment that reached to his feet, and that this vestment had a girdle; and that he carried his hair short with a tonsure on the head in the manner of a priest; and that he walked solemnly, and that he carried in his hands a certain thing which today seems to remind them of the breviary that the priests carry in their hands. And this is the account I received on this subject, according to what the Indians told me. . . .

There is no clear agreement as to where Con-Tici Viracocha came from, however. The chronicler Andagoya, who also took part in the conquest, wrote:

> . . . There is no record of whence he came, except that Viracocha, in the language of the people, means 'Foam of the Sea'. He was a white and bearded man like a Spaniard. The natives of Cuzco, seeing his great valour, took it for something divine and received him as their chief. . . .

The chronicler Zárate cites Lake Titicaca as a possible beginning point for Viracocha and writes:

> . . . Some mean to say that he was called Inga Viracocha, which is 'froth or grease of the sea', since, not knowing where the land lay whence he came, (they) believed him to have been formed out of that lagoon.

Gómara, however, recorded:

> Some aged Indians also say that he was called Viracocha, which is to say 'grease of the sea', and that he brought his people by sea.

The very name, Con-Tici Viracocha, is a composite of three names *Ills. 87, 177–179* for the same white and bearded deity. In pre-Inca times, he was known as Con on the coast of Peru and as Tici or Ticci in the highlands, but when Inca rule and the Inca language (Quechua) spread to encompass the entire territory, the Incas recognized that the names Con and Ticci referred to the same deity as the one they themselves called Viracocha. They thus grouped together the three names, to the satisfaction of all the people of their empire. Legends among the Chimu Indians of the north coast of Peru relate the interesting tale of this deity's having arrived by sea along the coast from even farther north. Whereas most of the highland legends have him appearing suddenly, at Lake Titicaca, as a personification of the sun, less reverent legends on the coast directly below Titicaca speak of a white-skinned, blond Viracocha who came sailing from the north and paused briefly among the coastal Indians before ascending to Lake Titicaca, where he established a hegemony through fraud: by introducing his fair-haired children to the Indians as supernatural offspring of the sun.

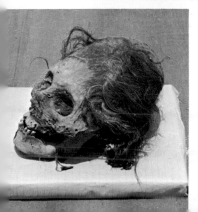

*Ills. 182–184.* Fair hair had always been a sign of high social status among the black-haired, pre-Columbian Indians of South America, as it was among the Polynesians at the time of Captain Cook's voyage across the Pacific. This mummy bundle from Paracas in coastal Peru (above), which is more than 2,000 years old, has been opened to expose the head wearing a wig with two long braids of blond, human hair. The two skulls (left and right) show specimens of European-like hair on pre-Inca heads. Both are from Maket Tempu near Lima. The hair is of a very light colour, fine texture and waviness.

*Ills. 185, 186.* The name of Quetzalcoatl, the culture god of pre-Columbian Mexico, is composed of the two words 'quetzal', the *trogon splendens*, a bird of vivid green plumage, and 'coatl', snake. Quetzal feathers were much used in the feather mosaics of the Aztecs and were one of the emblems of the emperor. The headdress above, over four feet high, and decorated with gold discs and blue, crimson and white feathers, was given to Cortés by Montezuma as a gift for his sovereign. The painting (left) in Diego Durán's *Historia de las Indias*, shows Montezuma wearing the royal standard of quetzal feathers strapped to his back.

The human aspect of Viracocha is also revealed in a highland legend that says that Viracocha 'was very shrewd and wise and said he was a child of the sun'. All the highland traditions agree that his first place of residence was on Titicaca Island, before he set forth with a fleet of reed boats to a site on the south shore of the lake, where he built the megalithic city of Tiahuanaco. He and his white and bearded followers were expressly referred to as *Mitimas*, the Inca word for colonists or settlers. They introduced cultivated crops and taught the Indians how to grow them in irrigated terraces; they showed the Indians how to build stone houses and live in organized communities with law and order; they introduced cotton clothing, sun worship, and megalithic carving; they built step-pyramids and erected monolithic statues said to represent the ancestors of each individual tribe over which they claimed dominion.

From Tiahuanaco, according to legend, Viracocha sent his white and bearded messengers into all parts of Peru to teach people that he was their god and creator. However, dissatisfied at length with the bad conduct and hostility of the local Indians, Viracocha, sun-king of Tiahuanaco, which had become the religious and cultural centre of the pre-Inca empire, decided to leave. Throughout the vast Inca empire, the Indians recalled until the Spanish arrival the routes of departure followed by Viracocha and his two principal disciples. On Viracocha's instructions, one disciple followed the inland mountain range northwards from Lake Titicaca, preaching as he went, while the other, in the same manner, followed the lowland coast. Con-Tici Viracocha himself took the middle route northward by way of Cacha (where the St Bartholomew-like statue was made in his honour) and Cuzco (whose megalithic walls he is credited with having built). After instructing the Indians of Cuzco in how to behave after his departure, he descended to the Pacific coast and gathered with his Viracocha followers near the port of Manta in Equador, from whence these sun-worshippers sailed westward into the Pacific, departing from almost the exact point where the Equator crosses the South American continent.

*Ills. 187, 188*

As we have seen, the Indians of Peru's north coast relate that the pan-Peruvian culture bringer disappeared towards the west, that is, towards Polynesia, although he had originally come from the north. North of the Inca empire, on the mountain plateau of Colombia, the Chibchas, another astonishingly advanced people, had distinguished themselves by a high degree of civilization by the time of European discovery. The traditional history of the Chibchas attributed their cultural attainments as well to the teachings of a foreign migrant, generally known to them as Bochica or Xue. He, too, was remembered as a white man dressed in long, flowing robes and with a beard that fell to his waist. He taught the savage Chibchas to build, to sow, and to live in village communities with organized government and laws. He ruled for many years, then departed, appointing a successor, whom he urged to govern justly. Bochica was also known as Sua, the local word for sun, and when the Spaniards first arrived, they were taken to be his envoys and were called Sua—or Gagua, which also meant sun.

According to tradition, Bochica, alias Sua, had come from the east. East of Chibcha territory, in Venezuela and adjacent territories, we once again encounter memories of the migrant culture-hero. He is referred to by various names, such as Tsuma or Zume, and he is always credited with introducing the people to agriculture and other benefits of his knowledge. According to one legend, he was accustomed to gathering the people around a lofty rock while he stood above them on its summit delivering his instructions and his laws. He lived a certain length of time with the people and then left them. In some areas, legend has him leaving of his own accord; in others, he is driven away by his stiff-necked and unwilling audience, which has become tired of his advice.

Immediately north of Colombia and Venezuela, the Cuna Indians of Panama, who practised writing on wooden tablets, had a tradition that after a devastating flood, '. . . there appeared a great personage who . . . taught the people how to behave, what to name things, and how to use them. He was followed by a number of disciples who spread his teachings. . . .' (D. B. Stout, *Handbook of South American Indians*, vol. IV, p. 267.)

North of Panama, in Mexico, yet another highly advanced civilization, that of the Aztecs, was flourishing at the time of the Spanish arrival. The vast military empire of the Aztecs—like that of the Incas —was far larger than Spain or any other contemporary European nation. Yet, when Hernando Cortés landed in Mexico in 1519, his

*Ill. 188.* Right, early Chimu art shows culture heroes travelling on a serpent raft. This may refer to one of the many versions of Viracocha's departure by sea—promising to return—and is similar to the legend of the departure of Quetzalcoatl from Mexico (*cf. p. 213*). The hero is accompanied by a bird-headed attendant, much like those which appear on the Gateway of the Sun at Tiahuanaco (*cf. Ill. 179*).

*Ill. 189*

*Ill. 187.* A Peruvian deity riding in a reed boat is shown on this early Chimu pot. Similar boats are still used in Peru and Bolivia around the Lake Titicaca area (*cf. Ills. 107, 117*).

*Ills. 204, 205*
*Ill. 176*

small band of medieval troops marched unmolested through the jungle and up to the Aztec capital in the distant highlands, where they subdued the mighty emperor and subjugated his nation with the same surprising ease as Pizarro was to experience when he reached the Inca empire a few years later. These events were due neither to Spanish military supremacy nor to Indian incompetence, but rather to religious confusion on the part of the Indians as to the nature of these 'returning' white and bearded strangers. All the way from Anahuac in Texas to the borders of Yucatán, the Aztecs spoke of a white and bearded Quetzalcoatl as the Incas spoke of Viracocha. And from the moment of their arrival on the beach in Mexico, the white and bearded Spaniards were regarded by the Aztecs as the returning people of Quetzalcoatl.

In his *Carta Segunda* (1520), Cortés personally recorded the speech delivered to him by the Aztec emperor, Montezuma, after the Aztecs had anointed the Spaniards with blood from a human sacrifice:

> We have known for a long time, by the writings handed down by our forefathers, that neither I nor any who inhabit this land are natives of it, but foreigners who came here from remote parts. We also know that we were led here by a ruler, whose subjects we all were, who returned to his country, and after a long time came here again and wished to take his people away. But they had married wives and built houses, and they would neither go with him nor recognize him as their king; therefore he went back. We have ever believed that those who were of his lineage would some time come and claim this land as his, and us as his vassals. From the direction whence you come, which is where the sun rises, and from what you tell me of this great lord who sent you, we believe and

think it certain that he is our natural ruler, especially since you say that for a long time he has known about us. Therefore you may feel certain that we shall obey you, and shall respect you as holding the place of that great lord, and in all the land I rule, you may give what orders you wish, and they shall be obeyed, and everything we have shall be put at your service. And since you are thus in your own heritage and your own house, take your ease and rest from the fatigue of the journey and the wars you have had on the way.

In his study of aboriginal American religions (1882, p. 140), Brinton comments:

> Such was the extraordinary address with which the Spaniard, with his handful of men, was received by the most powerful war chief of the American continent. It confessed complete submission, without a struggle. But it was the expression of a general sentiment. When the Spanish ships for the first time reached the Mexican shores the natives kissed their sides and hailed the white and bearded strangers from the east as gods, sons and brothers of Quetzalcoatl, come back from their celestial home to claim their own on earth and bring again the days of Paradise; a hope, dryly observes Father Mendieta, which the poor Indians soon gave up when they came to feel the acts of their visitors.

Originally, Quetzalcoatl, as well as Viracocha, seems to have been the hereditary name, or rather title, of a hierarchical sequence of priest-kings, who worshipped—and claimed descent from—a supreme sun-god of the same name. Only with time were all Quetzalcoatls, like all Viracochas, amalgamated into one, single historic deity—god and creator, as well as human culture-hero and mortal benefactor.

The name Quetzalcoatl is a composite, often translated freely as Plumed Serpent—*quetzal* (*trogon splendens*) being the favourite bird of

*Ills. 185, 186, 190*

the Aztecs and *coatl* the serpent and sacred symbol of light and divinity both in Mexico and Peru. Quetzalcoatl was the supreme god of the Aztecs as Viracocha was of the Incas. Yet, as Brinton writes:

> . . . It was not Quetzalcoatl the god, the mysterious creator of the visible world, on whom the thoughts of the Aztec race delighted to dwell, but on Quetzalcoatl, high priest in the glorious city of Tollan (Tula), the teacher of the arts, the wise law-giver, the virtuous prince, the master builder, and the merciful judge.

*Ill. 191*

He forbade the sacrifice of human beings and animals, teaching that bread, flowers, and incense were all that the gods demanded. And he prohibited wars, fighting, robbery, and other forms of violence to such an extent that he was held in affectionate veneration, not only by his own people but by distant nations as well, who made pilgrimages to his capital. The fact that the Aztecs, who excelled in human sacrifice at their pyramids and temples, still recollected a benevolent, pacifist culture-bringer whose teachings closely paralleled the Biblical Commandments so impressed the Spanish friars that they identified Quetzalcoatl with the Apostle Thomas—an exact analogy to the confusion of Viracocha with St Bartholomew in Peru. Brinton goes on to say:

> The origin of the earthly Quetzalcoatl is variously given; one cycle of legends narrates his birth in Tollan in some extraordinary

*Ill. 190.* An Aztec representation of Quetzalcoatl, the feathered serpent. The literal depiction of the culture-hero and god's name was often used by Mexican artists (*cf. Ill. 238*).

*Ill. 191.* The Toltecs, who preceded the Aztecs, had a very strong devotion to Quetzalcoatl, whom they regarded as the original culture-bearer of their race. Even in later times, the Aztecs, when asked about the origins of Quetzalcoatl, referred to him as the 'high priest in the glorious city Tollan [Tula], teacher of the arts and wise law-giver'. The Toltecs erected a step-pyramid crowned by a temple in his honour at Tula; the roof of this temple was supported by huge 'Atlantes', said to represent the culture-bearer and his followers.

Ill. 192. Quetzalcoatl standing on the top of a step-pyramid, holding a staff and wearing a long, white robe covered with crosses, from an Aztec codex.

Ills. 188, 193

manner; a second cycle claims that he was not born in any country known to the Aztecs, but came to them as a stranger. ... Las Casas narrates his arrival from the east, from some part of Yucatán, he thinks, with a few followers, a tradition which is also repeated with definiteness by the native historian Alva Ixtlilxochitl, but leaving the locality uncertain.

The essence of the Quetzalcoatl traditions is that he was a white man, tall of stature, with a flowing beard—which, according to some chroniclers, was reddish in colour. He wore a strange dress, unlike the attire of the Indians who received him; the historian Veytia recorded that he was 'clothed in a long, white robe strewn with red crosses, and carrying a staff in his hand'. He was accompanied in his travels by builders, painters, astronomers, and craftsmen; he made roads, civilized the people, and passed thus from place to place until, in the end, he disappeared. According to some traditions, he died on the coast of the Gulf of Mexico and was buried there at the seashore by his followers after they had burned his body and all his treasures. Other traditions, however, insisted that Quetzalcoatl and his entourage embarked on a magic raft of serpents and thus sailed away after promising solemnly to return and take possession of the land.

The neighbours of the Aztecs were the Mayas of the tropical lowlands of the Yucatán peninsula, which juts into the Gulf of

Ill. 193. A page from the Aztec Codex *Nuttall*, depicting bearded men attacking a town by means of rafts. These bearded men may well have represented partisans or followers of Quetzalcoatl.

Mexico. Juan de Grijalva, passing from Cuba to the Yucatán Peninsula a year before Cortés landed on the Gulf of Mexico, got the same amazingly respectful reception from the otherwise warlike Indians as that accorded Cortés and Pizarro. The great Maya civilization had collapsed before the Spaniards arrived, but the scattered remnants of the people still possessed detailed traditions as to the origins of the culture that had flourished under their ancestors. They spoke of two distinct culture-heroes, Itzamná and Kukulcan—both bearded, although arriving at different times and from opposite directions, leading the Mayas' ancestors to Yucatán. Brinton says of the descendants of the Mayas:

> They did not pretend to be autochthonous, but claimed that their ancestors came from distant regions in two bands. The largest and most ancient immigration was from the east, across, or rather through, the ocean—for the gods had opened twelve paths through it—and this was conducted by the mythical civilizer, Itzamná. The second band, less in number and later in time, came in from the west, and with them was Kukulcan. The former was called the Great Arrival; the latter, the Lesser Arrival . . . To this ancient leader, Itzamná, the nation alluded as their guide, instructor, and civilizer. It was he who gave names to all the rivers and divisions of land; he was their first priest and taught them the proper rites wherewith to please the gods and appease their ill-will; he was the patron of the healers and diviners and had disclosed to them the mysterious virtues of plants . . . It was Itzamná who first invented the characters of letters in which the Mayas wrote their numerous books, and with which they carved in such profusion on the stone and wood of their edifices. He also devised their calendar, one more perfect even than that of the Mexicans, though in a general way similar to it. Thus Itzamná, regarded as ruler, priest, and teacher, was, no doubt, spoken of as an historical personage, and is so put down by various historians, even to the most recent.

> After the Great Arrival came the Lesser: the second important hero-myth of the Mayas was that of Kukulcan. This is in no way connected with that of Itzamná, and is probably later in date, and less national in character . . . The natives affirmed, says Las Casas, that in ancient times there came to that land twenty men, the chief of whom was called 'Cocolcan' . . . They wore flowing robes and sandals on their feet, they had long beards and their heads were bare, they ordered that the people should confess and fast. . . .

Kukulcan was remembered as a great architect and pyramid builder who founded the city of Mayapan and caused various important edifices to be built at Chichen Itzá. He taught the people to refrain from using arms—even for hunting—and under his beneficent rule, the nation enjoyed peace, prosperity, and abundant harvests.

224

*Ills. 194, 195.* Quetzalcoatl and his followers, according to the Toltec legends, were obliged to flee from Tula by the followers of the rival god Tezcatlipoca. At about the same time, the Mayas were being invaded by the Toltecs, and Maya tradition recalls the arrival of Kukulcan (which in Maya means plumed serpent) from the west. The Toltecs rebuilt the great Maya ceremonial centre of Chichen Itzá and on the pillars of the Temple of the Warriors (below and left) depicted fierce-looking, bearded warriors. The two doorjambs of the temple at the top of the pyramid represent large, plumed rattlesnakes (*cf. Ill. 238*).

*Ill. 194*

The mere idea of the cruel and bellicose Mayas' having invented such a peace-loving doctrine as that of Kukulcan, the immigrant priest-king, is as surprising as the insistence on the part of these beardless natives on the flowing beards, fair skin, and long robes of this cultured wanderer and his followers. Nevertheless, his humanitarian teachings and cultural activities coincide completely with those of Quetzalcoatl. Moreover, while Aztec tradition has Quetzalcoatl disappearing eastward in the direction of Yucatán, Maya tradition has Kukulcan coming from the west, from the direction of Mexico. Brinton points out that one of the Maya chronicles opens with a distinct reference to Tula and Nonoal—names inseparable from the Quetzalcoatl tradition—and he concludes:

The probability seems to be that Kukulcan was an original Maya divinity, one of their hero-gods, whose myth had in it so many similarities to that of Quetzalcoatl that the priests of the two nations came to regard the one as the same as the other.

In fact, the word *kukulcan* is simply a translation of *quetzalcoatl*. *Kukul* is the Maya word for quetzal bird, and *can* is a serpent. Eventually, as in Mexico and Peru, the white and bearded priest-king left. According to Brinton:

> He gathered the chiefs together and expounded to them his laws. From among them, he chose as his successor a member of the ancient and wealthy family of the Cocoms. His arrangements completed, he is said, by some, to have journeyed westward, to Mexico or to some other spot towards the sun-setting.

A westward migrant from Yucatán would necessarily enter the habitat of the Tzendals in the Tabasco and Chiapas jungles. Tzendal legend, centring around their culture-hero, Votan, who came from the direction of Yucatán, was originally recorded in the Tzendal language as dictated by a Tzendal native. Referring to this manuscript, Brinton says:

> Few of our hero-myths have given occasion for wilder speculation than that of Votan. . . . At some indefinitely remote epoch, Votan came from the far east. He was sent by the gods to divide out and assign to the different races of men the earth on which they dwell, and to give to each its own language. The land whence he came was vaguely called *valum votan*, the land of Votan. His message was especially to the Tzendals. Previous to his arrival, they were ignorant, barbarous, and without fixed habitations. He collected them into villages, taught them how to cultivate maize and cotton, and invented the hieroglyphic signs which they learned to carve on the walls of their temples. It is even said that he wrote his own history in them. He instructed civil laws for their government and imparted to them the proper ceremonials of religious worship. . . . They especially remembered him as the inventor of their calendar.

Also remembered as a city builder, he was spoken of as the founder of Palenque with its great stone pyramids, two of which contained burial chambers like those of ancient Egypt. The Tzendal text continues:

> Votan brought with him, according to one statement, or, according to another, was followed from his native land by, certain attendants or subordinates, called in the myth *tzequil*, petticoated, from the long and flowing robes they wore. These aided him in the work of civilization . . . . When at last the time came for his final departure, he did not pass through the valley of death, as must all mortals, but he penetrated through a cave into the under-earth, and found his way to 'the root of heaven'.

*Ill. 196.* Throughout Central America legend tells of bearded wanderers, such as those shown on the Mixtec Codex *Dorenberg*.

With this mysterious expression, the native myth closes its account of him.

We do not have to go further down from the high plateau of Chiapas into the under-earth than to the coastal lowlands of the Zoques before Votan reappears, this time with the name of Condoy. Brinton says:

> The Zoques, whose mythology we unfortunately know little or nothing about, adjoined the Tzendals, and were in constant intercourse with them. We have but faint traces of the early mythology of these tribes; but they preserved some legends which showed that they also partook of the belief, so general among their neighbours, of a beneficent culture-god. This myth relates that their first father, who was also their Supreme God, came forth from a cave in a lofty mountain in their country, to govern and direct them . . . . They did not believe that he had died, but that after a certain length of time, he, with his servants and captives, all laden with bright, gleaming gold, retired into the cave and closed its mouth, not to remain there, but to reappear at some other part of the world and confer similar favours on other nations.

*Ill. 196*

South of the Mayas, Tzendals, and Zoques lived the Kiches of Guatemala, whose culture shows a root relationship to that of the Mayas. Their traditions have been preserved for posterity by a re-script of their original national book, the *Popul Vuh*. From this aboriginal source, we learn that in Yucatán—the gateway from southern Mexico to central America—the inhabitants were well acquainted with the 'wanderer', who seems to have passed through their territory more than once. Known in Guatemala under various names, one of which was Gucumatz, he educated and cultured the local savages, teaching them to develop their own civilization. Brinton concludes:

> But, like Viracocha, Quetzalcoatl, and others of these worthies, the story goes that they treated him with scant courtesy, and in

anger at their ingratitude, he left them forever, in order to seek a nobler people.

Although the Spaniards encountered the same traditions of white and bearded culture bearers throughout the Americas, from the Mexican highlands, through the central American jungles, down to the mountain plateaus of Peru and Bolivia—that is, precisely where they encountered spectacular ruins of pre-Columbian origin—many modern commentators, used to train, car, and aeroplane travel, find it difficult to imagine that any 'wanderer' can have covered such vast areas in pre-Columbian times. They forget that the medieval Spaniards had no access to trains, cars, or aeroplanes either. Yet, within merely two decades of their first landing in Mexico, the relatively few Spaniards had explored virtually all the New World territory from the Atlantic to the Pacific, from Kansas to Argentina. Within the same few years, Cabeza de Vaca and three companions became shipwrecked in the surf of the Florida coast, and for eight years (1528–36) they walked—unarmed, barefoot, and almost naked—through unmapped swamps, deserts, and mountains, from one Indian tribe to the next, right across the continent to the Gulf of California, where they finally reached the newly established Spanish settlements there.

Before the same two decades were over, Orellana, sailing from Spain, had crossed the Panama Isthmus and climbed the Andes from the Pacific side, from whence he descended to the sources of the Amazon, following the river across the continent to its mouth on the Atlantic side before returning home to Spain. To believe that a few Spaniards could walk in two decades across mountains and jungles while thinking that the founders of the pre-Columbian empires could not have traversed them in two centuries or even two millennia, is grossly to under-estimate the latter's capabilities.

Throughout the ensuing years, desperate attempts have been made to account for the paradoxical presence of white-skinned, long-robed, bearded men in the traditions and legends of the brown-skinned, loincloth-wearing, beardless Indians of tropical America. Some theorized that the flowing beards and robes spoken of in the Indian traditions were allegorical references among sun-worshippers to the rays of the sun. Others attempted to explain away these traditions by claiming that they were not, in fact, truly ancient, but that they postdated—and, indeed, had even been inspired by—the early Spanish arrivals.

With the progress of modern archaeology, these nineteenth- and early twentieth-century speculations have proved quite untenable, since highly realistic sculptures and paintings of bearded men have been found in tombs and ruins—and these not only antedate Spanish arrival, but in a great many cases even antedate the Aztec, Maya, and Inca civilizations. The stories encountered by the early Spaniards were not only recited to them orally upon their arrival, but they were already recorded in the written texts of the New World, as the Aztec emperor Montezuma himself emphasized in his speech of welcome to Cortés, and they were illustrated in the art of the very people who founded the civilizations from Mexico to Peru.

As we have seen, when the Spaniards entered the main temples of the Incas in Peru, they found gold and stone statues of the traditional culture-bringer, Viracocha, bearing a confusing resemblance to depictions of one of their own Apostles, with his beard and eastern-Mediterranean-style robe and sandals.

The majority of the great number of statues found by the Spaniards among the ruins of Tiahuanaco and said to represent the progenitors of the various tribes in the realm of Con-Tici Viracocha were destroyed as heathen relics by the Catholic Conquistadores. But a few were hidden by the Indians and thus escaped destruction. In 1932, while the American archaeologist, W. C. Bennett, was carrying out excavations in Tiahuanaco, he unearthed a complete statue undoubtedly representing *Ill. 87* Con-Tici Viracocha, with beard and long, girdled robe. The flowing garment was decorated by a horned serpent and two pumas, symbols of the supreme god in both Mexico and Peru. Bennett shows that this statue was almost identical to another bearded statue found on the shore of Lake Titicaca, on the very peninsula, next to the Island of Titicaca, where Viracocha must have landed when he left his refuge there to make his way to Tiahuanaco. Other bearded statues, similarly of pre-Inca origin, have been found at various archaeological sites *Ill. 178* around Lake Titicaca. Stone suitable for sculpture was almost non-existent on the Pacific desert coast of Peru, but there, among the Chimu and Nazca cultures, illustrations of the early culture-hero were either moulded in or painted on ceramic, showing him with moustache and chin beard. These representations of Viracocha, originally known locally as Con, are especially common on the north coast of Peru, where legend has it that the bearded god, arriving from the north, entered the area subsequently ruled by the Incas. These ceramic vessels date from the Early Chimu or Mochicas, the earliest founders of local civilization and builders of the finest pyramids in Peru. They *Ill. 172* depict a person wearing a turban and full-length robe, with a most realistic moustache and long, pointed beard reaching down to his chest.

Ceramic heads and figurines realistically depicting the same bearded personage are common northward from the coast of Peru through Ecuador and Colombia, and they reappear sporadically up through the Isthmus of Panama into Mexico. In fact, highly realistic illustra- *Ils. 196–201* tions of the bearded and often almost Arabo-Semitic ethnic type are extremely common all the way across Mexico, from Guerrero into Yucatán, from the Mexican high plateau and the northern jungles of

Vera Cruz to Chiapas, and from there into Guatemala and El Salvador. He is depicted in free-standing statues, carved in reliefs on flat stone stelae, moulded in clay, shaped in gold, painted on ceramic vessels and stucco walls, and represented in the picture writings of pre-Columbian paper folding books. His beard could be long or short; trimmed or natural; pointed, round, or even forked and curled as commonly seen in art from ancient Mesopotamia. In some instances, the Maya priests and other important personages, who could not grow beards themselves, would wear false beards in imitation of the divine founders of their religion.

Modern archaeology has come to the conclusion that the oldest civilization in Mexico, and the one that inspired and gave rise to the subsequent civilizations of the Toltecs, Mayas, and Aztecs, originated in the tropical jungle lowlands on the Gulf Coast of Mexico. This, as we have shown earlier, is precisely where the strong current comes in from across the Atlantic and where, in fact, the Spaniards themselves landed under Cortés. Here on the coast, in a highly unfavourable climate, archaeology has revealed that American civilization began abruptly with the sudden appearance of hieroglyphic script, a highly evolved calendar system, megalithic art, adobe manufacture, ceramic skills, pyramid building, and most sophisticated sculpture. Since the creators of this amazing cultural revolution are utterly unknown, modern science has merely assigned a name to them: Olmecs.

Lacking suitable stone in their jungle habitat, the Olmecs would fetch stones weighing up to 25 tons and drag them back over 50 miles through swamps and jungles to their temple sites. With unsurpassed skill, they sculpted human heads and full figures—in the

*Ills. 202, 203*

230

*Ills. 197-201.* Representations of bearded individuals abound throughout Mexico although the pure bred Indian is remarkable for his absence of facial hair. Examples from Rio Balsas (far left), Vera Cruz (centre left), Tres Zapotes ( left ), as well as representations of Huehueteotl, the old god of fire, with a brazier on his head (below), and Tlaloc, the rain god, from Oaxaca (right), seem to indicate that beards in different styles must have been familiar to artists at one point, even though later examples have become extremely stylized through being copied.

round and in relief—so realistically that we today have a very good indication of what the Olmecs looked like.

To judge from their art, the Olmecs comprised two contrasting ethnic types: one was remarkably Negroid, with thick lips, flat broad nose, and a round face bearing a naïve, unsophisticated, and rather sullen expression. This type has been popularly referred to among archaeologists as 'baby face'. The other Olmec type is strikingly different, sometimes representing an almost Semitic type, with narrow face, sharp profile, strongly hooked nose, thin lips, and a beard that can vary from a small goatee to a full beard reaching such a length that this type has sometimes been jokingly referred to among archaeologists as 'Uncle Sam'. Since neither of the two contrasting Olmec types—the Negroid and the Semitic—bears the slightest resemblance to any ethnic group known to have existed in aboriginal America, whereas both represent physical types characteristic of the ancient civilizations of the Old World, their sudden appearance as culture-bringers in the New World, just in the area where the natural ocean conveyor arrives from Africa, has led to a flurry of speculations. Like the early Spanish friars, religious sects even in our own modern days have jumped to the conclusion that Biblical or Mormon personages—not to mention the whole Lost Tribe of Israel—were the founders of Olmec civilization. Such mystical claims on the part of laymen have not furthered the Diffusionist cause, as they have frightened many serious scholars into remaining in the seemingly less incautious Isolationist camp. But is it really less incautious to ignore—and even attempt to explain away—available botanical, archaeological, and historical evidence than to face the fact that voyagers from Asia Minor were sailing beyond Gibraltar with astronomers, masons, and other experts aboard on organized colonizing expeditions—in the very centuries when Olmec civilization was beginning on the Gulf of Mexico? The Phoenicians and their unknown predecessors, who founded such megalithic cities on the Atlantic coast of Africa as Lixus, were navigating more than a thousand years before Christ in literally the same water as the Mayas of Yucatán, because just as the Moroccan sun becomes the Mexican sun in a matter of hours, so Moroccan water becomes Mexican water in a matter of weeks.

In one of the most important Maya pyramids, at Chichen Itzá in Yucatán, an entrance was found leading to interior chambers with walls and rectangular columns covered by stucco and painted with coloured frescoes, all strikingly reminiscent of eastern Mediterranean royal tombs. These coloured paintings, copied in detail by the archaeologists E. H. Morris, J. Charlot, and A. A. Morris (1931), have subsequently been destroyed by humidity and tourists. Among the most important motifs of these frescoes was a seashore battle involving two different racial types. One of these, represented as having

*Ill. 202*

*Ill. 203*

*Ill. 195*

*Ill. 206*

*Ills. 202, 203.* The two contrasting ethnic types in the art of the Olmec civilization are shown here. Above, the remarkably negroid 'baby face', and right, the semitic 'Uncle Sam' type. The Olmec civilization seems to have emerged fully formed in the jungle lowlands around the Gulf of Mexico. Although their cultural influence was felt throughout Mexico, they disappeared without leaving any written records, and our knowledge of their civilization is still very incomplete.

*Ills. 204, 205.* Left, two panels from a set painted in 1698, depicting the Conquest of Mexico and now in the Museo de América in Madrid. They show Cortés, accompanied by Spaniards, riding to meet Montezuma, who is carried on a litter. Montezuma's own reasons for welcoming the invading Spaniards were recorded by Cortés in his *Carta Segunda* of 1520 (*cf. p. 219*).

white skin and long, flowing, yellow hair, is shown either arriving or departing by boat on the ocean, which is symbolized by blue waves and crabs, rays, and other marine creatures. The white mariners are shown either nude and circumcised or dressed in tunics. One of them is shown with a distinct beard. Morris, Charlot, and Morris cautiously state that the unusual appearance of the yellow-haired mariners '. . . gives rise to much interesting speculation as to their identity'. The other ethnic type, in contrast, is represented as dark-skinned and wearing feathered headdresses and loincloths. These dark-skinned men are shown waging war against the light-skinned ones, several of whom they are leading away as bound captives. In another panel, one of these white prisoners, his long, yellow hair reaching to his waist, is being sacrificed by two black men, whereas another, his vessel capsized, is trying to escape by swimming, pursued by carnivorous fish, while his extremely long golden hair floats in the waves. In one of these mural panels, a white mariner is walking peacefully away, carrying a rolled bundle and other possessions on his back while his empty boat is shown offshore, yellow in colour and with the highly raised bow and stern strongly suggestive of a Lake Titicaca reed boat.

Reed boats have been recorded in post-Columbian times in eight different Mexican states, although they are not reported from Yucatán. The vessel depicted in the Mayan pyramid also recalls the reed boats used until modern times at Lixus on the Atlantic coast of Morocco. Similar mural paintings in ancient Egyptian tombs show crescent-shaped reed boats, sometimes involved in battles on the Nile. A relief in ancient Nineveh, however, shows Mesopotamians using reed boats in a battle on the sea; bearded men with long, flowing hair are shown swimming for their lives in an ocean, which, as in the mural at Chichen Itzá, is symbolized by large crabs and marine creatures. In the Nineveh relief, however, some of the reed boats are depicted as crowded with both men and women escaping across the sea, their arms raised in prayer to the sun.

Battle and escape have possibly brought as many mariners to grips with unknown seas and currents as have fogs and offshore gales. What happened to the fleeing sun-worshippers in the Nineveh relief happened to countless other mariners in Asia Minor and Africa from the very dawn of civilization. Basic similarities in human nature make history repeat itself. Thus we shall never know whether it was war, accidental drift, or planned exploration that brought tall, blond, and bearded men across the open sea from Africa to the Canary Islands long before European arrival there. We know from written accounts of the discovery of the Canary Islands a few generations before Columbus that these remote Atlantic islands were inhabited by an ethnically mixed population called Guanches; some of these aboriginal Canary Islanders were small, swarthy, and Negroid, whereas others

*Ills. 206–208*

*Ill. 117*

*Ill. 118*

*Ill. 209*

were tall, white-skinned, and blond. An early watercolour by Torriani (1590), showing six aboriginal Guanches, depicts them with extremely white skin and yellow hair and beards. Their beards are shown either extremely long and uncut or trimmed and pointed, whereas their long, yellow hair flows far down their backs—just like the hair of the blond mariners in the frescoes of the Mayan pyramid at Yucatán.

Linguistic traces and cultural vestiges—including the art of trepanning—clearly link the Guanches with the ancient civilizations that extended from Mesopotamia to the Atlantic coast of Morocco. Thus, the Berbers of Morocco, also a people of composite ethnic origins, included small, Negroid tribes as well as a tall, blond, and blue-eyed racial element which appeared at random from the Atlas Mountains to the Atlantic coast before the Arabs arrived. Blond and fair people are often erroneously associated only with Northern Europe, although such physical types have survived sporadically into historic times all the way from Asia Minor to the Atlas Mountains. Individuals with brown and even blond hair are frequently depicted

*Ills. 206–208.* The reconstruction of one of the mural paintings from the Temple of the Warriors at Chichen Itzá (left) shows white-skinned prisoners being led away naked by dark-skinned captors while others are preparing to retreat by sea. It is interesting to note that the captives—shown on another part of the same mural as being fair-haired—are circumcised, a practice which was not prevalent in high-culture areas of the Americas. A pottery vessel from northern Peru (right), however, shows a similar scene: white-skinned, naked captives, also circumcised, being led by fully armed, dark-skinned warriors. It is possible that the practice of circumcision was brought to the New World by cultural contact at a very early period (*cf. Chapter 4*). Below, a scene from the 'Tomb of the Doctor' at Saqqara, showing circumcision being performed in Egypt.

among both gods and naked reed-boat navigators on ancient Egyptian tomb wall-paintings. And the daughter-in-law of Pharaoh Cheops was found pictured with yellow hair and blue eyes when her tomb was opened at the foot of the pyramid of her husband, Pharaoh Chephren.

Trepanning, known from ancient Mexico and extremely important in ancient Peru, was almost absent from Europe until the nineteenth century AD and was not at all known in Asia except in Mesopotamia. In the Old World, its distribution thus coincided with ancient civilizations: from Mesopotamia and Egypt to the Atlantic coast of Morocco, reappearing surprisingly on the Canary Islands.

Who brought the art of trepanning to these Atlantic islands, where all traces of the art of boat-building had been lost by the time Europeans arrived? Both history and archaeology have shown that the Phoenicians, with their home ports in Asia Minor and North Africa, had established firm colonies on the Canary Islands centuries before the birth of Christ. They used these distant islands as staging areas on their difficult sailings to their purple dye manufacturing

colonies, of which vestiges have been found as far beyond Morocco as the coast of present-day Senegal.

It has been frequently suggested—rightly or wrongly—that the Phoenicians were light-skinned and blond. If this is true, there is no problem in explaining the presence of the light-skinned, blond Guanches on the Canary Islands. If it is not true, then some other early mariners—fair-skinned, blond, and bearded—must have reached the Canary Islands by navigating in the powerful Canary Current.

As we have seen (p. 120), anybody navigating in this current—as we did, twice—finds himself on a perpetual conveyor belt that will, if he does not fight it successfully, deposit him on the shores of tropical America. As we have also seen, white-skinned mariners with long, yellow hair, resembling the Canary Islanders, were depicted in frescoes by the Mayas on the very peninsula where this Canary Current comes in. Indeed, both among the Mayas and their Mexican neighbours, the Aztecs, consistent traditions related that white and bearded men had arrived by sea, from across the Atlantic, instructing their food-gathering, tribal ancestors in the sophisticated arts of civilization before departing, promising some day to return. Hence, the arriving Spaniards caused no surprise and were received as the awaited fulfilment of ancient promises. Today's Isolationist, then, having failed to find any visible centre of cultural evolution in the New World and contradicted by gradually accumulating objective evidence from botany, physical anthropology, archaeology, and navigation, finds himself bereft of concrete support for his position. Although neither Isolationist nor Diffusionist can as yet adduce absolute evidence for his position, the burden of proof has now clearly shifted to those who reject the very possibility of pre-Columbian, trans-Atlantic inspiration.

*Ill. 209.* The mummified body of a Canary Island Guanche. Mummification occurs in civilizations of the eastern Mediterranean, the Canary Islands, and the high-culture areas of Mexico and Peru and in Polynesia (*cf. Ills. 174, 175*). These areas are linked by direct ocean currents; mummification is but one of the cultural traits shared by all of them. The reed boat, another common trait, might well have been their means of diffusion (*cf. Chapter 4*). Although the body illustrated above has dark hair, the Guanches were often blond.

# 8         Contacts from Asia

Betty J. Meggers

THE EXCITEMENT OF DISCOVERY is one of the spices of life, particularly if one stumbles on to something that the experts appear to have missed. Since the criteria for judging the validity of data are seldom made explicit outside scientific circles, however, an enthusiastic layman is often puzzled, frustrated, or angered by the failure of the 'establishment' to take account of his 'revolutionary' observation. This kind of impasse stimulated Thor Heyerdahl to undertake the Kon-Tiki voyage, which dramatized his hypothesis of trans-Pacific contact so spectacularly that anthropologists could no longer ignore it. Some who looked into the matter in order to prove it false found themselves won over. Others have continued to deny adamantly that any evidence exists of outside influence on cultural development in the New World. One reason for prolongation of the controversy is the disagreement about what can be expected in the way of evidence.

To take an example, a demonstration that similar types of objects were used on both sides of the Pacific is not sufficient grounds for concluding that communication took place. The transmission of an object from one group to another is only one of three major possible explanations. The other two are independent invention and convergence from dissimilar origins. All three alternatives are equally probable and the correct explanation must be sought in each case. Often the evidence is inconclusive, either because the archaeological record is poor or because the trait is of a type that leaves no archaeological record. On the other hand, introduced traits may remain unrecognized because they were modified by the receiving culture to the extent that resemblances have been generalized or muted. Opponents of trans-Pacific contact have specified a number of conditions that must be satisfied before similarities between cultural traits on opposite sides of an ocean can be interpreted as resulting from trans-Pacific contact. A review of these will bring out some of the complications that are involved in evaluation of the evidence.

First, the traits being compared must be of the same age. Often this is difficult to determine with precision because archaeological sequences are incomplete or the object has been removed from its context and therefore cannot be accurately dated. Many comparisons are invalidated by this criterion, since they involve items that are centuries or even millennia older in Asia than in America, and died out in the former area long before they appeared in the latter. Careful examination of the evolution of such non-contemporary traits generally shows that independent invention or convergence is the probable explanation, particularly when art motifs are involved.

Secondly, a review of the history of the trait should reveal a long period of evolution in the donor region and a sudden appearance fully developed in the receiver region, if intrusion by trans-Pacific contact is responsible for the resemblance. Unfortunately, this situation may be impossible to demonstrate, either because the compared items have been preserved without sufficiently detailed documentation, or because one or both areas are too poorly known archaeologically to provide the required information. Failure to meet this criterion is one of the most common grounds for rejection of striking similarities.

Thirdly, along with greater antiquity, one would expect wider geographical distribution of the trait or complex in the donor area, since traits tend to diffuse from the place of origin to neighbouring groups with the passage of time. In fact, this correlation between age and area is one method of judging the relative antiquity of cultural traits. On this basis, it would be expected that an introduced trait would be found in a much smaller geographical area on the receiving side of the ocean than on the donor side. If the introduction was ancient, however, so that the trait had a long time to spread, or if it was popular and rapidly disseminated, the areas of distribution on both sides of the ocean might not differ significantly in size.

Fourthly, the argument for introduction is strengthened if the character of the trait is not determined by its function. The efficiency of an axe, for example, is related to material, form, weight, contour of the blade, etc. It is increased in effectiveness if hafted, and there are few practical ways to accomplish this. Consequently, repeated convergence towards a similar size, proportions, and materials is likely to occur independently. Independent invention or convergence may also result from similarities in the environment, whether in the form of raw materials, subsistence resources, or climatic excesses, which stimulate the manufacture of objects with similar functions. On the other hand, convergence must be demonstrated to be the most probable explanation. The theoretical possibility that it occurred is not basis for rejecting other alternatives.

Fifth, the improbability of independent invention is increased if a complex rather than a single trait is involved. A complex may consist either of several different kinds of objects that occur together or a

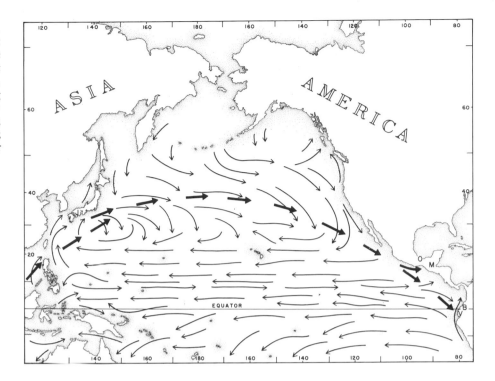

*Ill. 212.* The North Pacific Ocean, showing major currents (light arrows) and the Great Circle Route (heavy arrows), which is the shortest distance for trans-Pacific voyages. Letters designate the following archaeological complexes: J = Jomon, Japan; O = Olmec, Mexico; M = Maya, Mexico and Guatemala; B = Bagia and V = Valdivia, Ecuador (*cf. also Ills. 92–94*).

◀ *Ills. 210, 211.* A tetrapod bowl with incised decoration on a red slipped surface (above left), typical of the well made pottery of the early Valdivia Phase, coastal Ecuador, *c.* 3000 BC, and a small jar with incised, punctated, and appliqué fillet decoration from the Valdivia Phase (below left). The form and decoration of these vessels is remarkably similar to contemporary pottery of Early Middle Jomon sites in western Japan.

number of elements that combine to produce a distinctive result, such as a ceramic style or a complicated game. Although the individual components may appear to be simple and readily reinvented, the chances of their being independently combined in the same manner are infinitesimal.

Another extremely important but rarely mentioned factor is the nature of the trait. All resemblances are not equally significant quite aside from whether or not the foregoing criteria can be met, because certain kinds of socio-political and religious traits cannot be introduced from the outside but can only evolve. Social stratification, for example, cannot develop until a certain level of population concentration has been achieved and this in turn depends upon the productivity of subsistence resources. Without an elite, elaboration of scientific knowledge does not occur. Without occupational division of labour and the resultant opportunity to become skilled in the execution of a craft, certain complicated ideas and techniques cannot be adopted even if they become available for observation. By the same token, the presence of divine monarchs, social classes, clan organization, differential treatment of the dead, standing armies, and other such characteristics cannot be used as evidence of cultural contact.

Theoretically, a professional anthropologist who accepts or rejects a trait or complex presented as evidence of trans-Pacific contact bases his decision on all of the considerations just outlined. In reality, a careful evaluation is rarely made. Frequently, the incompleteness of the archaeological record on both sides of the Pacific Ocean prevents satisfaction of several of the criteria, so that the case can be rejected as 'not proven'. Often too the criteria are applied so rigidly that they can never be met because archaeological evidence simply cannot provide the required details. Nevertheless, a growing number of complexes cannot be explained except as the result of contact, and many anthropologists are convinced not only that trans-Pacific contact took place, but that it occurred repeatedly and independently at different times on different parts of the western coast of the Americas. It should be emphasized that these contacts did not contribute significantly to the population of the New World, since such immigrants must have been few and their genetic composition would have been swamped by interbreeding with the local inhabitants, who were descendants of much earlier immigrants over land via the Bering Strait. It seems increasingly probable, however, that trans-Pacific introductions played an important part in shaping the civilizations that existed at the time of European discovery.

Traits and complexes that have been cited as evidence of trans-Pacific contact include the manufacture of bark cloth, the game of parcheesi (known in Mexico as patolli), the use of a litter to transport persons of high rank, cylindrical pottery vessels with rectanguloid tripod feet and a conical lid, the lost-wax process and other metallurgical techniques, the concept of the zero, animal associations with days of the week, and a variety of other specific and often intricate features. These traits have different distributions in space and time, but several tend to cluster in two geographical areas. One is the coast of Ecuador; the other is the Maya homeland in Guatemala and Mexico. The nature of the resemblances in these two areas is different, largely because of differences in the level of cultural development at the time the introduction occurred. A review of the evidence thus provides some insight into the kinds of traits that appear to be of trans-Pacific origin and the manner in which they have been reshaped during incorporation into the new context.

One of the most astounding archaeological discoveries of the past decade was made by an Ecuadorian amateur archaeologist, who noticed similarities between the earliest pottery on the coast of Ecuador and prehistoric pottery of western Japan. Their significance could not be evaluated immediately, however, because evidence was missing on a number of crucial points. Specifically, there was no assurance that the Japanese and Ecuadorian complexes were contemporary, or that developmental antecedents were absent in the New World but present in Japan. However, the fact that the traits in question were not linked to functional or environmental imperatives, that they formed a complex in both areas, and had a more restricted distribution in the receiving area, favoured the possibility of trans-

*Ills. 213, 214.* Right, typical decorated pottery of the Valdivia Phase, coastal Ecuador: a, excised I; b, two rows of fingernail marks parallel to the rim; c, rocker stamping in depressed rows; d, all-over application of rocker stamping; e–g, drag-and-jab punctation with a toothed implement; h, incision in zigzag pattern; i, row of punctation at the lower margin of the incised zone; j, incision in cross-hatched pattern; k, incision applied in cross-hatch on rim; parallel horizontal lines on neck and zigzag on body; l, rim ornamentation with vertical nicks; m, zone of punctation bounded by zones of incised lines; n, finger pressed grooves with gashes between; o–q, shell scraping in patterns; r, incised interlocking elements on a polished surface; v, folded-over rim. Far right, typical decoration of Middle Jomon pottery, central and western Japan. The arrangement corresponds to that of the Valdivia Phase pottery from Ecuador.

*Ill. 212*

Pacific introduction. Because of the potential significance of such an interpretation, efforts were made to obtain the missing information. As a result, it now seems probable that New World pottery was not independently invented, but is instead an offshoot of an ancient ceramic tradition in Japan.

At around 3000 BC, the Pacific coasts of Japan and America were occupied by small groups of people who derived their food supply from both sea and land. Their dwelling places were easily recognized by the accumulation of shells discarded during decades or centuries of subsistence on marine molluscs. They also fished, hunted, and probably collected edible wild plants. Their tools were made of stone, bone, and shell, and were relatively simple but effective. There was one outstanding difference, however, in the material culture. In Japan, pottery vessels were used for cooking, eating, and perhaps storage, while in the New World containers were made of perishable materials like wood, gourds, or skins.

Pottery has been used in Japan for a long time. When carbon-14 dates were first obtained from the earliest Jomon sites, they were rejected as unreasonably early. A number of sites have now been dated, however, permitting a reconstruction of the evolution of ceramic form and decoration from around 7500 BC up to historic times. Initially, vessel shapes were limited to deep conical-based jars, but as the centuries passed other forms evolved and rim treatments became varied. The earliest pottery was decorated with a few simple techniques, such as brushing, shell stamping, and rouletting. Little by little, these were joined by finger grooving, incising, excising, punctation, appliqué, rocker stamping, and red slipping. By the beginning of the Middle Jomon Period, around 3000 BC, a broad spectrum of vessel shapes and decorative techniques and motifs was being made and used throughout the Japanese islands.

About 3000 BC (the earliest carbon-14 date for the Valdivia complex is 3200 ± 150 BC), shellfish gatherers living on the coast of Ecuador suddenly began to make pottery. In spite of its early date, Valdivia pottery has several remarkable features. First, it is symmetrical, well polished, and tastefully decorated in a wide variety of techniques—a far cry from the crude products of untutored potters. Second, most of the decorative techniques and vessel shapes from the earliest Valdivia levels are identical to those from contemporary Early Middle Jomon sites of Kyushu, Japan. Duplication occurs in surface finish, technique of decoration, motif, combinations of motifs, and variations in rim treatment, to the extent that without reference to the catalogue numbers it is impossible to distinguish fragments originating from sites in Japan from those obtained in Ecuador.

*Ills. 210, 211*

Illustrated are samples of the kinds of similarities involved. Features of special interest include excised I-shaped elements on a polished surface, fingernail marks in parallel horizontal rows, rocker stamping either in an unusual dragged execution forming independent horizontal parallel rows or as an overall pattern, manipulation of a multi-toothed implement in a drag and jab motion to produce adjacent narrow grooves of varying texture, slap-dash incision with

*Ills. 213, 214*

*Ills. 215, 216.* A pottery neckrest of the Bahia culture, Manabí, Ecuador (left), and a wooden neckrest from New Guinea (right). The introduction of neckrests in the New World, where they were unknown, implies contact with Southeast Asia, where they are widely distributed.

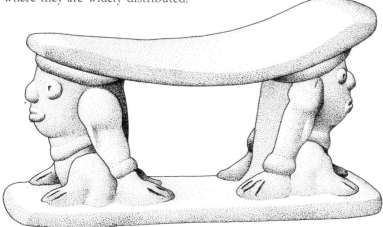

*Ills. 217, 218.* Left, a pottery figurine of the Bahia culture, Manabí, Ecuador, holding panpipes graduated from both sides towards the centre. Right, a pottery figurine from Esmeraldas, Ecuador, playing panpipes of the Asiatic type.

a pointed tool in zigzag or cross-hatch patterns, use of a row of punctates to delimit the lower edge of the incised portion of the vessel, combination of incised motifs in the same manner (cross-hatch on the rim exterior, horizontal lines on the neck, and zigzag on the body), ornament of the rim exterior with parallel vertical slashes, zones filled with punctations bounded by zones filled with parallel incisions, grooves made with the fingertip with the intervening surface embellished with slashes or punctations, scraping of the exterior surface with a multi-toothed implement, interlocking patterns of broad incised lines on a polished surface, broad square-ended incisions arranged in patterns of zoned parallel lines, and rims with an exterior thickening produced by addition of a coil of clay. (Numerous other parallels are described and illustrated in Meggers, Evans, and Estrada, 1965, Pls. 160–186, figs. 99–102.)

In spite of the overwhelming number of similarities, and even identities, between the ceramic complexes of early Valdivia and early Middle Jomon, many archaeologists refuse to accept the conclusion that a trans-Pacific contact is responsible. Two principal objections are raised. One is that the traits involved are all 'simple', and consequently susceptible to independent invention. It is asserted that a person wishing to decorate a plastic surface like clay will experiment with sharp sticks, fingers, and other universally available tools to make lines or rows of marks. Although reasonable in theory, this objection is not supported by fact. One of the reasons that pottery is a valuable indicator of temporal and cultural differences is that it is infinitely variable. Duplications of the kind exhibited by Jomon and Valdivia ceramics simply do not develop in the absence of communication. In fact, whenever they occur within a continent, however distant from one another, they are usually cited as evidence of cultural relationship. Were the Valdivia and Jomon cultures on the same side of the ocean, no one would question that one was derived from the other.

The second common objection is that the ocean is too formidable a barrier to have been crossed by primitive peoples. It is significant that this point is never raised by persons who have visited the Pacific islands or who are amateur sailors, because it is only the landlubbers who view water as an obstacle rather than a convenience. The Jomon peoples of coastal Japan must have been equally at home on water and land, since much of their food came from the sea. Like the modern Micronesians, they were certainly capable of sustaining themselves for considerable periods without returning to land. The self-sufficiency that is crucial to survival at a primitive level of culture declines with the advent of civilization. Few of us cast adrift without food and water could live more than a few days. Five thousand years ago, however, the odds were much better for the coastal inhabitants of Japan or Ecuador. To be sure, the trip would have been long and hazardous and it is probable that many boatloads were lost for every one that reached the New World. The appearance of Jomon-like pottery on the coast of Ecuador, however, is evidence that someone not only survived but was welcomed into the community.

Interestingly, there is evidence that a second contact occurred some 2,500 years later on the same part of the Ecuadorian coast. By this time, the population was living in larger villages and deriving its subsistence primarily from agriculture. Social stratification had begun to develop, occupational specialization probably existed on a small scale, and the need to assure a good harvest was reflected in intensification of religious practices. During this developmental period, a culture is more receptive to certain kinds of outside influence than it is at an earlier or later stage. In this context, the incorporation into the Bahia culture of several kinds of objects previously unknown in the New World but very widely distributed in southeast Asia and Indonesia is intriguing. Most striking are small neckrests, panpipes graduated from both sides towards the centre, models of houses with saddle roofs, columns and other un-American features, and figurines seated with legs crossed so that the right foot rests on the left knee. Structural parallels are numerous. For example, headrests in both continents are constructed with one large support, two or three slender columns, or two human figures uniting the flat base with the curved upper surface. The same peculiar anatomical distortion, in which the shoulders are displaced upward to the side of the head, is represented in both areas.

This evidence for contact differs from the Jomon-Valdivia case in several respects. Whereas a new technology was introduced to Valdivia as well as specific stylistic features, most of the kinds of objects involved in the Bahia complex were already present in the New World. Figurines date back to Valdivia times, pottery models of houses have been found in Peru and Mexico, panpipes are ancient

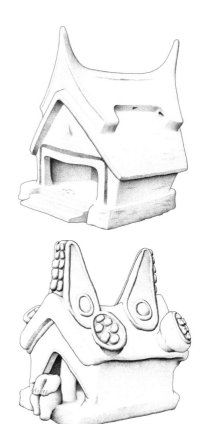

*Ills. 219, 220.* Pottery house models from La Tolita, Ecuador: above, with saddle ridge and double roof construction and, below, with elaborate ornamentation on the roof.

*Ills. 215–218*

*Ills. 219, 220, 222*

*Ills. 223, 224*

*Ills. 215, 216*

246

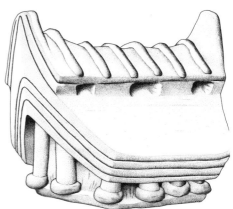

*Ills. 221, 222.* The Ise shrine, Uji-Yamada (above), represents typical Japanese architecture of the Archaic Period. The columns and logs lying horizontally across the ridge are duplicated on a pottery house model from the Bahía culture of Ecuador (right). This pottery vessel (spouts not shown on this drawing) from Esmeraldas has a double roof, a saddle ridge with transverse elements, and a row of columns instead of a wall.

and widespread; only neckrests seem to be something new. Asiatic influence is expressed in stylistic details and modifications in structure or form. New World panpipes are graduated from one side to the other, except on the coast of Ecuador, and even here the double graduated type occurs only for a few centuries. Figurines are particularly abundant in Meso-America, but they rarely show the Asiatic leg position, and when they do the context suggests that influence from Ecuador is responsible. Models of houses elsewhere always have a straight ridge and other characteristics of local architecture; the saddle ridge, gable decoration, roof ornaments, columns, double roof, and other features of the Bahia houses do not occur. Since all of these elements tend to occur in ritual contexts in Asia, it seems probable Ill. 221 that they reflect religious concepts and practices of an intangible nature that were introduced to the prehistoric Ecuadorians from a point of origin somewhere in southeast Asia.

If these two cases, which are relatively simple and which satisfy most of the criteria for judging the significance of cultural similarities, have not received universal acceptance—and they have not—then it is not surprising that instances where much of the evidence is ambiguous are often dismissed as unworthy of serious consideration. This is the attitude towards most of the parallels that have been cited between Meso-America and Asia, beginning with the Olmec culture around 1800 BC and continuing through the Maya civilization after the beginning of the Christian Era. Although numerous specific duplications occur in the calendar, mythology, art, architecture and ceramics, Asiatic influence has been rejected on the grounds that the function is different, that perishable antecedents probably existed, that the elements do not form a complex on either side of the ocean,

*Ills. 223, 224.* A stone figure of a seated Buddha from Campa (Annam), dating from the tenth century AD (left). The position of the legs and arms, the heavy ear ornaments, and the peaked headdress are reminiscent of the Bahia figurines, such as the one illustrated right, which is seated in the position utilized in Asia for religious meditation. The tooth-like necklace pendant, broad bracelets, large ear plugs, and peaked cap are characteristic of this type of figurine.

*Ill. 225.* The west gate of the Great Stupa, Sanci, India, erected during the early part of the first century AD, shows atlantean figures supporting the lintel which are similar to those in *Ill. 226.*

that contemporaneity has not been demonstrated, and failing all else, that it is an insult to the intelligence of the American Indian to suggest that he might not have invented all of these things himself. The unscientific nature of these kinds of objections becomes evident if one takes a closer look at the problems surrounding an attempt to trace the origin of the constituent elements of any high civilization.

One way of achieving perspective is to look at situations where we know that cultural development was strongly and repeatedly influenced from the outside. How would we interpret the rise of civilization in France, for example, if Paris were in ruins, there were no written records, and we had to rely solely on the archaeological

*Ill. 226.* An Olmec altar supported by atlantean figures, from Potrero Nuevo, Mexico.

*Ills. 227, 228.* The tiered construction, steep staircase, small temple and soaring roof of Temple I at Tikal, Guatemala (left) are Asiatic features, as can be seen from the stepped pyramid with a small temple on the summit at Baksei Chamkrong, Angkor, Cambodia (right).

remains? Would we recognize architectural details as the result of Greek or Roman influence or would we consider them independently derived? Even a superficial consideration makes it evident that incorporation of new elements into a flourishing culture involves amalgamation, redefinition, modification, and distortion that alters the original forms and obscures their foreign origin. It is also clear that introductions came piecemeal over centuries from different sources, so that it is impossible to identify a single place of origin, or to isolate similar complexes of features in both donor and receiver areas. Because history tells us that contacts of varying types, including trading, colonization, warfare, political domination, and missionary activity, took place over several millennia, we seldom stop to consider how difficult it would be to reconstruct the story if the only evidence consisted of objects of stone, pottery, or metal.

Another example of the manner in which cultural contact expresses itself in a high culture is provided by comparing modern Spain and

Mexico. We know that Mexico was colonized primarily by Spain, and that Spanish culture was superimposed on the indigenous population. The result is not a faithful reproduction of Spanish art and architecture, however, but something that might be considered independently developed if attention were directed to the differences rather than the similarities and the ocean were conceived as an impassable obstacle.

The Asiatic-appearing elements in Maya culture must be evaluated in this kind of context. The distinctive Maya civilization crystallized around AD 200 from the generalized Meso-American Formative. During the Formative period, which extended from approximately 2000 BC to the beginning of the Christian Era, a number of elements with Asiatic counterparts make their appearance. Many are represented in Olmec art, including the tiger or jaguar as a religious motif, atlantean figures, persons seated in niches beneath the mask of a jawless face, and a predilection for jade. Fortunately, the Olmec carved in stone, so that a large sample of their art is preserved. As yet there is no agreement on the origin of this remarkable early culture and little interest in solving the problem, to judge from the absence of commentary in recent publications (*e.g.* Benson, 1968; Bernal, 1969). When one looks to Asia, the parallels are scattered through China, Indonesia, and India, and date from 2000 BC to AD 1500. While the existing data are not sufficient to warrant the conclusion that contact rather than independent invention is involved, one may suspect that the fault is more with the incompleteness of our knowledge than with the weakness of the case.

*Ill. 226*

*Ills. 202, 203*

*Ill. 225*

*Ills. 229, 230.* The courtyard of the Palace at Palenque (left) shows the typical roof construction of Maya buildings. Similar roof shapes can be seen on the stucco architectural ornamentation of the façade of Lankatilaka Temple, Polonnaruwa, Ceylon, twelfth century AD (right).

During the Formative, Olmec influence permeated much of Meso-America in varying strength and always with some modification due to amalgamation with distinct local traditions. This cultural ferment and regional interaction stimulated the development of urban civilization in several parts of the area. Around the beginning of the Christian Era, Teotihuacán was already a metropolis of 100,000 people. The great Pyramid of the Sun had been built, along with an impressive assemblage of smaller pyramids, plazas, and ceremonial structures. These buildings, like those of other parts of highland Mexico, are relatively unadorned on the exterior and rely upon architectural details like tiers, staircases, and projecting cornices for embellishment.

*Ill. 103*

To the south, in Guatemala and Yucatán, contemporary Maya ceremonial centres look quite different. The Olmec predilection for stone carving has been elaborated not only in the form of stelae and smaller free-standing sculptures, but also applied to the decoration of buildings, where it is combined with mosaic. The jawless face, atlantean figures, and use of jade remain popular, but are submerged into a profusion of other details so that they no longer stand out.

Among these other details are many with Asiatic counterparts, particularly in the construction of the Maya buildings. The solid pyramidal temple substructure is a counterpart of the Hindu stupa and the stepped pyramids of Cambodia; the corbelled arch, resulting in long narrow corridors, is paralleled in southeast Asian temples; the distinctive Mayan roof shape, characterized by a gently rounded top, steeply sloping side, and short projecting eave is depicted on a

*Ill. 227*
*Ill. 228*

*Ills. 229, 230*

temple in Ceylon. Both Mayan and southeast Asian pyramids were scaled via steep staircases, with narrow treads and high risers; both were topped with small massive structures, with space inside only for an image and a few officiating priests; in both cases the roof height was increased beyond functional requirements to achieve a more graceful and impressive appearance.

There are also numerous specific parallels in details of execution. A comparison of the doorway and façade of the east wing of the Nunnery at Chichen Itzá with that of a temple at Prah-Khan, Cambodia reveals the following similarities: inset doorway, rectangular panel above lintel, figure surrounded by a curved 'frame', walls of building covered with ornamentation. The mask or face lacking a lower jaw appears frequently on Maya buildings and also on temples of southeastern Asia. In Asia, it is an ancient motif, depicted on Shang bronzes. In both areas, a serpent-like head with open jaws ornaments the base of columns, door jambs, or balustrades; sometimes a human head or figure appears in the mouth. Interestingly, the creature on Asiatic buildings, although in some respects resembling a snake, often has a long nose. Could this be the origin of the Mayan 'long-nosed god'?

Long noses inevitably lead to speculations about elephants. If elephants could be recognized on Mayan monuments, trans-Pacific contact disputes would immediately cease, since this animal became

*Ills. 231, 232.* The doorway in the east façade of the Annex to the Monjas (Nunnery) at Chichen Itzá (left), a Late Classic Maya construction, shows striking similarities with the Temple at Prah-Khan, Cambodia (above), which was built about AD 1000.

*Ills. 231, 232*

*Ill. 235*
*Ill. 234*

*Ills. 237, 238*

*Ill. 236*

extinct in the New World millennia before the rise of Maya civilization. Proponents have consequently searched for and found elements that look like elephants; opponents have ingeniously and adamantly rationalized them away. One of the most famous battles has raged over the significance of the design above the head of Stela B at Copán, Honduras. To Sir Grafton Elliot Smith, who wrote a book on the matter (*Elephants and Ethnologists,* 1924), it was obvious that the heads of two elephants are shown in profile, each mounted by mahouts; to American archaeologists like Alfred Tozzer and Herbert Spinden, it was equally evident that nothing more exotic was depicted than large-beaked macaws. Logic would appear to be on the side of the elephant-backers, since macaws do not have disproportionately large beaks. It also seems peculiar that the 'macaw' images lack the under part of the beak. Other long-nosed creatures, like that shown on the emblem glyph for Copán, look even less like macaws.

Close examination of the figure shown on Stela B reveals a number of Asiatic parallels in posture, dress and ornament. Comparison with a portrait statue from Madjakerta, East Java is hampered by the ornateness of the Copán stela, but it is evident that the position of the hands, the brim of the headdress, the broad bracelets and upper arm ornaments, ear pendants, heavy collar, and heavily encrusted central panel reaching to the ground are very similar. A Vishnu figure from Bengal dating from the eleventh to twelfth century AD is also reminiscent of exuberant Maya carvings. On the other hand, if one wishes to make an argument for independent origins, there are innumerable differences that can be pointed out. In addition there can be no denying that these two Asiatic statues come from widely separated places and are more recent in date than Stela B at Copán.

Ills. 239, 240

Ill. 233. An emblem glyph for the Maya city of Copán, depicting a creature with a trunk-like nose.

Ill. 242

Ills. 234, 235. The masks of a jawless face ornamenting the façade of the Annex to the Monjas, Chichen Itzá (right), bear a striking resemblance to the two jawless faces which decorate a Shang Dynasty bronze vessel from An-yang, twelfth to eleventh century BC (left).

In spite of a vast literature pointing out parallels between Maya and southeast Asiatic culture emanating from art historians, laymen, and increasingly in recent years from anthropologists, a Maya expert recently stated that 'it should be categorically emphasized that . . . theories involving trans-Pacific or trans-Atlantic contact have never survived scientific scrutiny' (Coe, 1966, p. 52). Yet the supporting material evidence is as strong as that linking Indonesia with India or Europe with the Middle East. Rather than conclude that theories of trans-Pacific contact have failed to survive scientific scrutiny, one might ponder the fact that such theories *have* survived in spite of unscientific scrutiny and grow more rather than less persuasive with the passage of time.

Opponents of trans-Pacific contacts often conclude by magnanimously declaring that 'we could concede them all without affecting the integrity of Nuclear American civilization in a strictly developmental sense' (Phillips, 1966, p. 314). The validity of this assertion, however, is debatable because we have no unequivocal example of a civilization that did develop in complete isolation. All of the Old World centres were in communication, and there is no way of demonstrating that any would have achieved the same level of development without this interfertilization. Nor is there any way of proving that this could not have happened, in our present state of knowledge. We simply do not know what are the crucial factors in the development of civilization, and it is quite possible that features that seem to us to be trivial play a fundamental role.

*Ills. 236–238.* Could the three superimposed representations of the Long-nosed God ornamenting the corner of the Platform of Venus at Chichen Itzá (left) derive from Asiatic features such as the pilasters (above) terminating in a serpent-like long-nosed creature, Chandi Sari, Java, ninth century AD? The niche is surmounted by a jawless face. El Castillo at Chichen Itzá (right) is framed by a similar serpent-based column on the summit of the Temple of the Warriors (*cf. Ill. 195*).

*Ills. 239, 240.* Left, Stela B from Copán, erected during the eighth century AD, and a drawing of the headdress (above) showing a pair of elements that have been interpreted as elephants with mahouts or as stylized macaws.

The acrimonious nature of the debate about trans-Pacific influences on New World cultural development reflects the subconscious realization that more is at stake than the inventiveness of the American Indian. If New World civilizations are part of the Old World diffusion sphere, then civilization has developed only once on this planet. Such a conclusion forces us to recognize that culture is not the free creation of the human intellect, but a unique product of the complicated interaction over many millennia between man's needs and the resources of the environment. If destroyed, there is no assurance that it would rise again in a similar form. Nor is there any ground for assuming that something comparable exists elsewhere in the universe. Although many people find this point of view intolerable, its acceptance is not an admission of defeat for mankind but a sign of long delayed maturity. By paving the way for a rational and realistic appraisal of man's place in nature, it offers the only hope for the continued survival of both nature and man.

*Ills. 241, 242.* The royal portrait statue from Madjakerta, Late East Javanese style (right), and the statue of Vishnu Trivikrama, Bengal, eleventh to twelfth century AD (far right), resemble Maya carvings in general ornateness of execution and in details of dress and ornament.

# The Historic Discovery of America

## 9

**Geoffrey Ashe**

ONE OF THE STRANGEST ASPECTS of all this history is the way the image of the New World, projected three or four times on European minds, faded back into nothingness during the Middle Ages. Islands were still believed in, but no continent. Plato's Atlantis was remembered dimly (by Honorius of Autun, for instance, in the twelfth century), but not the mainland said to lie on the far side of it. The Norsemen lost interest in Vinland; they recalled it merely as another island of vague extent, or as a cape of Africa. Greenlanders were still going over to Markland for timber in 1347, but the Greenland colonies lost touch with Europe, and succumbed to migrant Eskimos. Meanwhile the romance of St Brendan's voyage ought to have immortalized that Promised Land over the ocean, even if it was only a baseless fabric. Yet nobody took much notice of this either. Europeans clung to the vivid, if ill-located, St Brandan's Isle or Isles—not the Promised Land, but far smaller places visited by the saint on his quest—and to the other Irish figment, Brazil. From Hibernian sources, no more.

*Ill. 243*

As map-making improved, imaginations did not rest idle. One modern Russian geographer, Samuel Varshavsky, has even argued that Nicholas of Lynn, an English Minorite friar, somehow had a notion of America in the 1380s. But the only certain result of bolder and better cartography, and of bolder if not better guesswork, was the multiplication of islands already described (Chapter 1). Among them, 'Antillia' and the 'Island of the Seven Cities', whether distinguished or identified, were the most popular. By the fifteenth century both were generally held to exist, though no one could say where the knowledge of either had come from.

Speculation might have remained in this impasse much longer, if it had not been for economic and political pressures. After the Moslem conquests, a real decline had begun depressing the once dominant Mediterranean lands. With the Crusades came a partial recovery and counter-attack, bringing a renewal of eastern commerce, especially by

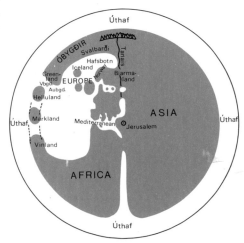

*Ill. 243.* A Norse map of the 'World Circle' showing Vinland as a promontory of Africa.

*Ill. 244.* A detail of a painting by Nuno Conçalves (?) depicting Henry the Navigator, under whose patronage the 'Age of Discovery' began.

*Ill. 245*

Venetians. The Crusades failed and Turks barred the road to India; but by then, Europeans were better equipped to respond. On the west, non-Mediterranean nations—notably the English and Portuguese—had risen in stature and were looking outward. On the east, merchant venturers who found it hard to penetrate Asia by the old routes were no longer disposed to acquiesce; a few, but an energetic few, began looking for new ones.

In 1271 the Polo expedition crossed central Asia to the court of Kublai Khan, and in 1295, after numerous adventures, Marco came home to describe China and other lands. Ship-owners of Genoa were improving the arts of navigation. In 1291 the Vivaldi brothers sailed out through the Straits of Gibraltar, apparently in hopes of reconnoitring a new way to India, and got some distance down the African coast. About twenty years later another Genoese ship reached the Canaries; the island of Lanzarote bears the name of its discoverer. The two impulses of progress, western and eastern, converged in 1317 when King Dinis of Portugal appointed a Genoese merchant, Manuel Pessagno, as 'admiral'. Pessagno was allotted a staff of twenty men from Genoa to serve the outward-looking Portuguese as maritime advisers and pilots.

Achievement did not follow at once, but it followed—largely through the efforts of one patron, Prince Henry, afterwards known as the Navigator (1394–1460). He was a son of King John I of Portugal and the English princess Philippa, daughter of John of Gaunt. Henry spent his own fortune and considerable public funds on the object of giving Portugal supremacy on the Atlantic, and exploring the ocean. He set up headquarters at Cape St Vincent, with a training school, an observatory, and a research institute and library, where he brought together all the experts he could, including Jews and Arabs. From 1416 onwards, the expeditions he sponsored were feeling their way into the open water and around Africa.

Prince Henry may already have cherished the hope which inspired subsequent Portuguese, about a sea-route to India. This did not dawn on him immediately, and perhaps he never saw it clearly at all, but his successors held on to it and pursued it to its final triumphant outcome. The main Portuguese enterprise was never westward. It led, however, to westward exploration. Columbus cannot be understood outside the context of this long search for the Indies, with its various by-products. The type of ship that finally made the crossing, the caravel, was developed to meet the needs of the long-drawn aspiration after Indian wealth.

In Henry's lifetime, progress round Africa was slow. At his death the most successful of Portuguese expeditions had scarcely got as far as Sierra Leone—reached, centuries before, by the Carthaginians (see pp. 81 ff). Coasting proved to be so difficult, the shoals and calms so baffling, the heat and thirst and disease so alarming, that the Portuguese gradually learned to swing farther and farther out into the Atlantic in a vast curve. Meanwhile, they were probing the ocean from other angles. They took possession of the Madeira group in 1418, rediscovered the Canaries in 1419, and settled them a few years later. Influenced, it is said, by the Brendan story, Henry ordered a western foray which took his ships to the nearer Azores about 1427. Colonization began in the 1430s. The remoter islands of the group, Flores and Corvo, were reached by Diogo de Teive in 1452. Always queries arose as to what was beyond. The Portuguese colonists were soon talking, as a matter of course, about such isles as San Borondon, their version of St Brandan's, which they sometimes caught sight of farther west still, but could never quite come up with; while on Tenerife, a legend about a visit by the Irish saint took root among the native Guanches as a 'local tradition'.

On Corvo the Portuguese found what they took to be a message from an earlier people. At the highest point stood a statue of a man on horseback. His left hand rested on the horse, his right pointed west. The pedestal bore an inscription in unknown characters. According to the received account, the sailors lugged the statue downhill and then lost it. More probably they noticed a rock formation which does resemble a rider pointing west, and the tale grew round their report. Columbus is supposed to have seen this natural 'statue'.

After exploring Corvo, Diogo de Teive sailed back northeast, yet with an intuitive conviction that something else lay beyond Corvo. Ten years later King Alfonso V, a nephew of Henry the Navigator, granted two phantasmal islands called Lovo and Capraria (both allegedly visited by Brendan) to a would-be colonist named Vogado . . . if he could find them. He never did. In 1473 a search for San Borondon was undertaken from the Canaries. All this time, other Portuguese were creeping ever farther round Africa. But they were still not round to the Indian Ocean when Columbus began urging that the best route to India was across the Atlantic.

The Portuguese were not alone in their maritime adventuring. Much less is known, however, of anybody else's achievements. The demand for cod and whale was drawing many fishermen, especially Basques and Bretons, out towards Canada. They may have got to the Newfoundland Banks ahead of any acknowledged explorer. Hearsay maintains that they glimpsed Newfoundland itself. But there is no tangible support. The fishermen put nothing in writing. They did not want to betray their secrets to rivals.

Bristol, also, was growing important as a base for far-ranging fisheries, and for voyages aimed frankly at exploration. In 1498 Pedro da Ayala, a Spanish envoy in England, sent a cipher dispatch to Ferdinand and Isabella, saying:

*Ill. 245.* No contemporary paintings exist of the *Santa Maria*, Columbus's flagship. However, this woodcut of a caravel is reproduced in a printed copy of the report which he wrote to Ferdinand and Isabella of Spain in 1493, announcing the results of his expedition.

The people of Bristol have, for the last seven years, sent out every year two, three, or four light ships in search of the island of Brazil and the Seven Cities.

Ayala thought these voyages had been inspired by the Genoese John Cabot. But it is doubtful whether he was in England early enough to account for a process beginning in 1491; and reason exists for suspecting that the Bristol ventures started before that, earlier than Ayala realized.

The terrestrial globe designed by Martin Behaim, a little before Columbus's sailing, shows how European minds were grappling with the Atlantic in the late fifteenth century. They were still not dreaming of any New World. They were thinking, in the first place, of additional islands; and in the second place, more and more insistently, of getting to the Indies and China by sailing west. The idea that the earth was still believed to be flat is untenable. All educated men knew its true shape. With that knowledge, some of them were now re-examining

*Ill. 246.* A planisphere, after the globe drawn by Martin Behaim in 1492.

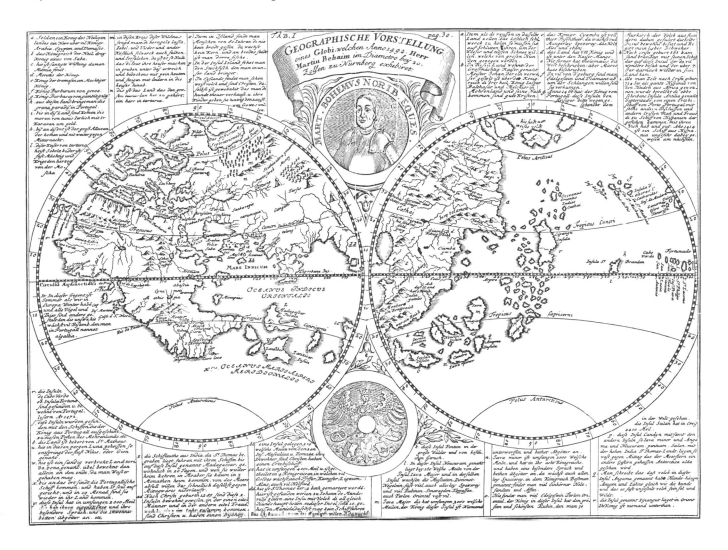

classical authorities such as Strabo, who had not only written of circumnavigation early in the Christian era, but hinted that sailors had actually tried it; and Aristotle, or rather a treatise ascribed to him, where they read that the westward passage from Spain to the Indies would require only a few days.

Was it so? How far would you need to sail: a possible or an impossible distance? That was the major question. The geography of Ptolemy, still commonly accepted, implied a magnitude for Asia from which it followed that the crossing—if unobstructed—would be immensely long. And Ptolemy, of course, was right. In the fifteenth century, however, a theory was gaining favour (based in part on Marco Polo) that Asia extended much farther east than Ptolemy thought, and thus came closer to Europe.

This theory had been expounded as far back as 1410 by Pierre d'Ailly, Cardinal of Cambrai, in a book entitled *Imago Mundi*. Those who endorsed it drew attention to such evidence as objects washed up on the beaches of the Azores and Europe by the Gulf Stream drift—corpses with features asserted to be Mongolian, and pieces of alien wood, sometimes with tool marks. The hard brazil wood which, in reality, came from Mexico, got over to Ireland in sufficient quantities for trade. 'Irish wood' was exported to France during the 1460s and employed to panel a library in the Louvre. Such things were certainly proof or near-proof of land to the west, and not colossally far off. Asia, said the enthusiasts. It seems not to have occurred to any of them that the land might be something hitherto unthought of.

One of them, the Florentine Paolo Toscanelli, was the chief theoretical inspirer of Columbus. On 25 June 1474 he sent Alfonso of Portugal a report which the King had asked for on the whole subject of getting to the Indies. In this Toscanelli spoke up for the hypothetical Atlantic route. He cited Marco Polo, grossly underestimated the distances, and argued that Antillia and Zipangu (Japan) could be stepping-stones. He made the distance from the Canaries to Japan only 3,000 nautical miles. It is 10,600. America was rediscovered through a monstrous miscalculation.

Even before obtaining Toscanelli's report, King Alfonso may have sponsored a western voyage. Some historians think he beat Columbus by twenty years but never followed up his success. Mystery shrouds this affair. It appears that Alfonso arranged with Christian I of Denmark for a joint Portuguese-Danish expedition. The principal Portuguese member was João Vaz Corte Real, governor of Terceira in the Azores from 1474. The voyage was made—if it was made—shortly before his appointment. Corte Real has a memorial in Lisbon as the discoverer of America, meaning—if anything—Newfoundland and a portion of mainland Canada. However, the documentation is late and dubious.*

*Ill. 247*

*Sophus Larsen, *The Discovery of North America Twenty Years before Columbus.*

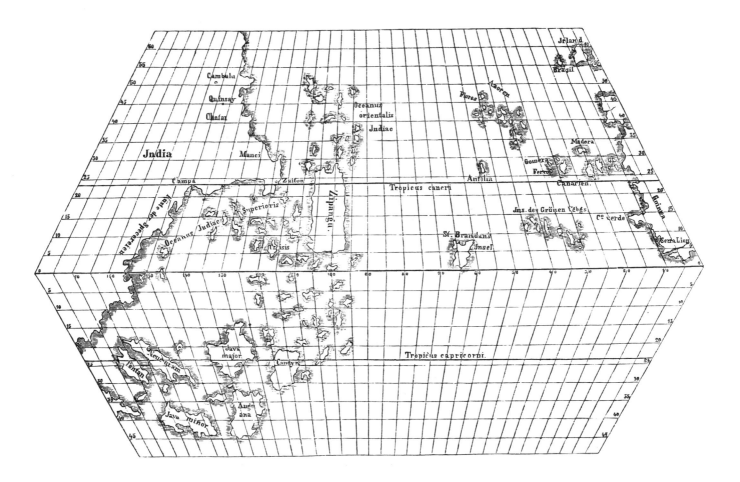

Ill. 247. A reproduction of Toscanelli's map of the world. This
fifteenth-century cartographer
argued that the Antilles, the mythical St Brendan's Isle and Zipangu
(Japan) were stepping-stones across
the Atlantic to the Indies.

*Ill. 249*

When Columbus himself began to be noticed, the two topics of
debate were firmly established: the hope of more islands, notably
Antillia, and the hope of a western sea route to the Orient. The
traditional view is that Columbus was concerned almost entirely with
the latter goal. Sceptical scholarship has tried to maintain that he
started out with the former, like so many others, and added the Indies
as an afterthought. However, his own words and contemporary
documents support tradition. His interest in potential islands was as
ports of call only. As for discovering a new continent, he had no more
notion of that than anybody else.

Columbus came from Genoa, the city which had supplied so much
invention and expertise already. His own vision, or obsession, sprang
from a mixture of motives. Some were spiritual. Despite signs of
renewal, much of Europe had succumbed to a dark mood. The
Church was corrupt, the Holy Roman Empire was futile, the Turks
had taken Constantinople and overrun the Balkans; morality was at
a low ebb and so, in most countries, were the arts. Columbus believed
that a kind of opening-to-the-west would revive Christendom, not

only through fresh activity and expansion, but through missionary work. A devout Christian, he saw his Occident-Orient as the field where the Church could regain purpose and fervour, and enlarge its shrunken ranks with millions of converts.

These dreams combined crusading faith with psychological foresight, and gave his propaganda a touch of mystique which the merely commercial arguments lacked. The case which he presented was a medley of sound reasoning, wishful thinking, biblical dogma, and sheer rationalization. It grew over the years, and he wandered from country to country gathering material to fuel the flame.

He went to Galway and studied the Atlantic flotsam. He may also have discussed legends with the natives. According to his son Ferdinand he was inspired partly by reports of 'the islands of St Brendan of which wonderful things are told'. On his own testimony, however, he heard of Brendan through Portuguese media, so he need not have picked up anything directly in Ireland; and a persistent belief that he took an Irishman with him in 1492 appears to be unfounded.

The same doubt about local inquiry applies to a visit he made to Iceland in 1477. It has been contended that he could have heard surviving traditions of Vinland, perhaps through a saga recital. But Ferdinand, when listing the supposed islands that were mentioned in his father's notes, says nothing of this. Columbus's discovery seems to have been independent of Leif's.

From Toscanelli, and later from Pierre d'Ailly, he adopted the 'big Asia' theory and the corresponding 'narrow Atlantic' theory. His reading of Marco Polo caused him to lay heavy stress on Japan, and he improved on even the sanguine Toscanelli by shifting Japan to within 2,400 miles of the Canaries. Among classical authors he was impressed (characteristically) by the poetic text in Seneca's tragedy *Medea,* quoted on p. 95. Ironically, the Roman with his 'new worlds' was more accurate than the Genoese.

Columbus, like generations of fellow-citizens before him, went first to Lisbon. It was still the logical place to promote his scheme. Late in 1484 he obtained an audience with King John II, a young and ruthless monarch with a truly Portuguese zeal for seafaring. John had just set up a Maritime Advisory Committee which was working on improved techniques for determining latitude. Also he had just secured his own throne by having several relatives made away with. He was able to devote a free and well-disposed mind to Columbus's proposals.

Their talks were indecisive. John thought the Genoese boastful and untrustworthy, and did not accept his exaggerated claims about Japan. Columbus was handed over to three members of the advisory committee, and they thought much the same. They regarded him as a re-hasher of Marco Polo, who was untrustworthy himself. Nothing

266

*Ill. 248.* A portrait of John II of Portugal (1455–95). The inscription on this portrait is believed to be false, as John Emanuel, who would have been King John IV of Portugal, never in fact reigned. John II was initially interested by Columbus's proposed expedition, but when Bartholomew Dias rounded the Cape of Good Hope in 1488, the Portuguese king ceased to back a western route to India in favour of an eastern one.

*Ill. 248*

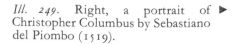

*Ill. 249.* Right, a portrait of ▶ Christopher Columbus by Sebastiano del Piombo (1519).

HAC·EST·EFFIGIES·LIGVRIS·MIRANDA·
RALE·QVI·PENETRAVIT·IN·

COLVMBI·ANTIPODVM·PRIMVS
ORBEM·

is more curious in this whole final debate than the way the sceptical experts were always right, and Columbus wrong.

Columbus asked John II to equip three caravels, with the specific aim of reaching Japan. John did not consent, but neither did he immediately refuse. He was impressed enough to encourage a foray by two of his subjects (at their own expense) with the limited objective of finding Antillia. Their caravels sailed from Terceira in the Azores on 1 March 1487, but they made the mistake (Columbus, later, did not) of starting too far north and running into the westerlies. Their failure did not quite destroy the King's interest. What did destroy it, in December 1488, was the return of Bartholomew Dias from his rounding of the Cape of Good Hope. At long last the eastward sea route to India was visibly opening, and Portuguese receptivity to a western project died away.

Meanwhile Columbus had been taking soundings in England and France, without result, but had also made his first real impact in a talk with Queen Isabella of Spain in May 1486. The Spanish negotiation was long-drawn and exasperating. Columbus put obstacles in his own path by his exorbitant demands for power and profit under the Spanish Crown in any lands he might win for it; his family had not been well off, and he was over-anxious to safeguard his own interests. Again he confronted experts, at the University of Salamanca, and again he met the rooted and right objection that he was understating the distance.

Yet he got his three caravels, went aboard on 3 August 1492, sailed to the Canaries, and then struck out to accomplish what we know. He made his landfall on San Salvador—Watlings Island in the Bahamas—on 12 October. From that moment the reunion of the worlds was an irreversible fact.

*Ills. 250, 251*

But it was still not a realized fact. Europe's awareness of America was still several years away. The closing chapter is an amazing tale of intellectual contortion and self-deception. The discoverer spent his remaining years struggling to prove, against mounting evidence, that he was not entitled to be so called. He had pinned his enterprise on Asia, and been appointed Admiral on that understanding. Asia, therefore, his discovery had to be. So it continued to be, through a series of four voyages and almost to his death. He said first that Cuba was Japan, and made hopeless attempts to reconcile the country and people with Marco Polo's account. Giving that up, he argued next that it was a promontory of China, and shrank from the action of sailing round it which would have refuted him. On his third voyage he touched the South American mainland, and decided (with an echo of the *Voyage of St Brendan*) that he had come to the confines of the Earthly Paradise as described in Genesis. On his fourth voyage he got to the isthmus of Panama and said it must be Malaya.

*Ills. 250, 251.* Left, this is the first graphic representation of American Indians and was reproduced in the first edition of Columbus's letter to Sanchez, Barcelona, 1493. It shows Columbus landing in America, while King Ferdinand of Spain looks on. An idealized version of the same scene, drawn two hundred years later by Theodor de Bry (above), shows Columbus being offered gifts by the natives of San Salvador while three members of his crew erect a cross.

The nearest he ever came to accepting the title of a discoverer, in the full sense, was a belated admission that South America was a continent unrecorded by Marco Polo. Still, however, he insisted that the West Indies were the East Indies. South America had to be fitted in as a sort of Australia. It was because of the Admiral's own stubbornness that the New World was not called Columbia. Instead it received the Latinized name of Amerigo Vespucci, an unimportant, dishonest, and none too loyal colleague but an excellent propagandist, whose sole distinction was that he published the truth which the Admiral resisted to the end of his days.

# Conclusion

**Geoffrey Ashe**

To SPEAK OF AMERICA as the goal of a Quest may sound misleading. So far as we can tell, a trans-Atlantic continent was never deliberately searched for by anyone. Explorers in other regions have had more precise objectives. The Polos searched for Cathay, and found it. Hudson searched for the North-West Passage, and failed to find it. Tasman searched for a southern continent, and found, not exactly that, but Australia and New Zealand. By contrast, those who were borne towards the New World, in mind or body, seem to have made the voyage in comparative vagueness and even delusion. Columbus himself never tried to find it. In a sense he tried not to.

However, a quest is more profound than a search. It is a spiritual adventure. It need not imply any exact idea of what one is looking for. Rather, it is rooted in a persistent unrest or yearning, a reaching out. The familiar life is unsatisfying; the familiar world is not all; somewhere *out there* is a mystery. There are those, like the speaker in Housman's poem, who feel the mystery but fear it, and turn away. There are others, the questers, who go forward to probe it.

For people in the Old World before Columbus, 'that-which-lies-across-the-Ocean' was a mystery which slowly acquired a character. The impulse to probe—even in imagination—never affected more than a few at any time; but it came and went and then came again, in different forms and with a variety of motives. Whether or not Plato *Ill. 8* and Plutarch drew on traditions of actual voyaging, their myths were *Ill. 10* the speculative flights of bold minds, unwilling to be enclosed in the Oecumene. The same dialogue of Plutarch that portrays his 'America' also discusses whether the Moon is inhabited. At the opposite extreme, the practical Norsemen were restless because of the scarcity of good land, the rigours of an arctic climate, the feeling that beyond Greenland there must be something better. Between those extremes we must place Columbus's weird mixture of religion, fantasy, greed and genius; and the Celtic imagination that carried real and fictitious curraghs into the sunset; and the obscure energies that drove anonymous seafarers outward from the ancient Mediterranean and Japan.

Always mystery lay beyond the horizon. The spirit which tried to pierce it was a questing spirit. And embedded in the mystery, as it turned out, was a continent.

What emerges from the inquiries outlined in this book? Have its contributors shown any clear advances in knowledge, whether positively by producing new arguments, or negatively by refuting old ones?

On the long-vexed question of the Viking discovery we now have a final 'yes', thanks to Helge Ingstad, in terms consistent with the sagas. As Canadian archaeology expands, it will be interesting to see if any more settlements come to light. But while research has substantiated Norsemen at one point, it gives no warrant for credulity about them elsewhere. The solidity of L'Anse aux Meadows does not improve the credentials of the Newport Tower or the Kensington Stone. On the contrary, as Birgitta Wallace makes clear, it is time to sweep aside a great deal of accumulated fantasy, and concentrate on our single fact.

Ill. 152
Ill. 147
Ill. 132

There is still an apparent loose end in the Norse evidence—the group of literary allusions to 'Great Ireland' or 'White Men's Land'. This place is as well documented as Markland or Helluland, and there are earlier references to it. Scholars' reluctance to admit as much, their eagerness to write off *Irland-ed-Mikla* as a fable, is due mainly to the asserted presence of Irishmen where no Irishmen should be. Zealots who have located this colony in America, and pointed to the utterly un-Irish North Salem ruins as evidence, have not helped matters. But I suggest that the neglected clue in Al-Idrisi is enough to remove the main obstacle. There need be no difficulty about an Irish or Irish-descended settlement in Greenland, and it would fit in with knowledge apparently revealed in the Brendan narrative. If that is granted, we may surely hope that the Great Ireland texts will be given due weight by future historians, that archaeologists in Greenland will bear them in mind, and that the extravagant claims based on them will be heard no more.

Ills. 148, 149

Dismissal of the case for an Irish colony in America is, I believe, another advance in knowledge which the authors of this book have achieved. But the loose end, though tied up, draws attention to a second loose end. The Great Ireland allusions still drive us back to the larger problem of the Irish as discoverers, and the legend of Brendan. Here also discussion has been bedevilled by wishful thinking, and an unwillingness to face the true issues. The insoluble question, 'What did St Brendan actually do?' can lead only to dead ends and uncritical fancies. The proper question to ask is 'What Irish geographical knowledge does the legend reveal?' Since the author of the *Navigatio Sancti Brendani* shows signs of having collected considerable Atlantic lore, including ideas about southwest Greenland, his glimpses of the farther ocean command respect.

Too much stress has been laid on the vast western country which the legendary saint finally reaches. It can be fully explained as a literary-religious figment, rooted in the fertile soil of classical and post-classical speculation. The river identified by enthusiasts as the Ohio is more likely to be the upper Euphrates. It is not the climax of the story that has geographical interest, but the loose end—the account of the pellucid sea and possible West Indies, with the flat island that could be in the Bahamas, and the semi-tropical one that could be Jamaica. Medieval agreement in ignoring the alleged paradisal continent, and picturing 'St Brandan's Isle' as much smaller and lying southwest, accords with the view that here if anywhere we have traces of a factual tradition.

*Ill. 19*

For the moment this puzzle must simply remain puzzling. Even if we accept that the *Navigatio* author heard some rumour of the West Indies, and incorporated it into the legend, we have no clue as to where it came from. It was not necessarily from the real St Brendan, or from any Irishman. Like several portions of the *Navigatio,* it may be a legacy from the classical world. When we turn to that world, to Plato and Plutarch and the rest, it is the loose ends yet again which are intriguing—the oddments, in admittedly mythical settings, which are not themselves myth-like.

Opinions of the Atlantic crossing in Plutarch are bound to be subjective to some extent. J. V. Luce, despite his own negative verdict, makes it clear that dogmatic rejection would be unwise. Half a dozen stubborn particulars snag the mind.

For example, Sulla says that the voyagers reach Ogygia by sailing five days west from Britain. As to the direction, this will work well enough if they go from Cape Wrath in Scotland to Cape Farewell in Greenland, coasting on afterwards; and even the too-brief transit has an eerie rightness-in-wrongness. Similar errors, for distances measured into the same quarter, occur in such undoubtedly factual works as those of Adam of Bremen, Ari Frode and Al-Idrisi. For some reason an understatement of the width of this part of the Atlantic is a chronic mistake, and Sulla's description fits a pattern.

Again, he indicates that in late autumn there are icy seas far west of Britain—a surprising guess if it is a guess, since nothing was then known of the climatic difference between Britain and Canada caused by the Gulf Stream. Sulla is also credible about the distance from Ogygia (if we take Ogygia as Greenland) to the farther continent; he speaks of a following wind, and floating ice and debris, exactly where these details belong—on the Labrador side of Davis Strait; and most startling of all, the latitude which he implies for the mouth of the bay containing Cronus's island is correct within a degree for the Gulf of St Lawrence.

If we compare the passage with a modern geographical text, we shall doubtless not be much impressed. But that is not the way to judge it. The fair comparison is with ancient geographical texts.

Within a few years of Plutarch's dialogue, Pliny the Elder published his *Natural History*. This contains a description of what is encountered if the Atlantic is navigated southwards instead of northwards—the African coast and neighbouring islands. Pliny is certainly using reports of real voyages. Yet he is less intelligible, harder to square with a modern map, than Plutarch.

The problems raised by Cronus, the banished Titan, are beyond the scope of a study of exploration. Elsewhere I have argued in detail that the Titans, Atlantis, and other westward-looking motifs in Greek myth, should be viewed in conjunction with the megalithic cultures. These flourished during the third and second millennia BC, and spread from Malta and Africa to the Iberian peninsula, Brittany, and the British Isles. Contact with America in that distant age would have been technologically feasible, though the gap between the megalith-builders and Plutarch is hard to bridge.

Everything shades off into obscurity, and there is no direct evidence. It is curious, however, that one further loose end in the data seems to be megalithic in implication if it is anything. We have seen how, apart from L'Anse aux Meadows, all the alleged archaeological traces in North America have collapsed under scrutiny: all but one. Mystery Hill, North Salem, remains to be finally accounted for.

*Ills. 148, 149*

My own impression of it (received in 1960, renewed in 1969) is that it is more cryptic than Birgitta Wallace suggests, and not in the same class with the other 'remains' which she refutes so conclusively and valuably. I have looked at one or two of the asserted parallel cases, as at Newton, and they are not parallel; they do not match the oddly megalithic effect, overall and in detail.

I retain reservations about this site, because I know the story. At the time of my first visit, expert opinion dismissed the whole thing contemptuously (and without inspection) as 'Pattee's Folly' and nothing more—the work of the nineteenth-century farmer who owned the hill. In my book *Land to the West* I offered reasons for thinking otherwise. I was reprimanded for this, but no refutation was forthcoming, and the Pattee theory was merely repeated as the truth.

Now, a decade later, the official orthodoxy has been tacitly dropped: Birgitta Wallace proposes an Indian-Early-Colonial-Pattee composite. Well enough; it may be so. But when the first iconoclasm quietly breaks down, I fail to see why a fair-minded inquirer should acquiesce uncritically in the second. Nothing has been proved except that the site deserves further study. That, however, has been proved amply. Whatever the eventual result, those who insisted, against ridicule, that Mystery Hill *was* more than Pattee's Folly have been vindicated.

So to Central and South America. Here the emphasis is reversed. It is the New World that supplies most of the evidence. The problem is to discover what to connect it with in the Old. And the effect—in reverse—is similar. We find the same disjointed impressiveness, the same difficulty in explaining everything away. There is one archaeological link-up which, if confirmed, corresponds to L'Anse aux Meadows . . . but nothing else that coheres; only an impression of 'something there'.

Betty Meggers's Jomon-Valdivia parallel seems to connect Ecuador with Japan in a remote past. Her other findings are deeply interesting, but, for the moment, indecisive. What they drive home most strongly is the general moral of this book—the need, not merely for more research, but for co-ordinated research, with wider and bolder communication among specialists in different fields.

Thor Heyerdahl underlines a paradox. The most haunting and baffling New World evidence faces the wrong way. We are told most circumstantially of the foreign gods—and they come from the Atlantic. The Japanese are no help with them. But neither (despite several efforts to establish a link) are the Irish or the Vikings.

Until fairly recently it was possible to dismiss Viracocha and Quetzalcoatl as pure myths. Some historians even hazarded the view that their beards and their general appearance were afterthoughts, added after the Spanish conquest, to improve the story. It may be that several details actually were added in this way. Certainly one is wary of exploits that sound too Christian (walking on the water, for instance), which could have been put into the Indians' minds by missionaries asking them leading questions. But we know now that the beards were not invented, nor were the god-men themselves, because, as Heyerdahl rightly insists, we have the art-works portraying them. Also, we can localize. There is good reason to believe that whatever events underlie the legend, its starting-point is on the Atlantic side, not the Pacific—on the coast of the Gulf of Mexico, probably its southern portion, the Gulf of Campeche.

Heyerdahl is an investigator with a style of his own. Nothing can shake the evidence of *Kon-Tiki* and *Ra,* as far as it goes. His practical proof that he knows what he is talking about must strengthen the credentials of his arguments, such as those drawn from the presence of beans, bottle-gourds and cotton in early America. But when he pursues the bearded gods, he is going over ground which I have traversed myself; and it seems to me that any summing-up must, in fairness, take note of an alternative possibility.

He and I agree on the main point. Somewhere in the New World—south of the Rio Grande, and before the Christian era—there were living human originals of the gods: pale-skinned men with beards, alien to the local stock, and higher in culture. Where I hesitate is in accepting his picture of these aliens as culture-bringers over an immense area and a long period—first landing in Mexico and influencing the natives there; then wandering east and south by stages, with the same effect (in varying degrees) at each halt; eventually climbing and civilizing the Bolivian heights; and, after that, sailing off into the Pacific.

This view of them is based chiefly on arguments from tradition and art. Heyerdahl implies that wherever we find the legend of white men firmly rooted, and wherever we find portrayals of men with beards, these facts point to his alien culture-bringers as having existed, historically, in that place.

Now evidence of the former type need not point to this at all. It only points to their having existed somewhere. Let us record a few parallels. The Hindu epic *Mahabharata* describes 'Yavanas' or Greeks taking part in a war north of Delhi, hundreds of years before the siege of Troy. The poet has transferred these Greeks from northwestern India, where Alexander the Great planted them in the fourth century BC, to another place and another time. Alexander himself was real enough, yet Arabian legend makes him go dragon-slaying in the Canary Islands, where he never was. The tales of King Arthur and his knights probably go back to a real British leader with an armed band; but when local lore talks of Arthur in Kincardine, the inference of his actual presence becomes dubious, and when it conveys him to Mount Etna, the inference breaks down entirely. A good story spreads; the fame of heroes spreads. A tribal legend, reported by Dr Manuel O. Zariquiey, locates Columbus himself at the bottom of a lake in the Venezuelan backwoods—for reasons which no biographer would accept.

Even when legendary figures are associated with known events or with standing structures, as at Tiahuanaco, the association proves nothing. Minnesinger fable ascribes much ancient architecture to 'Dietrich of Bern', *i.e.* the Gothic king Theodoric, quite erroneously. It is common knowledge that Stonehenge, England's Tiahuanaco, was built by Druids; common knowledge is mistaken.

On literary grounds it is more than conceivable that most of the stories gathered by Heyerdahl, and by Brinton before him, reflect mainly the spread of an American saga—the Saga of the Wonderful White Men. Somewhere this did indeed originate in actual events. Then it was diffused, orally and slowly, from tribe to tribe. Each nation adopted the heroes and related them to its own gods, its own myths, its own culture, with the diverse results that emerged into view after the Spanish Conquest. But the white visitors who inspired the saga need not have gone far, or stayed in the New World long. They might have been Norsemen if only the dates were right. The dates, however, are not right; and they are still not right if we try (as Irish authors have done in the past) to identify Quetzalcoatl with St Brendan.

The natural retort is to invoke the second class of evidence. What about those bearded faces in sculpture and ceramic work, all the way from Mexico to Bolivia? Do they not prove that the models were physically present?

As with Mystery Hill, I can only give my own impression, based on inspection of a wide range of these art-objects, in a short enough time for all of them to remain fairly fresh in my memory. During the journey on which the survey was made, it struck me that the same could happen with art as with story-telling. Bearded faces could have been copied from bearded faces. Only the prototypes would have required living models. The plain truth is that while some of the objects carry a vivid impact, most of them look more like copies than portraits.

For example, the museum at Oaxaca in southern Mexico displays several small figures of bearded men from the Zapotec site of Monte Alban. They are seated, and wear what appear to be showy head-dresses. Other figures of the same type have been unearthed at Mitla, a second Zapotec site nearby. Pots from El Salvador have similar faces on them. As to such peripheral items, guesswork in detail would be rash. But the Zapotec ones are quite clearly variations on a theme. If the prototype exists, it is probably the Olmec fire-god who squats cross-legged in the Museo Nacional in Mexico City, with a brazier on his head. The fire-god might well be the work of an artist who had seen bearded men. There is no reason to think that his stylized derivatives are.

*Ill. 200*

*Ill. 201*

In Bolivia and Peru the case for sculpture from life is weaker still. To a beard-hunter, the contrast between the archaeological museum in La Paz and its Mexican counterparts is obvious at once. As far as I know, the only beards in it which are even arguable are on some very worn figures from Titicaca Island, and these could be chinstraps or decorations. I cannot recall an entirely unequivocal sculptured beard in all the Viracocha country. With the alleged specimens, it seems to me that the legend may have put the idea into people's heads. Certainly there is nothing like the realistic and varied array of beards which can be assembled in parts of Mexico. The only good Peruvian items are the Chimu jars from the north coast. Some are fairly realistic, but all are stereotyped. That part of Peru is believed, on other grounds, to have been influenced from Central America. I cannot see that the jars have any feature which rules out copying from Central American designs. The ultimate model, once again, might be the Olmec fire-god; or perhaps the fine clay head from Tres Zapotes in Mexico which, as Heyerdahl observes, the Chimu effigies resemble.

*Ill. 172*

*Ill. 199*

Throughout the territory covered, these bearded images suggest living originals to me in one area only, and in one culture only. The Olmec specimens (plus one or two from places under the Olmecs' influence) carry conviction. If white men came, they came to this

*Ill. 203*

southern Mexican zone, during the age when the Olmecs flourished: a conclusion which agrees precisely with the shape of the legend. It is in this country, and in this period, that the oldest versions of it are placed. If we try picturing a saga of white men being transmitted through America, and an art-motif of bearded figures also being transmitted through America, we shall be guided back to the same probable origin by both routes. The coincidence is surely impressive.

With profoundest respect for Heyerdahl's theory of migrant culture-bringers, I cannot understand why portraiture should have faded out as their migration took them farther from Mexico. The ubiquitous legend might appear to support either theory equally. But does it, in fact? It never portrays the whites as forming a fixed clan, a recognized element in society. The culture-bringing which it ascribes to them is always a special mission, of limited duration. They come and go, they never settle for very long. No white women or children are mentioned. The only begetting in any form of the legend is with native women on Titicaca Island; and the mestizos thus produced are said to have driven their white progenitors out.

If the supposedly wandering white men were culture-bringers from the Old World, which culture did they bring? The classic civilizations of Mexico and Peru are not like any Old World culture, or like each other. The date which Heyerdahl assigns for the reed-boat crossings does not fit anything on the American side. Difficulties arise from the Mexicans' ignorance of metallurgy until far later times, and also from their strange use of the wheel.

This last matter is very strange indeed. They are often alleged not to have known the wheel at all. This is inaccurate; some of them did know it: yet in spite of the acute need for it, they made it a plaything *Ill. 114* only. Little toy dogs on wheels have been dug up at Vera Cruz. It is as if a few early Mexicans encountered people who showed them wheels, and the contact lasted just long enough for them to grasp the principle but not the potentialities. Lack of draught animals was no deterrent; the richer communities had plenty of slaves.

There is one observed parallel to this affair of the bearded gods, and it favours a temporary and limited sojourn rather than a prolonged penetration. During the first half of the twentieth century, and especially in the Second World War, various Pacific islands were visited by Europeans and Americans who did not settle. The islanders caught glimpses of the white man's technology and possessions, and were then left to reflect on what they had seen. Presently they were found to have invented a new religion. The so-called Cargo Cults were all centred on the idea that the foreigners would return bringing boundless wealth, and nobody would have to work any more.

One of the best attested cases was the cult of John Frum, on Tanna in the New Hebrides. John Frum, its god, was represented by an

image of a wh
come back. N
bottom of a v
from memory,
on the radio,
would bring '
work, and mc

If we apply
that pale-skin
people picked
them with aw
gods of them,
up residence i

I put forw
Heyerdahl's g
evidence he h
say where the
dwelling on t
problem of ea
same as the p
question is la
Meggers poin
tion has got
infectious abe
necessarily m
the window v
The theme of

Cultural di
contact. Diffu
however, do
diffusion. On
native Ameri
American cul
strably wrong

The proble
of the most
reality does r
them as cultu
be explained
without admi
however forc
more elusive
persons unkr
before the fir
existed.

HEYERDAHL, Thor: I *American Indians in the Pacific*, George Allen and Unwin, London 1952; II *Sea Routes to Polynesia*, George Allen and Unwin, London 1968.

HAKLUYT, Richard, *Principal Navigations, Voyages, Traffiques and Discoveries . . .*, 12 Vols., Hakluyt Society Publications, extra series, 1903–5.

HOLAND, Hjalmar R.: I *Explorations in America before Columbus*, Twayne Publishers, New York 1956; II *A Pre-Columbian Crusade to America*, Twayne Publishers, New York 1962; III *Westward from Vinland: an Account of Norse Discoveries and Explorations in America, 982–1362*, Duell, Sloan and Pearce, New York 1940.

IDRISI, Al-, *Geography*, edited and translated by P. A. Jaubert, Vol. 2, 1840.

INGSTAD, Helge, *Westward to Vinland*, Jonathan Cape, London; St. Martins Press, New York 1969.

MALLERY, Arlington H., *Lost America, the Story of Iron-Age Civilization Prior to Columbus*, 1951.

NANSEN, Fridtjof, *In Northern Mists*, translated by A. G. Chater, 2 Vols., Heinemann, London 1911.

O'DELL, Andrew C., *The Scandinavian World*, 1957.

OXENSTIERNA, Count Eric, *The Norsemen*, Greenwich (Conn.) 1965.

PLATO, *Timaeus* and *Critias*, in Vol. 3 of the *Dialogues*, translated by Benjamin Jowett, 1953.

PLUTARCH, *The Face in the Orb of the Moon*, edited and translated by A. O. Prickard, 1911.

POHL, Frederick J.: I *Atlantic Crossings before Columbus*, Norton & Co., New York 1961; II *The Lost Discovery: Uncovering the Track of the Vikings in America*, Norton & Co., New York 1952; III *The Viking Explorers: Their Lives, Customs, and Daring Voyages . . .*, Thomas Y. Crowell, New York 1966.

SAUER, Carl O., *Northern Mists*, 1968.

THOMSON, J. Oliver, *History of Ancient Geography*, Cambridge 1948.

WAUCHOPE, Robert, *Lost Tribes and Sunken Continents*, University of Chicago Press, Chicago 1962.

WESTROPP, T. J., *Brasil and the Legendary Islands of the North Atlantic*, 1912.

WILLIAMSON, Kenneth, *The Atlantic Islands*, 1948.

## Special Bibliographies

### CHAPTERS 1, 9

DEACON, Richard, *Madoc and the Discovery of America*, 1967.

DUNN, Joseph, 'The Brendan Problem', *Catholic Historical Review*, January 1921.

FISHER, James, *Rockall*, Geoffrey Bles, London 1956.

JOYCE, Patrick, *Old Celtic Romances*, 1961.

JUBINAL, *La Légende Latine de S. Brandaines*, 1836.

KENNEY, James F., *The Sources for the Early History of Ireland*, Vol. 1, 1929.

LARSEN, Sophus, *The Discovery of North America Twenty Years before Columbus*, 1924.

MAJOR, R. H., *The Voyages of the Venetian Brothers Nicolo and Antonio Zeno*, 1873.

MERRIEN, Jean, *Christopher Columbus*, 1958.

MEYER, Kuno, and NUTT, Alfred, *The Voyage of Bran*, 2 Vols., 1895, 1897.

MORISON, Samuel Eliot, *Christopher Columbus: Admiral of the Ocean Sea*, 1942.

O'DONAGHUE, Denis, *Brendaniana*, 1893.

PLUMMER, Charles: I *Bethada Naem Nerenn (Lives of the Saints of Ireland)*, 2 Vols., 1922; II *Vitae Sanctorum Hiberniae*, 1910.

RENAULT, Gilbert, *The Caravels of Christ*, 1959.

Schröder, Carl, *Sanct Brandan*, 1871.

Stephens, Thomas, *Madoc*, 1893.

Stokes, Whitley, *Lives of the Saints from the Book of Lismore*, 1890.

Thrall, William Flint, 'Clerical Sea Pilgrimages and the Immrama', *Manly Anniversary Studies in Language and Literature*, 1923.

Williamson, Kenneth, and Boyd, J. Morton, *St. Kilda Summer*, 1960.

Wright, John Kirtland, *The Geographical Lore of the Time of the Crusades*, 1925.


CHAPTER 2

Avienus, *Ora Maritima,* edited by A. Berthelot, Paris 1934.

Barnett, R. D., 'Early Shipping in the Near East', *Antiquity*, 1958.

Boardman, J.: I *The Greeks Overseas*, Penguin, Harmondsworth 1964; II *Cambridge Ancient History, revised edn.,* Vol. 11, chap. xxxvii (fasc. 57), 'The Western Mediterranean' by Glyn Daniel and J. D. Evans.

Culican, W., *The First Merchant Venturers: The Ancient Levant in History and Commerce,* Thames and Hudson, London; McGraw-Hill, New York 1966.

Dixon, L. P., *The Iberians of Spain*, Oxford University Press, Oxford 1940.

Dunbabin, T. J., *The Western Greeks*, Oxford University Press, Oxford 1948.

Finley, M. I., *A History of Sicily: Ancient Sicily to the Arab Conquest*, Chatto and Windus, London 1968.

Hamilton, W., 'The myth in Plutarch's *De Facie* (940f–945d)', *Classical Quarterly* 28, 1934.

Harden, D. B., *The Phoenicians,* Thames and Hudson, London; Praeger, New York 1962.

Hencken, H. O'N., *The Archaeology of Cornwall and Scilly*, Methuen, London 1932.

Hennig, R., *Terrae Incognitae*, 2 Vols., 2nd edn., Leiden 1944.

Hood, S., *The Home of the Heroes: The Aegean before the Greeks*, Thames and Hudson, London; McGraw-Hill, New York 1967.

Hutchinson, R. W., *Prehistoric Crete*, Penguin, Harmondsworth and New York 1962.

Hyde, W. W., *Ancient Greek Mariners,* Oxford University Press, New York 1947.

Kaeppel, C., *Off the Beaten Track in the Classics,* Melbourne 1936.

Luce, J. V., *The End of Atlantis: New Light on an Old Legend,* Thames and Hudson, London; McGraw-Hill, New York 1969.

Morrison, J. S., and Williams, R. T., *Greek Oared Ships 900–322 B.C.,* Cambridge University Press, Cambridge 1968.

Muller, C. (ed.), *Geographi Graeci Minores*, 2 Vols., Paris 1882.

Taylor, E. G. R., *The Haven-Finding Art: A History of Navigation from Odysseus to Captain Cook,* Hollis and Carter, London 1956.

Taylour, Lord William, *Mycenaean Pottery in Italy and Adjacent Areas,* Cambridge University Press, Cambridge 1958.

Torr, C., *Ancient Ships*, Cambridge University Press, Cambridge 1894. Edited by A. J. Podlecki, Argonaut, Chicago 1964.

Warmington, B. H., *Carthage,* Penguin, Harmondsworth 1964; revised edn., Robert Hale, London 1969.

Warmington, E. H., *Greek Geography*, J. M. Dent, London and Toronto 1934.

Woodhead, A. G., *The Greeks in the West*, Thames and Hudson, London; Praeger, New York 1962.


CHAPTERS 3, 6

Brøndsted, Johannes, *Vikingerne*, Copenhagen 1960; English edn., *The Vikings*, Baltimore 1960; revised 1965.

BRUUN, Daniel, *The Icelandic colonization of Greenland, and the finding of Vineland,* Copenhagen 1918.

FISCHER-MØLLER, K., 'Mediaeval Norse settlements in Greenland', *Medd. om Grønl.* 89, Copenhagen 1942.

GATHORNE-HARDY, G. M., *The Norse Discoverers of America.* The Wineland Sagas translated and discussed by G.M.G.-H., Oxford 1921.

GRAY, Edward F., *Leif Eriksson, discoverer of America A.D. 1003,* London 1930.

HAUGEN, Einar (tr.), *Voyages to Vinland,* New York 1942.

HERMANSSON, Halldór, *The Norsemen in America (982–c. 1500),* Ithaca (N.Y.) 1909.

INGSTAD, Anne Stine, 'The Norse Settlements at L'Anse aux Meadows, A preliminary Report of the Excavations', *Acta Archaeologica,* Vol. XLI, Copenhagen 1970.

INGSTAD, Helge, *Landet under Leidarstjernen. En ferd til Grønlands norrøne bygder,* Oslo 1959; English edn., *Land under the Pole Star,* Jonathan Cape, London 1966.

JONES, Gwyn, *The Norse Atlantic Saga,* London 1964.

JÓNSSON, Finnur, 'Eirik den Rødes Saga og Vinland', *Historisk Tidsskrift,* Christiania 1912.

KEJLBO, Ib Rønne, 'Claudius Clavus and the Vinland Map', *American-Scandinavian Review* 54, 1966.

MAGNUSSON, M., and PALSSON, Hermann (tr. and ed.), *The Vinland Sagas,* Baltimore 1965.

NANSEN, Fridtjof, 'The Norsemen in America', *Geographical Journal,* London 1911.

REEVES, Arthur Middleton (ed. and trans.), *The Finding of Wineland the Good. The History of the Icelandic Discovery of America,* London 1895.

REYNOLDS, Hans, *Grønland: Vestre Bygdi,* Oslo 1926.

ROUSSELL, Aage: I *Farms and churches in the mediaeval Norse settlements of Greenland,* Copenhagen 1941; II *Sandnes and the neighbouring farms,* Copenhagen 1936.

SCHREINER, Johan, 'Leiv Eiriksson og Vinland', *Aftenposten,* November 5, Oslo 1964.

SKELTON, R. A., MARSTON, Thomas E. and PAINTER, George D., *The Vinland Map and the Tartar Relation,* New Haven (Conn.) and London 1965.

STEENSBY, H. P., *The Norsemen's route from Greenland to Wineland,* Copenhagen 1918.

STORM, Gustav, *Studier over Vinlandsreisene, Vinlands geografi og ethnografi,* Copenhagen 1888.

THÓRDARSON, Matthias, *The Vinland Voyages,* New York 1930.

VILMUNDARSON, TÓRHALLUR, 'Reflections on the Vinland Map', *American–Scandinavian Review* 54, 1966.

## CHAPTERS 4, 7

BRINTON, D. G., *American Hero Myths,* Philadelphia 1882.

DAWSON, W. R., 'Mummification in Australia and in America', *Journal of the Royal Anthropological Institute,* Vol. LVIII, London 1928.

HEYERDAHL, Thor, *The Ra Expeditions,* George Allen and Unwin, London 1971.

HUTCHINSON, J. B., SILOW, R. A., and STEPHENS, S. G., *The Evolution of Gossypium and Differentiation of the Cultivated Cottons,* London, New York and Toronto 1947.

KUBLER, George, *The Art and Architecture of Ancient America,* Penguin, Harmondsworth 1962.

MORRIS, E. H., CHARLOT, J., and MORRIS, A. A., *The Temple of the Warriors at Chitzen Itzá, Yucatán,* Carnegie Institute Washington Publ. No. 406, Washington D.C. 1931.

ROWE, J. H., 'Diffusionism and Archaeology', *American Antiquity,* January 1966.

SAUER, C. O., 'Cultivated Plants of South and Central America', in *Steward*, 1950 (see below).

STEWARD, J. H. (ed.), *Handbook of South American Indians*, Vol. IV and Vol. VI, Smithsonian Institution Bur. Amer. Ethn. Bull. 143, Washington D.C. 1948, 1950.

STOUT, D. B., 'Handbook of South American Indians', Vol. IV of *Steward*, 1948 (see above).

TROTTER, M., 'Hair from Paracas Indian Mummies', *American Journal of Physical Anthropology*, Vol. I, 1943.

WILSON, D., *Prehistoric Man. Researches into the Origin of Civilization in the Old and New Worlds*, Vols. I and II, London 1862.


CHAPTER 5

ALBAUGH, William A., *Confederate Edged Weapons*, Harper & Brothers, New York 1960.

BLAIR, Claude, *European and American Arms, c. 1100–1850*, Bonanza Books, New York 1962.

BLEGEN, Theodore C., *The Kensington Rune Stone: New Light on an Old Riddle*, with a bibliography compiled by Michael Brooks, Minnesota Historical Society, St. Paul 1968.

GODFREY, William S., 'The Archaeology of the Old Stone Mill in Newport, Rhode Island', *American Antiquity*, Vol. XVII, No. 2, October 1951.

HENCKEN, Hugh O'Neill, 'What are Pattee's Caves? Are They Remains of a Medieval Irish Monastery in New Hampshire, as is Claimed?' *Scientific American*, November 1940.

HOEGH, Knut O., 'Kensington og Elbow Lake Stenene', *Symra*, Vol. 5, Decorah (Iowa) 1909.

HOLAND, Hjalmar R., *America, 1355–1364: a New Chapter in Pre-Columbian History*, Duell, Sloan and Pearce, New York 1946.

LANDSVERK, Ole G., *Ancient Norse Messages on American Stones*, Norseman Press, Glendale (Calif.) 1969.

LEE, Thomas E.: I 'Archaeological Discoveries, Payne Bay Region, Ungava, 1966', Centre d'Études Nordiques, *Travaux Divers*, No. 20, Université Laval, Quebec 1968; II 'Fort Chimo and Payne Lake, Ungava, Archaeology, 1965', Centre d'Études Nordiques, *Travaux Divers*, No. 16, Université Laval, Quebec 1966.

MEANS, Philip Ainsworth, *The Newport Tower*, H. Holt and Company, New York 1942.

Minnesota Historical Society Archives.

NEARA (New England Antiquities Research Association) Bulletins.

PETERSON, Harold L., 'American Indian Tomahawks', *Contributions*, Vol. XIX, Museum of the American Indian, Heye Foundation, New York 1965.

RAFN, Carl Christian: I 'Account of an Ancient Structure in Newport, Rhode Island, the Vinland of the Scandinavians, Communicated by Thomas H. Webb, M.D. in Letters to Professor Charles Rafn, with Remarks annexed by the Latter', *Mémoires de la Société Royale des Antiquaires du Nord*, Copenhagen 1836–9; II 'Antiquitates Americanae Sive Scriptores Septentrionalis Rerum Ante-Columbianarum in America. Samling af de i Nordens Oldskrifter Indeholdte Efterretninger om de Gamle Nordboers Opdagelsereiser til America fra det 10de til det 14de Aarundrede', *Societas Regia Antiqvariorum Septentrionalium*, Schultz, Copenhagen 1837; III Supplement to *Antiquitates Americanae*, Copenhagen 1841.

Royal Ontario Museum, the files pertaining to the Beardmore find.

RUSSELL, Carl P., *Firearms, Traps, and Tools of the Mountain Men,* a guide in pictures and text to the equipment of the trappers and fur traders who opened up the Old West from the 1820s to the 1840s, Alfred A. Knopf, New York 1967.

STRANDWOLD, Olaf, *Norse Inscriptions on American Stones Collected and Deciphered,* Magnus Bjørndal, Weehawken (N.J.) 1948.

VESCELIUS, G. S., *The Antiquity of Pattee's Caves,* typescript, 1955.

WAHLGREN, Erik, *The Kensington Stone, a Mystery Solved,* University of Wisconsin Press, 1958.


CHAPTER 8

EKHOLM, Gordon F., 'Transpacific Contacts', *Prehistoric Man in the New World,* ed. Jesse D. Jennings and Edward Norbeck, University of Chicago Press, Chicago 1964.

ESTRADA, Emilio and MEGGERS, Betty J., 'A Complex of Traits of Probable Transpacific Origin on the Coast of Ecuador', *American Anthropologist,* Vol. 63, pp. 913–939, 1961.

FERGUSSON, James, *History of Indian and Eastern Architecture,* Vol. II, Munshiram Manoharlal Oriental Publishers, Delhi 1967.

D'HARCOURT, Raoul, 'Archéologie de la Province d'Esmeraldas, Equateur', *Journal de la Société des Américanistes,* Vol 34, pp. 61–200, Paris 1942 (1947).

HEINE-GELDERN, Robert, 'The Problem of Transpacific Influences in Meso-America', *Handbook of Middle American Indians,* Vol. 4, pp. 277–295, University of Texas Press, Austin 1966.

KEMPERS, A. J. Bernet, *Ancient Indonesian Art,* Harvard University Press, Cambridge (Mass.) 1959.

KOOIJMAN, Simon, *Die Kunst van Nieuw-Guineas,* Service, The Hague 1959.

MEGGERS, Betty J., 'North and South American Cultural Connections and Convergences', *Prehistoric Man in the New World*, ed. Jesse D. Jennings and Edward Norbeck, University of Chicago Press, Chicago 1964.

MEGGERS, Betty J., EVANS, Clifford and ESTRADA, Emilio, *Early Formative Period of Coastal Ecuador; The Valdivia and Machalilla Phases,* Smithsonian Institution Press, Washington 1965.

PHILLIPS, Philip, 'The Role of Transpacific Contacts in the Development of New World Pre-Columbian Civilizations', *Handbook of Middle American Indians,* Vol. 4, pp. 296–315, University of Texas Press, Austin 1966.

POPE, John A., GETTENS, Rutherford J., CAHILL, James and BARNARD, Noel, *The Freer Chinese Bronzes,* Vol. 1, Catalogue, Freer Gallery of Art, Oriental Studies No. 7, Washington 1967.

PROSKOURIAKOFF, Tatiana, *A Study of Classic Maya Sculpture,* Carnegie Institution of Washington, Publication 593, Washington 1950.

ROWLAND, Benjamin, *The Art and Architecture of India,* Penguin Books, Harmondsworth and Baltimore 1967.

SMITH, G. Elliot, *Elephants and Ethnologists,* Kegan Paul, Trench, Trubner and Co., London; E. P. Dutton and Co., New York 1924.

STIRLING, Matthew W., 'Monumental Sculpture of Southern Veracruz and Tabasco', *Handbook of Middle American Indians,* Vol. 3, pp. 716–738, University of Texas Press, Austin 1965.

SWAAN, Wim, *Lost Cities of Asia,* Elek, London; G. P. Putnam's Sons, New York 1966.

ZIMMER, Heinrich, *The Art of Indian Asia, Its Mythology and Transformations,* Bollingen Series XXXIX, Pantheon Books, New York 1955.

# List of Illustrations, Maps and Tables

The contributors and publishers are grateful to the many official bodies, institutions and individuals mentioned below for their assistance in supplying illustrative material.

Frontispiece. Sunset. Photo: Tuggener.

Page 2. General Chronological Chart. Drawn by G. Jones.

1 Christian Krohg: *Leif Eiriksson sights America*, 1893. Photo: by courtesy of the Nasjonalgalleriet, Oslo.

2 Map showing the routes of the known and legendary discoverers of America. Drawn by G. Jones.

3 Portrait of Joseph Smith. Photo: by courtesy of the Church of Jesus Christ of Latter-Day Saints, Salt Lake City.

4 Title page and first page of the *Book of Mormon*. Photo: by courtesy of the Church of Jesus Christ of Latter-Day Saints, Salt Lake City.

5 St Brendan on the whale's back, from the medieval *St Brendan Codex*. Photo: by courtesy of the Universitätsbibliothek, Heidelberg.

6 A proto-Corinthian pyxis, 680–650 BC, showing Hercules capturing Geryon's cattle. Photo: by courtesy of the Trustees of the British Museum.

7 Sculpture showing Atlas bearing the heavens on his shoulders, Museo Nazionale, Naples. Photo: by courtesy of the Soprintendenza alle Antichità della Campania, Naples.

8 Plato, *c.* 427–347 BC, the head of an inscribed herm. Staatliche Museen, Berlin. Photo: Phaidon Press.

9 Reconstruction of the map of Atlantis: left, showing the centre of the city; right, superimposed on the shape of the island of Thera (modern Santorini).

10 Head of a sculpture which might have represented Plutarch. By courtesy of the Archaeological Museum, Delphi.

11 A modern curragh in Brandon Bay, County Kerry. Photo: by courtesy of the Irish Tourist Board.

12 Curragh carved on a stone pillar near Bantry, County Cork, eighth century AD. Photo: by courtesy of Paul Johnstone.

13 Sepia drawing by Captain Thomas Phillips: 'Portable vessel of wicker, ordinarily used by the wild Irish', *c.* 1685, from a book of prints and drawings of ships collected by Pepys. By courtesy of the Pepys Library, Magdalene College, Cambridge. Photo: Edward Leigh.

14 Map showing the Irish monks' sea-pilgrimages and settlements in the period between the sixth and eighth centuries AD. Drawn by G. Jones.

15 The island of Skellig Michael. Photo: by courtesy of the Irish Tourist Board.

16 A page from the *Book of Lismore*, fol. 74ʳ. Devonshire Collection, Chatsworth. By courtesy of the Trustees of the Chatsworth Settlement. Photo: Mottershaw.

17 The island of St Kilda. Photo: Tom Weir.

18 A volcanic spring in Furnas Valley, St Michael, Azores. Photo: by courtesy of the Portuguese Information Office.

19 The island of Exuma Cays in the Bahamas. Photo: by courtesy of the Bahama Islands Tourist Office.

20 The volcano on the island of Hekla. Photo: by courtesy of the Icelandic Photo and Press Service.

21 The Beerenberg volcano on the island of Jan Mayen. Photo: by courtesy of the Norsk Polarinstitutt, Oslo.

22 The island of Rockall. Photo: Ministry of Defence (Air Force Department). Crown copyright reserved.

181 Peruvian Indian holding a *quipu*, from the *Chronicle* of Huamán Poma de Ayalá.

182 Mummy bundle from Paracas, Peru. Museo Nacional de Antropologia y Arqueologia, Lima. Photo: Thor Heyerdahl.

183, 184 Specimens of European-like hair on pre-Inca heads from Makat Tempu, near Lima, Peru. Museo Nacional de Antropologia y Arqueologia, Lima. Photos: Thor Heyerdahl.

185 Headdress, over four feet high, mainly of green quetzal feathers and decorated with gold discs and blue, crimson and white feathers, brought to Europe from Mexico before 1524 by the Spanish conquerors. It has recently been established that, contrary to the caption, this headdress did not form part of Montezuma's gift to Cortés. Photo: by courtesy of the Museum für Völkerkunde, Vienna.

186 Montezuma wearing the royal standard of quetzal feathers strapped to his back, from Diego Durán: *Historia de las Indias*. Photo: by courtesy of the Biblioteca Nacional, Madrid.

187 A Peruvian deity riding in a reed boat, from an early Chimu pot. After Kutscher.

188 Early Chimu art showing culture heroes travelling on a serpent raft. After Kutscher.

189 Indians giving Cortés a bead necklace, from Diego Durán: *Historia de las Indias*. Photo: by courtesy of the Biblioteca Nacional, Madrid.

190 An Aztec sculpture of Quetzalcoatl, the feathered serpent. Photo: by courtesy of the Museo Nacional de Antropologia, Mexico City, D.F., I.N.A.H.

191 'Atlantes' from the temple of Quetzalcoatl at Tula. Photo: Thor Heyerdahl.

192 Quetzalcoatl standing on top of a step-pyramid, from an Aztec Codex.

193 Page from the Aztec Codex *Nuttall*, depicting bearded men attacking a town by means of rafts. Photo: by courtesy of the Trustees of the British Museum.

194 A bearded warrior on a pillar of the Temple of the Warriors, Chichen Itzá. By courtesy of Thor Heyerdahl. Photo: T. S. Ferguson.

195 The Temple of the Warriors at Chichen Itzá. Photo: by courtesy of T. G. Rosenthal.

196 Bearded wanderers, from the Mixtec Codex *Dorenberg*. After Seler.

197 Bearded pottery head from Rio Balsas, Guerrero, Mexico. American Museum of Natural History, New York. Photo: Thor Heyerdahl.

198 Bearded slate relief carved on the back of a prehistoric stone mirror from Vera Cruz, Mexico. American Museum of Natural History, New York. Photo: Thor Heyerdahl.

199 Clay head from Tres Zapotes, Vera Cruz. National Geographic Society, Washington, D.C. Photo: Thor Heyerdahl.

200 Clay representation of Huehueteotl, the old god of fire, with a brazier on his head, from Central Vera Cruz. Photo: by courtesy of the Museo Nacional de Antropologia, Mexico, D.F., I.N.A.H.

201 Stone statue of Tlaloc, the rain god, from Oaxaca, Mexico. Photo: by courtesy of the Musée de l'Homme, Paris.

202 Colossal basalt head, about eight feet high, from La Venta, now at Villahermosa, Tabasco. Photo: Thor Heyerdahl.

203 A semitic 'Uncle Sam' type of bearded relief from a large stela excavated in the Tabasco jungle. Photo: Thor Heyerdahl.

204, 205 Two panels from a set painted in 1698, showing Cortés riding to meet Montezuma. Photos: by courtesy of the Museo de América, Madrid. Photo: Oronoz.

206 Reconstruction of a mural painting from the Temple of the Warriors at Chichen Itzá, from Morris, Charlot and Morris: *The Temple of the Warriors at Chichen Itzá, Yucatán*, Carnegie Inst. Washington, Publ. No. 406, 1931. By courtesy of the Peabody Museum of Archaeology and Ethnology, Cambridge, Mass. Photo: Peter Davey.

207 Pottery vessel from Chimbote, north Peru, showing dark-skinned warriors leading white-skinned captives. Photo: Thor Heyerdahl.

208 Scene from the 'Tomb of the Doctor' at Saqqara, showing circumcision being performed in Egypt. Photo: Peter Clayton.

209 The mummified body of a Canary Island Guanche. Photo: by courtesy of the University Museum of Archaeology and Ethnology, Cambridge.

210 Tetrapod bowl from the early Valdivia Phase, coastal Ecuador, *c.* 3000 BC. Photo: C. Evans.

211 Small jar with incised, punctated, and appliqué fillet decoration from the Valdivia Phase, coastal Ecuador. Photo: C. Evans.

212 Map of the North Pacific Ocean showing major currents and the Great Circle Route. Drawn by George Robert Lewis.

213 Typical decorated pottery of the Valdivia Phase, coastal Ecuador. Photos: C. Evans.

214 Typical decoration of Middle Jomon pottery, central and western Japan. Photos: C. Evans.

215 Pottery neckrest of the Bahia culture, Manabí, Ecuador. Drawn by George Robert Lewis.

216 Wooden neckrest from New Guinea. Drawn by George Robert Lewis after Kooijman.

# Index

Numbers in *italic* refer to illustrations and their captions.